Schools of Reconciliation

Schools of Reconciliation

Issues in Joint Roman Catholic–Anglican Education

Priscilla Chadwick

CASSELL

Cassell
Villiers House, 41–47 Strand, London WC2N 5JE
387 Park Avenue South, New York, NY 10016–8810

First published 1994

British Library Cataloguing-in-Publication Data
A catalogue record for this book is available from the British Library.
Library of Congress Cataloging-in-Publication Data
Applied for.

ISBN 0–304–33140–6 (hardback)
        0–304–33142–2 (paperback)

Typeset by August Filmsetting St Helens
Printed and bound in Great Britain by
Biddles Ltd, Guildford and King's Lynn

Contents

Patri pacis fidelium amantissimo

Forewords

Reconciliation like ecumenism is the subject of heated opinion in Northern Ireland. Definition and sensitive understanding by adherent and critic alike are essential if full understanding of community co-operation is to be strengthened. Integrated education deserves that same care of definition and practical sensitivity if it is to be allowed an opportunity to make a real contribution to peace and understanding.

Priscilla Chadwick writes with sensitivity and care based on detailed research and knowledge of the pioneer efforts of Lagan College in Belfast and St Bede's at Redhill. Both schools represent the problems as well as the opportunities integration could offer. Her analysis of the ways in which these two projects speak of vision, practicalities and the diversity of religious/social/cultural interests which go to make up the agendas of each is fascinating. Her conclusions deserve most serious consideration by all who are interested in integrated education. But even more, her analysis demands attention by all who try to look to the future of this divided community in terms of reconciliation, justice and peace.

Robin Eames, Archbishop of Armagh
Primate of All Ireland

This is a most interesting, informative, thoughtful, and challenging study about Roman Catholic and Anglican approaches to Church schools in England and in Ireland. It is valuable for its careful analysis of what is seen to be the nature and purpose of Church schools, for its excellent outline of differing views of what RE in such schools should be, as well as for the detailed reflection on two joint Church schools, in Redhill and in Belfast.

Anyone concerned about Church schools (not just joint Church schools) can learn a great deal from this valuable and hopeful piece of research.

David Konstant, Bishop of Leeds
Chairman, Catholic Education Service of England and Wales

1

Introduction

1. PERSONAL PREFACE

My interest in ecumenical education began in Raffles Hotel, Singapore in 1978. Travelling overland in Asia, I received a letter from the chairman of governors of St Bede's joint Church School, Redhill, inviting me to apply for the post of head of religious education, and my professional experiences over the next few years proved the stimulus for action research into the area of ecumenical education. At the same time my involvement in the national Anglican/Roman Catholic Committee on ecumenical relations prompted further reflection on and dissemination of the St Bede's experience (Chadwick and Gladwell, 1987). The visit of two colleagues from Belfast to Redhill in preparation for the founding of Lagan College in 1981 marked the beginning of my interest in integrated education in Northern Ireland.

Back in the early 1980s there was, and even now is, very little published material on ecumenical education. The data on St Bede's came mainly from extensive interviews, diocesan and school documents, and personal experience. Similarly the initial studies on Lagan College were based on personal interviews across the community, with people ranging from taxi drivers to archbishops, since university researchers had not considered one (then independent) integrated school worth detailed review, and seemed preoccupied with analysing the effects of segregated education.[1]

[1]Even to the point of dismissing integrated education as not being a valid way forward (Gallagher and Worrall, 1982, p. 171).

In 1992 South Bank University offered me research time to revise, update and significantly reconstruct the pattern of data collected over the previous twelve years, as well as follow up new issues in the case studies in 1991–2. What started as snapshot case studies in the early 1980s became a more comprehensive survey of the development of two secondary schools over a decade, as they evolved from hesitant pioneers in an educational experiment to well-established, oversubscribed school communities providing exemplars of good practice in ecumenical education.

Three assumptions might be said to reflect a consensual perspective for those actively interested in such developments. First there is a conception of the 'ecumenical' which assumes ecumenical co-operation not only to be desirable but also an explicit response to Jesus' prayer in John 18:21; which is based on a unity that already exists (for example in 'common baptism') and which celebrates the enrichment of diversity rather than strives for uniformity. Secondly there is a conception of the 'educational' which is 'liberal-democratic'; encouraging pupils to be critical and independent-minded, rather than passive recipients of a body of knowledge and doctrine with the accompanying dangers of indoctrination. Thirdly there is a conception of the 'Church' which turns away from an inward-looking defensiveness to witness outward into the world as a leavening influence in promoting justice and peace.

Neither of the two ecumenical case-study schools would claim that it had 'got it right' and each is in the process of developing major initiatives as it moves forward to the twenty-first century. But both of them in different ways point a way forward for the Churches and for educationists who believe, reflecting the declaration of the 1952 Faith and Order Conference of the World Council of Churches at Lund, that Christians should not do separately what can be done together.

2. ECUMENICAL ISSUES

The ecumenical movement in this country has made more progress this century than anyone could have dared to expect. The anti-Roman-Catholic feelings stirred by the burning of Cranmer, Ridley and Latimer during Queen Mary's brief counter-reformation were no less influential than the execution of Thomas More and John Fisher in generating resentment and rivalry between two Christian communions. The Victorian age brought several additional problems. Irish labourers entered Britain, willing to accept lower wages and retaining a separate ghetto-like community, particularly in Liverpool and London: each Sinn Fein murder exacerbated anti-

Irish and therefore anti-Catholic feeling. Protestants were bewildered by the profound effects of the Tractarian movement in the Church of England on the one hand, and the influence of liberal theology on the other. At the same time, the decree of 'papal infallibility' at the Vatican Council of 1870 and Leo XIII's 1896 declaration against Anglican orders (*Apostolicae Curae*), served only to reinforce the feeling of division and of doors towards unity being abruptly slammed.

Yet the twentieth century has been marked by various attempts, not all successful, to move towards reconciliation between separated Churches. Tractarian theology, with its emphasis on the one visible body of the Church and on eucharistic sacrifice, reminded Anglicans that they shared a common heritage with Roman Catholics. The attempts, nervous at first but later mountingly confident, by Roman Catholic theologians to come fully to terms with historical criticism of the Bible have also removed barriers to mutual understanding. But the event of outstanding significance was the 1962 Second Vatican Council called by Pope John XXIII, which put the ecumenical movement unequivocally on the map, with a decree on Ecumenism that included a look of affection and longing towards the Anglican Communion. The Council not only established a Secretariat for Christian Unity within the Roman Curia, but also paved the way for the visit of the Archbishop of Canterbury, Michael Ramsey, to Pope Paul VI in 1966. The mutual concord then achieved led to the establishment of the first Anglican/Roman Catholic International Commission (ARCIC), whose work (1970–82) in uncovering common ground on eucharist, ministry and authority contributed much to increased ecumenical understanding. The Common Declaration signed by Pope John Paul II and Archbishop Runcie at Canterbury in 1982, unimaginable at the beginning of the century, showed how much progress had been made and provided the necessary endorsement to further ecumenical co-operation.

Although the Vatican's eventual response in 1991 to the Final Report of ARCIC I was not particularly encouraging, the Pope recognized that the ARCIC process had shown

> it is possible to go to the heart of the serious differences between Christians and still persevere in a fraternal and progressive dialogue.... . Ecumenism is not solely a matter for the highest Church authorities. It also involves a 'dialogue of life' at the level of exchanges and cooperation between believers at every level. (Address to the English Roman Catholic bishops, 17 March 1992)

3

3. CHURCH SCHOOLS

In education, Church schools have developed alongside state schools throughout the present century. The so-called 'dual system' has allowed the Churches the opportunity to develop their traditional involvement in education backed by financial assistance from the government. Their position has not been immune to criticism. The critics of Church schools urge that they are from a secular standpoint anachronistic, and from a social standpoint divisive.[2] Today's society is predominantly secular in tone; Church attendance figures are low; the multi-cultural emphasis in education makes a narrow focus on an exclusively Christian culture appear outdated; and the Churches suffer acute financial stringency. On the other hand, Church schools are usually oversubscribed; parents increasingly exercise their right to choose a religious school for their children; articulate Christian educationists are contributing fresh ideas to the current debate; and recent moves in ecumenical relations have provided additional incentive for schools to take the specifically religious and moral ingredient in Christian education seriously. Setting aside the apparent ambivalence of contemporary English society about its Christian inheritance, the coincidence in the past twenty years of ecumenical development with economic belt-tightening has prompted the creation of joint Church schools in several places in Britain. These schools have often been brought into being by the amalgamation of two denominational schools, preceded by local and national consultations, in order to provide a viable Christian school in the locality.

There is an important additional factor. Religious education in Church schools is drawn in two apparently different directions: on the one side towards catechetical instruction of children from committed Christian families; on the other side towards academic RE teaching which does not presuppose personal commitment but leads the pupil into an understanding of what the Christian faith is, what its history has been, and how burning contemporary issues can be looked at from a religious perspective.[3]

A series of questions arises here: how does the Christian school explicitly nurture the faith of its pupils while educating them to be intellectually critical? What should be the relationship between the Christian school and the nearby parish communities? In what ways, if any, will the ethos or community spirit of a Christian school be distinguished from that of a

[2]Discussed in *The Fourth R*, Durham Report (1970), para. 475 and Tilby (1979), ch. 5.

[3]The problems created by this polarization of the confessional and phenomenological approaches to RE are further explored in an article by Nicola Slee in *British Journal of Religious Education* (1989).

county school? To what extent will that ethos affect the teaching of non-religious subjects in the curriculum and the way in which members of the school relate to each other? If a clear strategy for the Church school is to be developed, for example to facilitate effective school appraisal, to implement the requirements of the National Curriculum and assessment, or to develop new patterns of relationship between schools and with local communities, Christian educationists need to address these issues.[4]

The 1988 and 1993 legislation set up administrative structures for grant-maintained schools, anticipating large numbers of schools 'opting out', driven by the principles of parental choice and market forces. Both Anglican and Catholic Church leaders were reluctant to see their local education authority (LEA) partners 'wither on the vine' or Church schools 'floating away' from their diocese. The grant-maintained debate has focused attention on the *raison d'être* of the contemporary Church school: is a grant-maintained school a Christian community in which parental choice should take precedence over diocesan authority[5] or a Christian enclave upholding values threatened by secular society (see Field, 1989)? Is a Christian school one which places a high priority on its role within the wider Christian community across a diocese or LEA, as advocated by both Roman Catholic and Anglican diocesan authorities? The debate raises serious questions about the future of the partnership between Church and state in education, which has seldom been under such pressure since 1944.

This study is concerned not merely with the coming together of two religious traditions which for 400 years have led independent lives, but also with the proper role of Christian education in equipping pupils to take their place in a society in which religion is often pushed to the periphery. These two themes are far from unrelated, since the marginalization of religion would be considerably less drastic if Christian communions, with a vast shared inheritance, felt the mutual confidence in each other to speak and act together both in worship and in relation to the world outside the church door.

A key question is whether or not different ecumenical schools manifest sufficient similarities to suggest certain shared answers to certain shared problems. Generalizations from one ecumenical school to another create doubts and difficulties, since each has its own history and context, particularly in England and Northern Ireland. It might be argued that, rather than being 'ecumenical', the two case-study schools are particular in their denominational focus. St Bede's is specifically Anglican/Roman Catholic,

---

[4]Cf. *On Appraisal in Catholic Schools* 2nd edn (Department of Catholic Education and Formation, 1991); Lankshear (1992c).

[5]See Sheila Lawlor, *Tablet*, 20 February 1988.

though with the Free Churches waiting in the wings. Lagan College involves families from most Protestant traditions alongside Roman Catholics, but is situated within the very specific religious context of the Northern Ireland Churches. If 'ecumenism' refers to a rather wider inter-Church dialogue than just Anglicans and Roman Catholics (such as is now possible within Churches Together in England or the World Council of Churches) or even to the broader context of inter-faith networks, then these two schools clearly have 'ecumenical' limitations; similarly, since both are secondary schools, their experience may not be usefully comparable with Church of England/Methodist foundations in first, primary or middle schools.[6]

As more school governors seek to explore the 'ecumenical' option, and as the already established schools are supported by their National Association formed in June 1992, common principles can more easily be identified. Religion can be the most divisive or the most uniting force in human society; moving from the former and towards the latter is an ideal that inspires widespread assent. If others come to contemplate embarking on similar projects in the future, this study may perhaps be of service in noticing points both where mistakes were made (usually with the noblest and best of intentions) and where a breakthrough on the path to success became possible.

[6]Of 55 Methodist schools, 23 are jointly managed with Anglicans.

2

The Nature and Purpose of a Christian School in England: a Survey of Views and Possibilities

1. INTRODUCTION

This chapter explores whether there is a common view of Christian education within an Anglican and Roman Catholic framework in England. Philosophical and theological concepts are never far from the surface but it is not
primarily a working out of the philosophy and theology of the Christian
school; rather, it focuses on the cultural and political opportuneness of
greater co-operation between Anglican and Roman Catholic schools and
particularly joint schools.

We start by reviewing the issues for Anglican and Roman Catholic
schools, looking predominantly at two dimensions of the schools' aims: the
'general' focus on service to the local and national community, and the
'domestic' focus concerned with support of primarily Christian families.
Although the distinction may initially seem more appropriate to Anglican
schools, this study suggests that these important issues are also increasingly
recognized by Roman Catholic educationists. Underpinning this bifocal
perspective lies a vision of Christian mission to the universal Church and the
wider world, rooted in an ecumenical confidence which embraces diversity,
maintains denominational integrity and strives for unity rather than uniformity. The evidence reflects a range of opinion from traditional evangelical
through to ultramontane Roman Catholic, from official Church statements
to individual parental views, and points up some areas where Anglican and
Roman Catholic views and concerns are clearly distinct from each other

7

though only rarely mutually exclusive; equally, it suggests areas for co-operation in matters of common concern for Christian education.

2. THE DISTINCTIVE ROLE OF THE CHRISTIAN SCHOOL

The Christian churches must provide a distinctive contribution, one that grows out of theological reflection on the nature and practice of education. (National Society, 1984, p. 105)

The process of education, teaching and learning is a holy act and, since the world in which we live is God's, all teaching and learning is somehow related to Him. (Bishops' Conference of England and Wales, 1988, p. A1)

The political climate of the 1990s demands that schools (especially Church schools) should have a distinctive ethos which is marketable to parents. But in clarifying their 'mission statement', to what extent do governing bodies give real consideration to the aims and purpose of a Christian school?[1] In considering these, how far do they take into account the strategic view of their respective diocesan or Church authorities in overall planning and development of Christian education? A distinction has traditionally been drawn by Anglicans between two differentiated aims of a Church school: the 'general' or 'inclusive' aim which is a school's responsibility to serve the community, and the 'domestic' or 'exclusive' aim to educate the children of its own Church. Anglican policy in general, though not every Anglican school, has usually attempted to maintain a balance between these two aims, while Roman Catholics have unequivocally favoured the 'domestic' approach.

Partly because the sixteenth century bequeathed the notion that literacy and Protestantism are a common cause,[2] one tradition of the Church of England has been to see Church schools as an integral yet distinctive part of

[1]Both Roman Catholic and Anglican national educational bodies have published support materials for teachers and governors e.g. *Development Materials for Catholic Schools* (CCIEA, 1990), and *Mission, Management and Appraisal* for Anglicans (National Society, 1992); the latter also suggests it may be 'of value to other denominations'.

[2]Sixteenth-century Erasmian Protestants regarded the cause of the Reformation as virtually synonymous with liberal education: the martyrologist John Foxe hailed the German invention of printing as a providential divine gift, since the accessibility of bibles undermined the medieval system of religious authority (*Acts and Monuments* 1563, ed. Pratt, vol. III, p. 718). Erasmus and his followers saw secular learning as preparation for sacred study.

the Christian mission to a secular society. This is not a mission that aims to convert and to gather into the well-walled sheepfold, but one that somehow assumes a common interest between national education and the national Church where every English citizen has the right to worship. The concepts underlying Roman Catholic understanding of what a Catholic school in Britain exists to do and to be are intimately bound up with the Roman Catholic doctrine of the Church as a body, entrusted by God with a dogmatic, coherently articulated faith to be proclaimed and defended, and in principle and practice independent of secular society.

The prospect of Church schools 'opting out' of local authority control under the 1988 and 1993 legislation has greatly concerned some Anglican diocesan authorities, who fear that the 'community focus' of Anglican schools may become a thing of the past. The fear expressed by Roman Catholic authorities has been quite different, almost opposite: namely that where one of their schools opts out, it may cease to be sufficiently Roman Catholic in its intake and character. Catholic authorities have indeed also expressed a more general concern at the weakening of the spirit of local co-operation and the sense of local community implicit in 'opting out', but it is fair to say that this has not been their main concern.

The balance sought and achieved between the 'general' and 'domestic' aims seems most evident in the ways in which schools view their *admissions policies* and, especially nowadays, *the rights of parents to choose*; in the form and extent of their *religious education and nurture*; and in the way they conceive the *Christian ethos, culture and values of the school*. After some analysis of the Churches' views on the distinctive nature of their schools, we shall consider each of these areas in more detail; an overview of general issues will be followed by the debate within the respective denominational traditions. Discussions in current literature, recent research surveys and numerous press articles throw into high relief the contemporary significance of these issues in educational debate. The various approaches to defining the nature and purpose of a 'Christian' school may then be related to the case study of an 'ecumenical' school.

Anglicans

The Church of England in the last century had little doubt that its task was the general education of the whole community, consequent upon a consciousness of its position as 'the Church of the nation'. It had a duty to provide Christian education for the nation's children since the nation itself acknowledged Christian values in political and public life. For the national Church, values of equipping the children of the Church to take their places in the Christian community and serving the nation through the moral formation of its children were hardly distinguishable.[3] Thus for Anglican schools the 'domestic' and the 'general' aims of providing a service for the Church and by the Church for the nation's children could be comfortably accommodated together.

The Church of England has always sought the ideal, never realized in practice, of holding together the idea of a national Church with that of the universal Church Catholic. That was what it had been before the Reformation; the very title 'Church of England' is medieval, not a product of the sixteenth-century changes which the main line regarded as reform, not revolution or rupture. (Only the radical Protestants wanted a sect or a 'gathered Church' ministering exclusively to committed believers.) The name of the National Society which, since its foundation in 1811 'to educate the children of the poor in the principles of the Established Church', has guided Anglican educational policy, reflects this aspiration. The Church of England has therefore tended to see its own catechetical task, often described as Christian nurture, as merging into its concern for the nation's general provision in education.

The Anglican schools brought into the dual system in 1870 continued their practice of teaching the local children in their neighbourhood school, and such arrangements were strengthened after 1944, when many became 'controlled' rather than 'aided', thereby enhancing the shared responsibilities with the LEAs. The Bishop of Hereford affirmed in 1968: 'The Church is privileged to work in partnership with the State. . . . We are in, and will remain in, education because that is where we belong' (quoted in Bander, 1968, p. 271). The 1981 Allington statement by Anglican secondary head-teachers in south-east England, reaffirmed in 1991, called for a clear Christian basis to the life of the school, for Church schools to be accountable to the Church as well as to society, and for closer liaison with local county schools, thus pushing in both traditional directions at once.

Yet how far is it possible to create a truly coherent educational policy reconciling the 'domestic' or internal role of Anglican Church schools in serving the Church with their more 'general' role of serving the nation? This issue has been hotly debated, particularly since the 1970 Durham Report[4]

[3]Psychologically this remained true even after the momentous constitutional changes enacted by Parliament between 1828 and 1832, and the opening of membership of the House of Commons to non-Anglicans. Otherwise there would not have been a row when in 1880 the militant atheist Bradlaugh claimed his seat. No one until recently had thought to repeal the requirement that the sovereign be in communion with the see of Canterbury.

[4]As one may see from the National Society's *A Future in Partnership* (1984), *The Church School* (Duncan, 1990) or *A Shared Vision* (Lankshear, 1992a) and O'Keeffe's *Faith, Culture and the Dual System* (1986).

(*The Fourth R*). The increasing pressures of secularization and free-market economics might be taken to argue that any such reconciliation, if not inherently impossible, is at least unlikely to be realized. As British society has changed, becoming more pluralistic and secular, so Church schools have had to put their 'general' aim under closer scrutiny.

The Anglican school is caught on the horns of a dilemma. It does not wish to separate itself from the secular world, since it is convinced that Christian values contribute to making society more morally responsible and sensitive. At the same time it claims to retain a distinctiveness over against secular society, contending that the Christian community has a unique gospel to proclaim, transcending, for example, what can be learnt from the media. However, the ever-increasing pluralism of contemporary society in the West creates enhanced pressures. John Hull has argued that the two-pronged pluralism of Britain today, partly a result of the increased number who claim to have no religious belief whatever, partly caused by those who adhere to a faith other than Christianity, makes it no longer possible to nurture children into the faith of their 'society' (Hull, 1984, p. 47). If county schools are predominantly liberal secular humanist institutions, some of which attempt to provide their pupils with a basic understanding of world religions and 'life-stances', whereas specifically religious schools (either aided or independent) make no apology for encouraging parents to value the nurture of their children within a specific faith tradition with a definite creed, those Anglican schools that attempt to avoid this polarization may find their *via media* a lonely path to travel.

The National Society and the diocesan education authorities are only too well aware of the difficulties. They have seen themselves in close partnership with secular government, yet they are convinced that Church schools need to be distinctive and unhesitatingly Christian to justify the massive expenditure on them. But it is far from easy to provide a totally convincing definition of their distinctiveness. *A Future in Partnership* (National Society, 1984) outlined ten characteristics of a good Church school, but many of the ten could be true of good and humane county schools with a predominantly Christian intake of pupils:

> an implicit Christian ethos, a sensitivity to different beliefs, a distinctive all-round excellence, links with the community, living out the concerns of the gospel, a learning process related to God's revelation, a selfless commitment in relationships, a beacon to the transcendent, an integrated view of knowledge, and a creative stimulus to teaching and learning. (p. 71)

In a more recent National Society booklet, *The Curriculum: a Christian View* (1990) Geoffrey Duncan affirmed without reservation that important educational values form common ground among professional teachers, whether Christian or not; for example personal integrity in respecting both their own and their pupils' commitment; the establishment of open and honest relationships; the importance of constructive discipline; an appropriate curriculum which respects Christian values; a coherent and balanced curricular view, and a commitment to develop pupils of all abilities to their full potential. But he insisted that Christian values cannot only be part of the 'hidden' curriculum:

> It would be difficult to affirm the Christian ethos of Church schools if the manifestation of Christian faith were not apparent in personal relationships, in admissions policies, in the relationship with local Christian communities. (National Society, 1990a, p. 8)

In other words, the 'implicit Christian ethos', of which *A Future in Partnership* spoke, must from time to time become altogether explicit or its presence might be seriously doubted.

Further indications of the current concern to identify ways in which Christian values can be made explicit may be found in Bernadette O'Keeffe's 1986 research, *Faith, Culture and the Dual System: a Comparative Study of Church and County Schools*. Comments on school worship or moral and religious education given by some of her Anglican respondents include the following:

on worship—

> 'Assembly is distinctively Anglican.' 'We follow the order of the Christian year.' 'Christianity is the religion of our country, and all children regardless of their backgrounds should be made aware of its significance' (pp. 77–8);

on moral teaching—

> 'I would hope their view of Christian morality would come from all subjects, not just RE. This is a Christian school, and Christian morality fuses all of the school' (p. 104);

on religious education—

> 'Our parents expect us to bring their children up in the Christian faith.' 'I am preparing them for a Christian lifestyle and a personal and detailed knowledge of Christ' (p. 95).

Such sentiments go some way towards answering the critics who feel that Anglican schools are not offering 'full service' (nor indeed value for money) to the Church that sponsors them. Many teachers in Church schools are aware that Christianity ought not to lose its quality of being *sui generis*: the salt must not lose its savour. But that cannot mean building ghetto-like walls to protect such values (Durham Report, 1970, paras 471, 482). For one thing, Christian values do still affect the moral assumptions of society far beyond the frontiers of the specifically worshipping community. John Haldane has commented that 'it is still the Churches that provide the main source of reflection upon the meaning of public virtue, and they are perhaps the only critics of government who are not simply regarded as self-interested' (1986, p. 176). This kind of observation raises the twin questions of whether it is truly realistic to suppose that the Church still exerts such an influence and whether it can exert it effectively within the Establishment without diluting the gospel and its responsibilities to its own Church members.

Roman Catholics

Until the Second Vatican Council, the Roman Catholic Church (especially in Britain) appeared, to most outsiders at any rate, to be an enclosed society erecting walls to defend the purity of faith and morals against hostile out-side forces at first Protestant, later secular. Since Vatican II, the characteristic attitude of Roman Catholic institutions, in Britain as in the West more generally, has come to seem more open. The pre-conciliar position insisted that the Catholic child from the Catholic home must receive education at the hands of Catholic teachers in a Catholic school.[5] In the code of canon law of 1917, canon 1374 declared against any education of Catholics in non-Catholic schools; and 'because of the risk of perversion' canon 2319 held over parents who arranged a non-Catholic education for their children the threat of excommunication. One chairman of the Catholic Education Council, Bishop George Beck of Brentwood, based this view on child psychology: the Catholic child in a non-Catholic environment was faced with divided loyalties leading 'either to moral irresponsibility or to acute moral tension' (1955, p. 55). Although the threats and penalties have gone, even the new code of canon law of 1983 insisted that Roman Catholic parents have a duty to send their children to Roman Catholic schools unless that is impossible (canon 798), and education 'must be based on the principles of Catholic doctrine' (canon 803).

The Church has the duty and the right to instruct children in the truth it has received and, moreover, acceptance of the truth defines a believer. Bishop Beck continued: 'The essence of true religious teaching is that the teacher should believe that which he teaches, and should be delivering, as he believes it, the whole message of truth.' The magisterial approach stressed the importance of catechetical teaching, handing on doctrine verifiable in authoritative collections of Catholic dogma or morals, and taught in an essentially didactic way, in which the pupils did not so much exercise a personal discernment as accept that, as members of the Catholic commu-

[5]Leo XIII's encyclical *Militantis Ecclesiae*, 1879 and Pius XI's *Divini Illius Magistri*, 1929.

nity, this was what they were committed to. Cardinal Heenan pointed to one defence of this approach by asking, 'Would our small flock remain the largest Church-going community if we were to abandon our schools?' (*Catholic Herald*, 29 April 1966).

A more refined version of this form of defence for specifically Roman Catholic education for Roman Catholics has proceeded empirically, by seeking to gather factual evidence on the relative effect of Catholic and non-Catholic schooling upon an individual's religious behaviour and practice. Greeley's research in America in 1963, replicated in 1974,[6] showed 'a moderate but significant association ... between Catholic education and adult religious behaviour' (1966, p. 219); 'Catholic schools do have an impact which is net of education, parental religiousness, spouse's religiousness, age, sex and educational attainment' (Greeley *et al.*, 1976, pp. 306ff.). Hornsby-Smith's research in England cautiously confirmed such findings:

> Catholic schools appear to be effective in producing adult religious outcomes, although the actual effect is small, especially in relation to the effects of variables like parental religiosity and spouse's religiosity which measure the impact of the home. (Hornsby-Smith and Lee, 1980, p.105)[7]

On the other hand, the admission that a Catholic school cannot achieve much without support in the home and family was at one time used by some to query the huge investment in separate schools. At the 1966 Downside Symposium, A.E.C.W. Spencer observed that if, for example, better attendance at mass were to be indicative of the results of Catholic schooling, then it had failed; one should be looking, he urged, to the supportive family background rather than to the school. From this he concluded that 'the empirical basis of the strategy of providing a place in a Catholic school for all Catholic children is extremely doubtful' (Jebb, 1968). In the same 1966

[6]Greeley and Rossi (1966); Greeley *et al.* (1976). The more the Church appeared to be undergoing an institutional crisis, the more important Catholic schools appeared to be in nurturing the Church of the future: 'Catholic schools are a tremendous asset for the changing Church. They tend to produce people who are change-oriented and flexible, but secure in both their world-view and their loyalty to past traditions and values' (p. 301).

[7]Hornsby-Smith and Lee argued that attention should also be paid to adult catechesis since this would help counteract the long-term decline in Catholic influence as children grew up, and would reinforce the family support for Catholic pupils at school. This priority was also advocated by the Bishops' Conference report in 1981, *Signposts and Homecomings* and is still on the Catholic agenda (cf. *Priests and People*, February 1993, vol. 7 no. 2). See also Hornsby-Smith (1978), p. 46.

symposium, Michael Gaine expressed the view that, although Catholics in the latter half of the twentieth century have generally ceased to speak about 'the danger of perversion', they appear to be needlessly defensive about the importance of a 'Catholic atmosphere' for their children's education. More moderately, Hornsby-Smith (1978, p. 139) later encouraged Catholic education policy-makers, faced with the falling school rolls of the 1980s, to turn their attention from the quantitative to the qualitative—to reassess their dominant perspective of expansion and to evaluate the effectiveness of Catholic education.

The desire to retain the system is sometimes linked with the feeling that Catholic schools are simply part of the inheritance which Catholic forefathers made huge sacrifices to keep, and which should, for that reason alone, be preserved at all costs. That is, the schools are the visible and public symbol of the essential distinctiveness of the Roman Catholic Church and of its determination to resist secularity and all attempts to dilute the faith into some undenominational flag-waving pageantry. The retention of Catholic schools is therefore a sign of that determination to be distinct, perhaps even awkward to the point of pertinacity, which tended to characterize English Catholics before Vatican II began to produce a different social attitude, and which is consciously and nostalgically felt by some as a proper manifestation of the uncompromising spirit (cf. *Tablet*, 14 September 1985).

Since the Second Vatican Council, there have been a number of thought-provoking publications, reflecting wide-ranging opinions, as theologians and educationists explored the implications of that Council for Catholic Education. The document on The *Catholic School* (Sacred Congregation, 1977) spoke of 'a problem requiring clear and positive thinking, courage, perseverance and cooperation to tackle the various measures without being overawed by the size of the difficulties from within and without, not by persistent and outdated slogans' (para. 64). The Catholic school's job is 'infinitely more difficult, more complex, since this is a time when Christianity demands to be clothed in fresh garments . . . when a pluralistic mentality dominates' (para. 66). The problem is to identify and lay down the conditions necessary for the Catholic school to fulfil its role 'in the saving mission of the Church, especially for education in the faith' (para. 9). The '*aggiornamento*' of Vatican II has moved the Roman Catholic Church into a close engagement with the modern world, thereby encouraging Catholics to develop a more world-involved perspective and opening up more radical theological discussion. The Council crucially balanced its reaffirmation of papal supremacy with an emphasis on collegiality (*Lumen Gentium*, paras 22ff.: Hastings, 1968), strengthened through the role of national bishops' conferences. This not only encouraged a stronger sense of national identity (for example the Dutch or American Church), but also enhanced lateral links across national boundaries (such as pan-European or pan-Latin

American and particularly between developed and developing countries). Again, the bishop of the local diocese is not to be seen merely as the delegate of the Pope, handing out to his obedient people the instructions of higher authority, but rather as himself representing the apostolic succession and performing a role in relation to his clergy and laity which best enables them to participate and to express their faith, always in eucharistic fellowship with the whole Catholic Church and never apart from it.

The acknowledgement of the local diocesan community as something active, and not merely a passive recipient of curial directives, has consequences for the understanding of catechesis and religious education generally. Vatican II described the laity not so much as belonging to the Church as being the Church: through the laity the Church is present in the world (Rahner, 1968, vol. 2, p. 355). Essential to that maturity is a personal and religious freedom to take responsibility for one's understanding of the faith as contrasted with an unreflective acceptance of a set of propositions.[8] In the field of biblical studies, the past three or four decades have seen an increasing rapprochement in method and results between Catholic and Protestant biblical scholars.[9] In contrast to the days of Vatican I, Bible-reading is now regarded as appropriate for laity as well as clergy (Constitution on Divine Revelation, *Dei Verbum*, 1965, para. 22: Hastings, 1968). The ability of Roman Catholic teachers to balance doctrinal with biblical study has become important in devising religious education appropriate to the Christian school: the inveterate Protestant prejudice that by policy Roman Catholics neglect the Bible is antiquated.

The decree of Vatican II on Ecumenism, *Unitatis Redintegratio* (November 1964: Hastings, 1968), gave concrete substance to many of the ideas reflected in other conciliar discussions and documents. 'The restoration of unity among all Christians' is one of the principal concerns of the Second Vatican Council' (para. 1). Such unity may be furthered by a renewal of the Church, e.g. by biblical and liturgical movements, catechetics, social teaching (para. 6); by prayer and discriminating use of common worship (para. 8); by the development of theology paying due regard to the ecumenical

[8]In *The Catholic School* (1977, para. 70) produced by the Sacred Congregation for Catholic Education, the Catholic school is to 'develop persons who are responsible and inner-directed, capable of choosing freely in conformity with their conscience' (para. 31).

[9]The virtual disappearance of the imprimatur except for catechetical handbooks means that it may not be easy to judge from a monograph itself whether the author is a Roman Catholic, Anglican, Methodist or Lutheran. The extent of contemporary liberation can be judged by a comparison of the caution shown in the notes of the 1968 edition of the English *Jerusalem Bible* with the freedom and learned candour of Roman Catholic biblical scholars manifested in the 1985 revision of the same book.

point of view (para. 10). The 'co-operation' and 'dialogue' advocated by the Council presupposes a massive change of direction from the suspicious reserve of the pre-conciliar period and, as we shall see, has brought Roman Catholic educational policy substantially closer to that traditional in the Church of England, thereby laying the foundations for innovative and co-operative developments in joint schools.

3. ADMISSIONS POLICIES AND PARENTAL CHOICE

The question of admissions policies is primary, for the decisions of the governors in this area have a profound influence on all the activities of the school. Does the policy place more emphasis on the 'domestic' priorities of church attendance and commitment, or on general principles of admitting children from the local community whose parents express a preference for Christian education though they have no specific parish affiliation and possibly an allegiance to a non-Christian faith?[10] Admissions criteria cannot, however, be considered in isolation. Contemporary political philosophy has made the issue of parental choice an overriding consideration in educational policy-making, from open enrolment through to grant-maintained status.

Before the 1980s, 'one nation' Conservatives and Labour party strategists held a more or less consensus view that children were entitled to the best education in a comprehensive system offering equality of opportunity for all. Church schools were sometimes seen as an historical anomaly in this age of equality, since they were operating a distinctive selection procedure, attaching particular weight to church attendance. Suspicions were inevitably fuelled by the fact that many Church schools remained oversubscribed at a time of falling pupil rolls in the 1980s. What then was the attraction of Church schools for parents?

In the 1970s and 1980s, reorganization for comprehensive education was the policy of the majority of LEAs in Britain. As 11-plus selection was dismantled, so the parents' desire to identify the 'best school' for their

[10]One aspect of the dilemma is summarized by an Anglican headteacher in O'Keeffe's 1986 survey: 'At the moment we are accused by those who do not like Church schools of not taking pupils who are not Christians. If we are undersubscribed and did not want to have unfilled places and then allowed more and more non-Christians in at a time of falling rolls when county schools are losing children, we could be accused of poaching children from them' (p. 24).

children (granted that private education was out of the question, for what-ever reason) was diverted into a choice between different state schools, including Church schools. Parental priorities might include smart uniform, regular homework, high academic examination results, setting or stream-ing, and a perception that the school's values coincided with those of the parents; in middle-class catchment areas, the comprehensive school tended to reinforce middle-class values.[11] Was the priority of those attracted to Church schools a good academic record, a caring environment, or the fact that religious faith was taken seriously? Again, how well did the parents applying to the Church school reflect the general social and ethnic back-ground of the school's local community?

As non-Christian faith communities have established themselves perma-nently in Britain, these parents' interest in the local Church school has in many instances been considerable, since the alternative is usually the secular environment of a county school based on the values of liberal humanism.[12] Ann Dummett (a Roman Catholic and distinguished activist in combating racism) commented:

> Many parents, whether Christian, Sikh, Muslim, or Hindu, take the attitude that a school which has some religious character is better than a completely secular school. There are great differences between religions, but none of these is so great as the gulf between people who practise a religion and people with no religion at all. (Dummett and McNeal, 1981, para. 23)

Church school headteachers are from time to time approached by families who are firm adherents of non-Christian faiths and who want a school where religious beliefs and their influence on daily life are taken seriously. This creates difficulties where admission policies are strictly based on the priority of Christian families but where the catchment area has substantial multi-ethnic communities; the problem also exists for the Church school in a mainly white area which wishes to admit ethnic-minority families and thus show its concern for the wider community and acknowledge the sig-nificance of other faiths.

It has become difficult for a Church school not to be flattered by oversub-

[11]Walford and Jones' survey showed comprehensive schools in Birmingham 'were suc-cessful and efficient and would ensure that there was a high chance of adequate certification to legitimate social class reproduction' (1986, p. 251).

[12]Understandably, the Muslim community found the government's reluctance in May 1990 to grant 'aided' status to its Islamia school in Brent incomprehensible, when that school had a thousand children on its waiting list: 'They are denying Muslim parents the rights that Christian and Jewish parents have', claimed the head, Dr Azambaig. The impression was given that the government was applying the principle of parental choice selectively.

scription, whatever the cause, especially at times of falling school rolls or pupil-led funding. The desire for a balance in social or ethnic background among pupils, even at the cost of turning away some parents who could make a positive commitment to the school and/or the parish, appears stronger among some diocesan administrators than among school governor practitioners.

The exercise of parental choice, enshrined in section 76 of the 1944 Act and considerably strengthened by the 1988 Education Reform Act, has raised important questions for Church schools. The Parliamentary Private Secretary to Kenneth Baker commented at a conference on the role of Church schools:

> The parent must be getting something extra besides the level of religious instruction being conveyed in your school. I think many parents expect, for one reason or another, a higher standard of dedication amongst the staff, a higher standard of discipline in the school, and that indefinable something extra, perhaps some form of teaching that will act as a guide through the difficult years of adolescence and give the child something more to cling to than might immediately be apparent in the teaching of the State sector. (Culham College Institute, 1987, p. 23)

Anglicans

When many Anglican schools are oversubscribed, the high priority in admissions criteria of regular Church attendance (87 per cent of Church secondary schools in O'Keeffe's 1986 survey made this a first priority)[13] can result in a bias toward the 'domestic' responsibility of the Church school; for if the majority of pupils are from practising Anglican or Christian homes, the effect on the school's ethos, its approach to religious education and school worship may be significantly more 'Church-orientated'. By comparison, other Anglican schools which give a higher priority in admissions to siblings or 'ease of access' to the school, are placing more emphasis on the local community and are likely to admit a larger proportion of children of other faiths if the catchment area reflects substantial ethnic minorities. An article in the *Church Times* (1 June 1990) published a feature on an Anglican primary school in Nottinghamshire with the headline: 'The Church school that turns Church children away'. The school's admissions policy had placed a higher priority on residence in the parish, time on the waiting list, and siblings at the school than on Church links or parents' desire for Christian education. The vicar, also chairman of the governors, commented:

> The Church school is part of our Church life and our work, and yet the people who are the very members of our Church family cannot get their children in. But

---

[13]Culham's 1991 survey of London diocesan primary schools confirms this high priority (Gay, 1991a, p. 16).

if we changed the criteria and put those people first, it would have difficulties for people who live around the school and cannot get their children in. It would be dynamite. Do they then start coming to Church just to get their children in? I think we have a real ministry to those who don't come to Church.

The dangers of a fragmented society, highlighted by the Archbishop of Canterbury's 1985 report *Faith in the City*, suggest that there is a clear need for Church schools to play a part in the reconciliation of different social and ethnic groups (para. 13.91). They cannot hope to do this unless they see their role as serving the community as a whole, rather than exclusively looking after their own interests as a community of faith; indeed that community of faith itself commits Christians to an openness towards those who are not members. Many Anglican schools have followed the National Society's recommendations, in *A Future in Partnership* (1984), that oversubscribed Anglican schools should differentiate between foundation and non-foundation places, thereby retaining some balance between children committed to the local parish church and those living nearby who have no specific Anglican affiliation but who are part of the parish's wider community. O'Keeffe's 1986 survey showed that 61 per cent of headteachers interviewed thought such differentiation beneficial, while 29 per cent found it unacceptable. Comments of the majority included the following:

> 'The whole purpose of Christianity is to go out to all children.' 'I do not want a monastic settlement of committed Christians.' 'Our original foundation was set up to instruct pupils in the Christian faith, not reinforce/teach those already so instructed.' (pp. 46–7)

It is difficult to assess with any accuracy how far such moves towards a more 'general' selection procedure were the response to state school accusations of divisiveness and selection, at a time of falling rolls. *A Future in Partnership*, however, offered a theological justification by suggesting the model of the Church as identified with the suffering servant, 'ministering rather than being ministered unto', being thrown back into the world; a Church which directs all its energies to itself is 'ceasing to be a sign of the Kingdom' (National Society, 1984, p. 65).

Nevertheless, 'equipping the children of the Church to take their place in the Christian community' has always been an accepted part of the Church's 'domestic' responsibility and, with so many Anglican schools closely linked to their local parish or deanery, it is hardly surprising to find admissions criteria linked to clergy references, with one consequence an 'unseemly enthusiasm' for churchgoing in the weeks preceding school applications. It is ultimately up to the aided school governors, in consultation with the LEA, to determine their own admissions criteria. Parish clergy, who are often chairs of the governors, have a strong loyalty to their own parishioners, who may be reluctant to adopt a policy of balancing 'foundation' places for Anglicans with 'non-foundation' places for others in the community if the result were to mean excluding Church-affiliated families. The additional pressures of parental right of appeal against the governors' decisions, possessed since the 1980 Education Act, have made it essential that admissions criteria are explicit, removing any powers of discretion previously exercised by governors' admissions panels and simultaneously reinforcing the need for references on family church attendance.

In O'Keeffe's survey of Anglican schools (1986, pp. 37–8), 48 per cent of the 139 parents interviewed put Christian or Anglican education as the top priority in their choice of school, while only 28 per cent placed academic reasons first. The fact that 44 per cent put 'academic' as their first or second priority shows that this is clearly an important issue for a substantial number of parents, but that is hardly surprising considering that they are choosing a school. Stephen Ball argued, from O'Keeffe's evidence, that

> The attraction of the Church school for many parents who choose to send their children lies in image (and the reality) of the Church school as holding out the 'modalities and voice' of the lost world of the grammar school, academic reputation. What many parents seek from these schools is not, or not solely, a religiously grounded education but educational and social advantage. (In O'Keeffe, 1988, pp. 15–16)

Such comments seem somewhat tendentious. On the one hand, they underplay the religious motive in choice; on the other hand, they cloud the fact that educational advantage is a natural objective of parents from all backgrounds.

The publicity in 1987 caused by the claim of parents in Dewsbury, Yorkshire that, for cultural rather than racial reasons, their white children ought to be transferred from one Anglican school to another, placed in sharp relief the contrast between the Church school with a predominantly white Anglican intake and the comparable Anglican school nearby whose intake reflected a substantial proportion of families from other faiths, and where the broader admissions policy was strongly defended by the local vicar (also chairman of the governors) as serving the community. The optimism of the 1970 Durham Report, *The Fourth R*, in suggesting that the difficulties caused by parental choice would disappear if Church schools focused on their 'general' rather than 'domestic' responsibilities (para. 526), here seemed overstated. The ensuing public debate polarized those who attacked such attitudes as 'institutional racism' (*Times Educational Supplement* [*TES*], 9 October 1987) and those who prioritized freedom of choice (Baroness Hooper in *Daily Telegraph*, 16 November 1987).

How far should response to parental choice go? Should, for example, a single-sex Anglican school in a Muslim area admit large numbers of Muslim girls whose parents require single-sex education, regardless of the possible undermining of the school's predominantly Christian ethos and support from the local Anglican parish community? Or even, as was proposed in Birmingham in 1987, should a mixed Anglican school reopen as a single-sex, multi-faith girls' school, providing a workshop of 'cooperation and creativity by different religious communities' (report in *Church Times*, 20 February 1987)? This latter scheme never materialized, but the debate showed that Church schools were taking seriously the challenge made by the National Society in 1984, that the Church of England should 'return to its historic role as *pioneer* and seek those points within the education service where new initiatives are required' (1984, p. 54).

Inherent contradictions appear in the policies advocated for responding to parental choice. On the one hand, those who place no limit on admitting practising Anglican families are criticized for creating 'ghetto-type huddles'; on the other hand, those who admit families committed to other faiths, and therefore turn away practising Anglicans, could be criticized for, among other reasons, not responding to legitimate parental choice. Anglican schools, eager to face the ugly phenomenon of racism in British society yet anxious to uphold the principle of parental choice, find themselves in some embarrassment. The Church school which finds itself with a very high proportion of Muslim children in a predominantly Asian area may, for understandable and high-minded motives, be creating only an alternative ghetto which does little or nothing to bring about greater tolerance between faith communities.

In addition to the tensions already noted, there is the local factor. While the Church school in a multi-ethnic community may find the 'non-foundation' admissions helpful in achieving more integration, another in suburbia may wish to retain Church affiliation as a high criterion precisely with the object of drawing children from more diverse social backgrounds across a wider area, and thereby encouraging greater social reconciliation as an integral part of its Christian witness. The 'general' aim of Church schools in serving the nation tends to be more common in Anglican primary schools serving a specific local community than in secondary schools which usually draw children from a wider catchment area. Each governing body has to take into account social, educational and theological considerations in formulating an admissions policy appropriate to its own circumstances, while recognizing the important influence that such a policy will inevitably have on the entire ethos of the school.

Roman Catholics

The *Declaration on Christian Education* issued by the Second Vatican

Council on 28 October 1965 (Hastings, 1969) reiterated the importance of Catholic parents choosing Catholic education for their children, and of ensuring the availability of Catholic schools as of right. It pointed out that the aim of the Roman Catholic school was to create 'an atmosphere animated by the spirit of liberty and charity based on the Gospel' (Flannery, 1981, p. 732). The document left much unexplored. The pressure of other priorities, resulting in a short statement of principles in Catholic education, made it impossible for anything either radical or distinguished to be produced. The Council did not address itself to the question of the diversity of Catholic education: it passed over the purpose of education, its methods, philosophy and sociology. The document strongly stated that Christian education is 'for the world and in the world' but this was not costed out in terms of balancing the traditional purpose of educating Catholics with a Christian duty towards other children. More exactly, there was an acknowledgement, even an insistence, that Catholic schools would serve as a beacon to the wider society, but no consideration of the possibility of deliberately admitting other children to Catholic schools. The one important departure from previous stances was the document's emphasis on the need to recognize the Church's responsibility for the one-third of Roman Catholic pupils not taught in denominational schools (para. 7). It was frankly realized that, in the world as a whole, there were insufficient Catholic schools for the Church to maintain its previous canonical position. One could not threaten Catholic parents with excommunication if there was no school for them to send their child to.

To what extent are the premises of Roman Catholic schools' admissions policies similar to those of Anglican schools? Once a child has been baptized as a Roman Catholic, later attendance at church is not always a necessary criterion for admission to a Catholic school unless the school is oversubscribed: a high priority is often the parents' desire for Catholic education.[14] As Cardinal Hume commented, 'I believe in parental choice ... the right of Catholic parents to choose Catholic schools' (Hume, 1991b). Roman Catholic schools may not be faced with the exact equivalent of the nominally Anglican family which feels it has a right to send its child to the local Anglican school because being English means being Church of England, but the 'once a Catholic, always a Catholic' rationale is not unusual and there are many Catholic children from non-practising families in Catholic schools.

[14]The Department for Education (DfE) has based its forecasts for Catholic school places on parish baptismal register numbers. In Hornsby-Smith and Lee's survey (1980), 73 per cent of parents cited their own Catholic upbringing and the desire for a Catholic education as more influential factors in choosing a school for their children than the favoured school's ethos or academic standards.

Roman Catholics also have to address the issue of 'divisiveness' relating to their reluctance to admit non-Catholics. As in Anglican aided schools, selection on denominational criteria has led to allegations of being 'divisive by definition'. An additional accusation has been that many Catholic grammar schools were entrusted to religious orders, while the vast majority of Catholic children in secondary moderns were left to the laity. When Eric Bolton, then Chief HMI, asked the headteacher of a large Roman Catholic comprehensive why his exam results were better than those of neighbouring schools, he replied, 'There are good Catholics and bad Catholics; faced with oversubscription, we only choose good Catholics!' implying the use of unofficial academic selection criteria.

Roman Catholic admissions policies were challenged in 1991–2 when one Muslim and one Hindu girl were refused admission to an oversubscribed Catholic girls' comprehensive in Tower Hamlets and took their case to court. The policy of placing the criterion of Catholic and Christian affiliation higher than parental preference was deemed unlawful since it had not been formally agreed by the LEA (required under section 6(6) of the Education Act 1980). This decision was overturned on appeal in the House of Lords (June 1992), since the school was heavily oversubscribed. The diocesan director, it might be noted, was keen to point out that the school was 'happy to offer places to non-Christian children if there are available spaces'.

Ann Dummett is one Roman Catholic who has positively advocated a policy wider than the normal Catholic view that their schools are primarily for Roman Catholics. She has suggested that the modern Church school, as a service provided by, rather than for, the Church, should take less cognizance of the pupils' religious affiliations. Admitting Sikh or Muslim pupils, she argued, was 'a more important service to the local community in a racist society than to admit white ones' (Dummett and McNeal, 1981, p. 18). But she acknowledged that there is great danger in 'prescription' and the imposition of a single formula, because of the vast diversity of schools and catchment areas.

It is fair to say that there is some uncertainty and debate among Catholics about their traditional admissions policy. Cardinal Hume himself claimed that Catholics 'have much to contribute to the principles and practice of education in our society' (Hume, 1991b). Yet in insisting that Catholic parents should take their responsibilities seriously, he commented:

> It is not sufficient for Catholics to choose to send their children to a Catholic school simply because that school has a good academic record or good discipline . . . parents should also be embracing all that the school stands for in terms of the Catholic faith and practice. (Speech to the first National Conference on Catholic Education, 13 July 1992)

Catholic parents send their children to Catholic schools for a host of reasons other than catechesis. In the *Tablet* (17 August 1985) Mary Kenny even relegated 'Christian formation' to a subordinate clause, and concentrated on the importance of harmony between home and school values; and she suggested that most Catholic parents probably try to get their children admitted to Catholic schools for more practical reasons, such as impressive examination results or fewer ethnic-minority pupils. Kenny's article was followed by Anne Rogers' letter the following week, which suggested that the majority paid only lip-service even to 'shared Christian values', and that it remained the task of a minority of committed staff and parents to 'retrieve the situation and evangelise their own education system'; the huge investment of resources in schools for motives of evangelization and catechesis was misplaced. Cardinal Hume, addressing headteachers in September 1991, acknowledged their difficulties:

> Many of the families from which your pupils come are lapsed. Either they do not practise their faith or it is low among their priorities... I strongly urge you never to cease to strive to win for God the minds and hearts of the young under your care nor to lose sight of what a Catholic school should be.

There is also some evidence to suggest that Roman Catholic parents may not always be placing Catholic schools as their first choice, that their 'brand loyalty' is not holding up under market pressure. The then director of the Catholic Education Service noted in a personal interview in 1992 that, although 90 per cent of children in Roman Catholic primary schools were Catholics, in Catholic secondary schools the proportion fell to 62 per cent, a drop of 10–12 per cent over the last decade; the figures gave him cause for concern. Even if much of the drop may be explicable in terms of falling rolls and attracting non-Catholic families to make good the shortfall, some of it may be due to an increase in the Catholic families who choose non-Catholic schools.

This relatively new presence of significant numbers of non-Catholic children in Catholic schools creates an interesting situation. A number of studies have been undertaken, particularly by Leslie Francis (Francis, 1986; Francis and Egan, 1987, 1990) in Britain, Australia and America (following on the work of Greeley and others; see Flynn, 1979; O'Neill, 1979), to assess the influence of widening admissions on the effectiveness of a Catholic school. He identified three particular groups of pupils—practising Catholics, non-practising Catholics and non-Catholics—and noted that, while practising Catholics appreciated Catholic education, the other two groups without the congruence of home, school and parish were not so favourably disposed; he suggested that this arose from 'the incompatibility between their own religious background and the doctrinal, liturgical and catechetical assumptions of the schools'. Francis recommended two possible solutions: either the Catholic school should restrict its entry to practising Catholics, thereby strengthening 'the inculturation of the faith community' but excluding others who might benefit from Catholic educational provision; or it could recognize the contribution of the other groups and restructure its assumptions – 'far from weakening the distinctiveness of Catholic schools, such a strategy could help to secure a significant and appropriate Christian presence in education in a fast changing world'.

This latter view was supported by staff at St Philip's sixth form college in Birmingham when the Oratorian Fathers, as trustees, proposed in September 1992 that, because Roman Catholics amounted to less than 30 per cent of the student body, the college should close. Although it taught the largest number of Roman Catholics in any Birmingham sixth form, the trustees felt that the school could no longer claim to be 'Catholic'; their fear was exacerbated by new legislation which could not safeguard the college's religious identity. However, the Catholic staff argued that the measure of Catholicity 'cannot simply be confined to measures of religious practice, but must take into account the spiritual life of the school as a whole, witnessed to by the majority of those who come to it' (*Tablet*, 10 October 1992). The inter-faith environment encouraged Catholics to look beyond their own interests to the needs of the community at large and (as one Muslim student at St Philip's commented) others to learn from Catholics how to respect different religions.

Such examples throw into sharp focus the question of admission policies for Catholic schools. To what extent must the schools preserve or even protect their Catholic identity by allowing in only practising Catholics who will be responsive to Catholic formation and instruction? Or, in the spirit of the main thrust of Vatican II teaching, can they open their doors to the outside world, confident in the value and contribution of their own distinctive ethos and tradition? For both Anglicans and Roman Catholics addressing issues of admissions and parental choice, there is a fundamental difference between a school whose main aim is to preserve and to defend and one whose mission is to witness to the world.

4. RELIGIOUS EDUCATION AND CHRISTIAN NURTURE

To educate children in the Christian tradition as they have received it is the privilege and responsibility of both Anglican and Roman Catholic Church schools, enshrined in the legislation of 1944. But to what extent should such education nowadays be 'denominational'? Should it imply for example that a prime objective is to make Anglican children aware of what distinguishes their Church from, say, Roman Catholicism, or vice versa?

The Roman Catholic Church has traditionally held the view that its schools exist to teach Roman Catholic faith and morals to Roman Catholic children: the schools are the vehicle of catechetical instruction intended to bring the pupils to faith. Although Roman Catholic theologians would say that a proposition is defined by the Church because it is true, not true because defined by the Church, nevertheless the principal emphasis in school catechesis lay in the passing on of what authority has defined.

Many Anglican schools have reflected as strong a conviction that Christian nurture through the schools is integral to their role of serving the Church by encouraging Christian commitment, based upon proper knowledge and understanding.[15] Just as Roman Catholic schools would be unlikely to have hesitations about the importance of teaching their pupils the meaning of baptism or eucharist, so also Anglican schools may not be reticent, whether about the sacraments or the gospel or about providing specific instruction in the essentials of faith and Christian morality. The pupils' spiritual development is best nurtured within a particular faith community: 'religion is caught rather than taught' (Dean Inge).[16] If there are strong links to the local parish church, the school may be able to enrich the pupils' experience by encouraging participation in worship and exposition of the tenets that give form to religious faith. Indeed the expectation of many parish clergy is that the local Church school will be responding to their investment in the school of much time and parishioners' money by encouraging pupils to be active participants in parish worship on Sundays. An unhappy obverse tendency is for the clergy to blame the Church secondary school when pupils from the parish turn away from the Church in adolescence and treat their confirmation as a rite of passage signifying abandonment rather than acceptance of their baptismal contract.[17]

[15]During the debate in the General Synod in 1985 a delegate from the diocese of Chester, anxious that Anglican schools should be clear about their purpose, sought to table an amendment requiring Anglican Church schools to provide a 'definite and distinctive Christian environment, including a Christian education as reflected in the Church's creeds and historic formularies' (Kerfoot, 1985, p. 656). His amendment was rejected because his claim that the Church of England's role in education was 'uniquely significant' was considered by the Bishop of London to be unjust to schools of other Christian denominations.

[16]*Speculum Animae* (1911), p. 38. Inge continues: 'It is the religious teacher, not the religious lesson, that helps the pupil to believe.'

[17]This phenomenon can, of course, be found throughout Europe, and is not confined to Anglican situations. Leslie Francis' research *Rural Anglicanism* (1985), noted that the majority of Anglican clergy visited their local schools to take assemblies, but he regretted that too many Anglican clergy appointments are made to benefices containing Church schools without reference to the person's ability or interest in education (p. 99).

Expectations at the local level are echoed in national debate. The Earl of Arran, a Conservative whip speaking on behalf of the government in a parliamentary debate on 26 February 1988, commented that the option of sending children to aided denominational schools was open to parents who 'wish to have exclusively Christian education' (*Hansard*, col. 1484), and 'specifically want their children to participate in an entirely Christian act of worship' (ibid., col. 1495). The implication is clear: parents expecting an explicitly Christian nurture can and should turn to Church schools.

The results of Leslie Francis' research of 1986, *Partnership in Rural Education*, however, questioned the effectiveness of Anglican schools in nurturing their pupils, and indicated that children educated in Roman Catholic schools or even some county schools were likely to have a more informed and favourable attitude to Christianity. It seemed almost as if teachers in Anglican schools had become so hesitant about expressing their Christian values and convictions that the effect was more to inoculate than to nurture their pupils. Roman Catholic schools which uninhibitedly emphasized their commitment to their faith community appeared to gain a higher degree of response and commitment from their pupils. If so, it could readily be argued that Anglican schools ought to be more explicit in teaching their faith. Edward Norman commented that 'there is a groundswell sense that religious education should be precise, recognisable, unadulterated ... faithful belief in exact truths' (*The Times*, 16 December 1987).

O'Keeffe reflected that if the RE teacher in an Anglican Church school 'is not explicitly teaching for commitment on the part of the pupils, then R.E. will not differ significantly from that provided in county schools: one justification for Church schools would then be called in question' (1986, p. 117). The assumption in this comment, that 'teaching for commitment' is appropriate in RE classes, is not shared by all Christian educationists, Anglican or Catholic. A submerged ambiguity needs to be brought to the surface. A teacher of RE is not a preacher or an evangelist: the primary task is to inform, to bring to the pupils an awareness of historical facts, of moral and philosophical debates that have engaged the greatest minds, of the social as well as the individual significance of religious allegiance. Education is like an initiation into a journey of discovery in which both teacher and pupils co-operate and evaluate progress together: 'Such a philosophy of education presents those committed to teaching a revealed religion with quite new and special problems' (Bishops' Conference, 1981, p. 12).

Anglicans and Roman Catholics face similar questions in considering their approach to issues of pedagogy, religious education, nurture and catechetics. Should the phenomenological and confessional approaches to RE be categorically distinguished or do the assumptions inherent in such a polarization in recent years 'betray the poverty of our thinking' (Slee, 1989)? The long overdue rapprochement between the two may provide the opportunity to develop an RE programme which draws on the strengths of each, a model for which may already be found in joint Anglican/Roman Catholic schools.[18]

Anglicans

Religious education in Anglican schools 'will be of the highest possible quality' ... it 'may enable children to come to understand more fully what they believe' ... but 'religious nurture is the task of the parents and faith communities' (Lankshear, 1992a, p. 52).

This statement from the Church of England schools officer reflects both policy and practice in most Anglican schools, many of which are 'controlled' and therefore legally required to teach their LEA agreed RE syllabus. Even in 'aided' schools, where the RE programme is in accordance with the trust deeds and diocesan guidelines, the priority is to ensure good-quality RE teaching and learning, rather than to nurture pupils into Anglican doctrine.

> As in other areas of the curriculum, children and young people will be encouraged to develop attitudes of openness and enquiry and to engage in a search for truth. In this way they will come to understand what they believe and ... enter into the joys and challenges of an adult Christian faith.[19]

An education which is content-based, and primarily concerned with the transmission of ready-made formulae and solutions, may be unlikely also to focus on the process of bringing out the pupil's capacity to learn with understanding and personal autonomy. A contrast is often unconsciously assumed by which Christianity (or, for that matter, Judaism or Islam) is a religion of revelation and authority given by God and therefore is to be blindly received by the believer as a totality, whereas educating people is initiating them into a lifelong process of growth, development and change.[20]

[18]Such a rapprochement is advocated by John Hull (1984), Nicola Slee (1989), and contributors to Francis and Thatcher (1990).

[19]Cf. Lankshear (1992c), p. 10. Interestingly, St Augustine's little tract *On Catechizing the Uneducated* differentiated catechism from ordinary education in literature with the observation that learning by heart was inappropriate in teaching the faith, whereas it was normal in other subjects.

[20]In his 1852 lectures on *The Idea of a University*, Newman rejected as intolerable the submissive learning by rote and dictation in which the pupil is merely passive: serious education means that people learn to use their minds, to weigh evidence, to see inner connections (see Discourse 6). His *Essay on Development* (1845) discusses the notion of change and development in the understanding and formulation of Christian doctrine.

John Hull has argued that a polarization of nurture and education is misleading, since both Christian nurture and religious education require a degree of 'critical openness': for the former to ensure the continued vitality and relevance of Christian faith, for the latter to encourage people to think for themselves as autonomous individuals (Hull, 1984, ch. 18). As far back as 1976 the British Council of Churches attempted to tackle these questions in *The Child in the Church*,[21] advocating a theology in which critical openness is inherent in Christian commitment (para. 44).

> 'Christian nurture occupies a middle position between closed and authoritative instruction on the one hand, and open enquiring education on the other' (para. 57). 'Christian growth is not a matter of simply taking over the tradition ... but rather of responding to what is offered' (para. 73). 'Christian faith is constantly critical of itself. . . . There is no fixed form of nurture into it' (para. 60). 'What we pass on to our children is not the painting but the paint box' (para. 63).

In 1981 the British Council of Churches developed these ideas further in *Understanding Christian Nurture*. While Christian doctrine is important, the Church is not seen as issuing commands as if it embodied power, but as a community informing the conscience and providing a moral and spiritual atmosphere, an ethos of values rather than a sharply defined system of dogmas (paras 59, 287).

In reassessing their approach to Christian nurture, the school's contribution cannot be seen in isolation. The Anglican school may in practice achieve little in bringing about the moral formation of its pupils unless the individual pupil concerned is also within the Christian community. In the triangle formed by home, Church, and school, the task of the school, including the Church school, is education. In comparison with home and Church, school will always be an inefficient instrument for specific religious or moral instruction, for which it can at best be only supportive. This is not to suggest that this support will be unimportant, but rather that home and parish must be the primacy locus for faith development. The point is sharply made by the Anglican Bishop of Blackburn, Alan Chesters, that while the Church school has some responsibility to involve children in the worshipping life of the Church, 'only in the home can Christian parents be sure that a child is nurtured for Christ'.[22]

This perspective does not diminish the responsibility of the Church school to be and to be felt to be Christian, but merely removes the unrealis-

---

[21]The British Council of Churches (BCC) included representatives from the mainstream Protestant Churches. Roman Catholics, although not part of the BCC, became full members of its successor body Churches Together in England and its regional counterparts.

[22]His paper of 1988 is in Francis and Thatcher (1990), p. 290.

tic expectations of those who think such a school fails if it does not produce a body of practising Anglicans. Nothing is more damaging to the intellectual standing of religious education and to the open relationship between teacher and pupil than undue pressure which produces instinctive resistance and even long-lasting prejudice against religion.[23]

Religious education concerns an area of human life, thought and action where a commitment involving the entire personality of the individual is never far from the surface. It follows that there is a stronger consciousness here than in some other areas of the curriculum that unexamined prejudices can influence presentation, and this can invite the accusation of indoctrination. This is taken to mean, first, that the content of what is taught rests on assumptions and evidence which are not generally accepted as unshakeably true; secondly, that in inculcating belief it tends to appeal to authority rather than rational methods of enquiry; thirdly, that the teacher has the conscious intention of persuading the children to accept particular beliefs irrespective of evidence or argument, and this inhibits their development as autonomous persons with critical powers. Edwin Cox has written that

> teaching, however well intended, which closes minds to cogent considerations and to valid arguments, as indoctrination does, ought not to have a place in any establishment which claims to give education.[24]

The suspicion of indoctrination cannot be confined to Church schools. The prevailing secular humanism which claims to adopt a value-free neutrality based on objective and rational thinking may also incur the charge of indoctrination. A balanced view of the world accepts the validity of emotional and intuitive sensitiveness or individual interpretations of literature, for example, even though a scientific rationalism may be dismissive of these phenomena. There is also a powerful pressure on young people from the peer group and from the media.[25] The 'hidden curriculum', through which pupils absorb the sense of values that will stay with them for life, is often more deeply influential (in spite of its lack of quantitative accountability) than the overt, official curriculum.

Through this minefield, Edwin Cox outlined three ways for RE to move forward (1983, p. 108): first by marking a distinction between facts and beliefs, so that, when exploring the latter, pupils learn to respect views and

[23] A view shared by Michael Donley, 'Teaching discernment' in Watson (1992).

[24] Cox (1983), p. 106. See also e.g. Mitchell (1970), pp. 353–8; Hull (1984), p. 103; E. Thiessen in Francis and Thatcher (1990), pp. 215ff.; and Watson (1992), pp. 6, 7, 17, 128.

[25] A classic psychological analysis of the influence of the peer group occurs in the second book of St Augustine's *Confessions*. On his adolescent gang who stole pears, he writes: 'Alone I would never have done it' (viii, 16).

judgements which they may not share themselves; secondly, recognizing our pluralist culture in which differing beliefs can be examined sympathetically and openly; thirdly, by awareness of the possible influence of the teacher's own beliefs upon the presentation of the subject-matter. He also warned against the opposite danger that, in an effort to avert any charge of indoctrination, the RE teacher may resort to a sterile teaching of dry facts and lose 'the sense of adventure and commitment which is characteristic of religion' (ibid., p. 109).

Is it possible for the personally committed teacher to distinguish between enthusiasm for a subject and attempts to persuade pupils into one way of life rather than another? (See Sealey, 1985, p. 74.) Or might the seriously searching agnostic do a better job by sharing in the pupils' enquiry and quest? Since Edward Hulmes' book *Commitment and Neutrality in Religious Education* (1979), the pendulum seems to have swung away from detached neutrality towards a recognition that all teachers, whether of religion, science or technology, can prove most effective when their personal interest and commitment inspires the children to become actively involved in the learning process. The 'search for a faith by which to live' is more likely to be taken seriously if convictions are acknowledged and respected; greater toleration and understanding are encouraged by 'a frank declaration of commitment and an open recognition of continuing religious and philosophical differences'.[26] Hulmes has also argued that 'commitment is both the point of departure and the final goal of religious education. The seeking, the questing, the finding, the revising are all stages in commitment' (1979, p. 87). The teacher's sense of commitment is therefore a factor in moving the pupil to take religion seriously.

Proselytizing may be inappropriate in the classroom in Church schools. But the teacher's personal commitment may rightly encourage pupils to explore religious and moral issues across the curriculum (e.g. in literature or history), and at the same time enrich their understanding of their own faith through a genuine encounter with religious beliefs as practised by others coming from families of different world faiths. Pupils who already know from inside something of what religion is about have a vantage point from which to look sympathetically at beliefs and practices of other faiths.

One problem for the teaching of religion in Anglican schools emerges from the climate of misty liberalism which can make Anglican teaching seem elusive. It is not characteristic of many Anglicans to be strongly aware of what their faith is in contrast with that of other Christian bodies, or at least to be able to state with any accuracy and precision what makes Angli-

[26]E. Hulmes in Cole (1978). Edwin Cox has a comparable comment that the teachers' confident but unaggressive belief should be matched with 'a commitment to the belief that genuine study and critical search for understanding will lead to truth' (1983, p. 56).

cans different from Roman Catholics or Baptists. However, the recent revisions of agreed syllabuses have encouraged the publication of more RE textbooks which provide useful accounts of belief and practice in different Christian denominations.[27]

There are Anglican schools which see themselves as primarily serving the local community rather than the Church of England, and these may be drawn more to general religious and moral education in preference to specific Anglican instruction. Because Anglican schools have usually had a more 'general' focus then Roman Catholic schools, the debate on an appropriate approach to RE has not seemed dissimilar to that in county schools, especially in relation to indoctrination and nurture. One RE teacher in O'Keeffe's 1986 survey suggested: 'It is much easier in Roman Catholic schools—their schools are for Catholic children. Our schools have to cope with materialist youngsters from materialist homes' (p. 99).

Where Church schools have a high proportion of Muslim pupils for example, the question presses whether it is appropriate to provide Christian education at all, or whether it is right to adopt a general theistic approach, exploring areas of common belief between Christianity and Islam. By working with themes that are characteristically but not distinctively Christian, yet avoiding the accusation of multi-faith 'mishmash', the teacher may promote mutual respect and understanding in the local community. In the *Church Times* (20 February 1987) the Director of Education for the Anglican diocese of Birmingham commented on this:

> The Church of England has never been, and is not, in education to make a denominational point, but rather nowadays to contribute to, and perhaps influence, the whole. Church of England schools play an important role in multi-ethnic and multi-faith areas in bringing the religious communities face to face, dispelling ignorance and prejudice, and so enabling non-Christian children to gain a more positive outlook on Christianity.[28]

By contrast, this 'open' approach was unacceptable to the vicar of St Matthew's Church, Blackburn, who resigned as chairman of governors of his Church primary school because he could not rely on diocesan support, or that of other governors, for his proposal that Muslim parents ought to agree to their children receiving some instruction in Christianity if they were admitted to the school (*TES*, 21 June 1986). The view of the Blackburn diocese was also reflected by teachers of religious education: one teacher from a school where 85 per cent of the pupils came from Christian homes said: 'Most pupils do not have a personal faith. It is the job of the Church.

[27]For example the Chichester Project materials (Lutterworth Press).

[28]See also Meakin (1988): RE has a significant role in 'fostering tolerance'.

The school is not a pew-filler for the Church of England. Religious Studies is an academic subject' (O'Keeffe, 1986, p. 99).[29]

The national debate on the curriculum has been gathering momentum since 1988, and Church schools should be in a position to take a lead in the development of the 'spiritual' dimension within the curriculum following the DfE Circular 1/94. As the National Society has said:

> In a society which generally preaches a secular materialistic ethic, particularly through the media and commercial activity, some form of positive discrimination in favour of the religious dimension of life is required in curricular provision in schools. (1984, p. 81)

In the 1989 Culham survey of Church primary schools in the diocese of London, one headteacher described the role of the Anglican school as

> witness in its wider sense. The state system is either secular or too multi-faith to have a clear message. . . . While not seeking to evangelize, it is hoped that children will look back on their school days with pleasure and regard the Church as significant in their lives and grow up with a sense of God as their heavenly Father. A deeper faith than this is the responsibility of the Church, not the school. (Gay, 1989, p. 11)

A Church school RE teacher in O'Keeffe's survey took up the challenge: 'I am not trying to turn out good Anglicans, but to show them that a religious outlook on life is still a viable option in the twentieth century' (1986, p. 96). The Anglican school which succeeds in this aim could be said to have scored a noteworthy achievement.

Roman Catholics

By contrast with Anglican schools, the task of the Catholic school has traditionally been explicit catechetical instruction, ensuring that by the time children leave they have already moved beyond first communion and con-

---

[29]It is often assumed that for county schools teaching for religious commitment is inappropriate. Yet O'Keeffe's survey also showed that as many as 18 per cent of RE teachers in county schools saw their task as Christian nurture and their school as 'a Christian community as much as a Church school would be' (1986, p. 118). Surprisingly, 36 per cent of county schools understood their approach to religious education to be 'confessional', while 55 per cent of Church schools considered their approach to be open-ended in 'enabling pupils to become aware of the relevance of a religious interpretation to life'. Such varieties of approach suggest that there is considerable diversity in interpreting the role of Christian nurture in schools in general.

firmation; in short, by the time they reach the 'outside world', they are signed-up Church members. However, we shall see that in recent years a number of influential Catholic educationists in England have also manifested a certain hesitation about the appropriateness of the catechetical role for today's Catholic schools.

The traditional catechesis based on the Creed, the seven sacraments and the Ten Commandments was modified in the 1960s as interest increased in the biblical and liturgical movements rooted in the traditions of the early Church and reflected in the work of theologians such as Jungmann. By the late 1970s the shift to a more 'implicit' approach can be seen in the development of an 'experiential' or 'incarnational' model of catechetics (see O'Leary and Sallnow, 1982) not dissimilar to the 'implicit' phase of British RE and influenced by the theology of Gabriel Moran. The Veritas catechetical programme also incorporated much of Kohlberg's work on moral development. At the same time, the increasingly positive view of the contribution of other Christian Churches and world faiths, alongside the developments in liberation theology, encouraged Roman Catholic teachers to broaden their understanding and experience of approaches to religious education and theological developments in Europe and America. The work of Kevin Nichols in reassessing the appropriateness of catechetics to the British RE classroom was also highly influential in the 1980s. However, tensions between those who want a return to more traditional catechetics and the many Catholic RE teachers who have adopted a more pupil-centred approach to RE, seem to have emerged in the 1990s.

In 1979 Pope John Paul II declared: 'The school provides catechesis with possibilities that are not to be neglected.' A Catholic school would no longer deserve this title if 'there were justification for reproaching it for negligence or deviation in strictly religious education. Let it not be said that such education will always be given implicitly and indirectly. The special character of the Catholic school, the underlying reason for it, the reason why Catholic parents should prefer it, is precisely the quality of the religious instruction integrated into the education of the pupils' (Sacred Congregation, 1979, para. 69).

At the same time the family was clearly recognized by Catholic authority as the place in which catechesis had to be rooted. The school was not expected to take over this role from the parents, nor should the parents expect the school to do so, however inadequately trained they might feel. The parish had to support the parents in their difficult task.[30] Pope John Paul II stated: 'Family catechesis precedes, accompanies and enriches all forms of catechesis' (ibid., para. 68).

In the statement *The Catholic School* (1977), issued under the authority

[30]This view is restated by Cardinal Hume (1988a).

of the Sacred Congregation for Catholic Education, this idea was developed:

> It is recognised that the proper place for catechesis is the family helped by other Christian communities, especially the local parish. But the importance and need for catechetical instruction in Catholic schools cannot be sufficiently emphasised. Here young people are helped to grow towards maturity in faith. (para. 51)[31]

How have Roman Catholic educationists attempted to apply general principles from Rome and Westminster to the reality of English classrooms? If catechesis is a 'dialogue between believers', and presupposes faith (however immature) on the part of the catechumen, to what extent is it appropriate, when even among Roman Catholic pupils it is doubtful whether personal belief can or should be presumed any longer? While committed Catholic parents will send their children to Catholic schools,[32] the pupils themselves may not necessarily share that commitment, and cannot have it forced upon them. A captive audience is no guarantee of successful catechesis; in fact, the result is only too likely to be a generation of lapsed Catholics (as prophesied by Dr Jack Dominian in *The Tablet*, 31 August 1985).

Roman Catholic educationists have had to reassess the place of catechesis in education, guided by the work of theologians such as Jungmann,[33] and Moran.[34] A certain progression in this questioning over time can be observed, particularly by comparing the views of three successive national advisers to the Catholic bishops on catechesis.

[31]Among the major statements from Rome since Vatican II, the *General Catechetical Directory* (Sacred Congregation, 1971) surprisingly discussed children's catechesis with scarcely a reference to Roman Catholic schools as having a part to play. It focused rather on the role of parents and of trained catechists. Either the document took it for granted that trained catechists would work among young people within their schools and so did not mention the matter, or else perhaps we may infer that the Sacred Congregation had come to consider catechesis to be appropriate primarily for the parish and the home.

The relationship between religious education and catechesis is further discussed in Moran (1989), p. 157.

[32]Yet in their 1977 survey of Roman Catholic opinion, Hornsby-Smith and Lee found that of the 31.5 per cent of parents who chose Catholic schools for their children because they wanted to 'ground them in the faith', some 20 per cent rarely or never attended mass (Hornsby-Smith and Lee, 1980).

[33]*The Good News and Our Proclamation of the Faith* (1936) criticized contemporary catechetics for its narrow doctrinal focus, advocating a return to the early apostolic Church's 'kerygmatic' theology. See also Rahner (1968): catechesis is 'the proclamation of the word of God in view of the education of man to faith' (vol. 1, pp. 263ff.).

In the late 1970s Monsignor Kevin Nichols, the first national adviser, published two influential books, *Cornerstone* (1978) and *Orientations* (1979). He recognized the dilemma of attempting to catechize pupils in Catholic schools when many were clearly at the pre-catechetical stage; but he resisted the temptation to polarize religious education and catechesis.[35] Rather he insisted that

religious education is a particular mode or style of catechesis. It is the educational mode, the one which stresses the development of understanding, analysis, and thoughtfulness in faith. There is no essential reason why religious education properly so called should not go on within a community of faith such as our Church. (Nichols, 1978, p. 15)

Catechesis can take an educational form which respects freedom, encourages growth and personal development. (Ibid., p. 26)

He went on to emphasize that the catechist, in handing on a living tradition of faith, must make it relevant to the pupils, allowing them 'free adherence to God in faith'. At the same time, other elements of catechesis will be present in a Church school through 'the quality of relationships and pastoral care, the school community and its liturgy' (Nichols, 1979, p. 20).

The 1981 report to the Bishops' Conference of England and Wales, *Signposts and Homecomings* (produced by a three-year study group chaired by Bishop David Konstant[36]), made no attempt to define religious education or catechesis, sensing perhaps that Nichols had already attempted that for them. It acknowledged the use of 'religious education' when speaking of 'some formal process of learning and instruction', and 'catechesis' when emphasising 'the development of faith itself' (p. 25). But it recognized that

for Catholics traditionally the idea of handing on the faith in its cultural context has been an overriding educational aim. The notion of promoting critical reflection in pupils seems at odds with this, for it would encourage questioning rather than loyalty to tradition. (p. 65)

The report went on to suggest that RE, like catechesis, is part of the process

---

[34] *God Still Speaks* (1967) criticized the traditional catechists' appeal through 'sentimentality and fear' (p. 42) and argued that their task 'is not the divine task of saving children, but rather the human task of freeing men for life in the Spirit by awakening intelligence and freedom'. See also Moran (1966), p. 135 and (1968), p. 13.

[35] See also K. Nichols, in Watson (1992), pp. 116ff.

[36] Chairman of the Catholic Education and Formation Council and involved in preparing the English text of the *Catechism of the Catholic Church* first promulgated in December 1992.

of inducting pupils into a way of life, which in a Catholic context will of course be Catholic,[37] and argued for a higher priority for adult catechesis. While the new directions of Vatican II were clearly discernible in this document, there were doubts however that the report could offer constructive and realistic assistance to the classroom teacher caught between the apparently conflicting demands of catechesis and RE.[38] Roman Catholic views on this central subject were already beginning to shift from thinking of classroom RE as explicit catechesis, or vice versa, to a position more attuned to the reality facing the teacher. Catechetical instruction presupposes faith, and should be a voluntary activity if conducted within denominational schools; the Catholic school will want to support catechesis in the parish (RE teachers may even be involved in the classes outside school hours), and students may attend in their own time voluntarily. This minimizes any confusion deriving from the juxtaposition of catechesis and RE on the timetable, and allows each to develop along its own lines.[39] Both could still be regarded as 'education in a Christian context' but, from the pupils' point of view, the 'handing down of a living tradition' to nurture faith would be distinguishable from a more general study of religion, which we have noted is normally characteristic of much RE in Anglican schools.

This distinction is worrying to some Roman Catholics. Paddy Walsh of the London Institute put it in an acute form:

[37]To paraphrase the document's development of this point: Catholic education has to reflect four elements to ensure 'the opportunity to grow towards responsible freedom according to the mind of Christ' (p. 121). First, a perspective—centred on faith in Christ as Saviour of all men—is essential and among other ways may be given in explicit religious teaching. Secondly, a deep respect for the individuality and integrity of all human beings must allow room for personal growth and development. Thirdly, Catholic education recognizes 'that all men and women without exception are the children of God and included in the scope of Christ's redemptive love'. Fourthly, 'education is part of the Church's mission to the world, perpetuating the salvific work of Christ'.

[38]See Paul Hirst (1981) and (1974), p. 80. John Hull (1976) argued that Christian theology and educational theory should not be polarized.

[39]'The parish is in essence the principal catechetical centre ... our expectations of home and school have been unrealistic' (Sector E Report of the National Pastoral Congress, 1981, pp. 213ff.). The Bishops' Report continued: 'What can be expected of a Catholic school are a knowledge and understanding of the content of the faith, the experience of a Christian caring community and the experience of a living liturgy' (National Pastoral Congress, 1981, para. 136). Lay Catholics in Schools (Sacred Congregation, 1982) emphasized that 'the teaching of the Catholic religion, distinct from and at the same time complementary to catechesis ... ought to form a part of the curriculum in every school' (para. 56).

If ever we who are Catholics did come to accept a sharp form of this distinction [between education and catechesis], we should have lost a large part of our rationale for having Catholic schools. (O'Leary, 1983, p. 12)

If the language seems strong, it is defended and justified by the considerations that nurture in Christian truth and relationships is a profound educational experience for the pupils, that schools are better staffed than parish catechetical classes could ever be, and that nurturing RE should have an enriching effect on other subjects in the curriculum.

The good Church school will be quite simple and straightforward about having as its ideal the nurturing in its pupils of a faith in God and in Christ that is explicit, clear, intelligent, articulate, open-minded and sincere. (Ibid., p. 13)

At the same time it will 'respect the unbelievers and searchers in its own midst—and that goes also for teachers in this position'; it will avoid indoctrination by encouraging freedom of speech and acknowledging 'the validity of non-commitment' (p. 14).

It must be a question whether these comments did not presuppose the time when Catholic schools were comparatively easy to fill with committed Catholic teachers and pupils.[40] *Signposts and Homecomings* (Bishops' Conference, 1981, p. 32) showed that in maintained Catholic secondary schools in 1980, 33.6 per cent of all staff were non-Catholic, in independent Catholic schools 34.6 per cent.[41] Of course the proportion of Catholic RE staff is likely to be higher, but the Vatican has not traditionally singled out RE in this way, insisting instead that the whole curriculum should reflect Catholic teaching. Moreover, evidence suggests that the explicit confessional environment has come, at least in some cases, to antagonize rather than to nurture. Hornsby-Smith and Lee's (1980) survey, *Roman Catholic Opinion*, showed that 32 per cent of those questioned who would not choose a Roman Catholic school for themselves, if given a second chance, gave as their reason 'too much emphasis on religion'; 23 per cent felt that Catholic schools were 'too much of a closed community', 'too narrow', or even 'too bigoted', perhaps reflecting the more indoctrinatory approach of the past.

The same survey also revealed that the majority considered religious education to be the responsibility of the parents, not of the school.[42] Fur-

[40]Further criticism of Walsh's views is found in McLaughlin (1992).

[41]A two to one majority is no doubt substantial, but the figures point to increasing difficulty in finding practising Catholics to teach in these schools; in 1970 it was 26.3 per cent in maintained Catholic schools.

[42]Of the 74 per cent who agreed with this, 18 per cent agreed strongly; of the 11.4 per cent who disagreed, only 1 per cent disagreed strongly.

thermore, while just over a third of those questioned thought that Catholics should be taught in separate schools, significantly just under half thought they should not be segregated.[43] These half-articulate feelings raise the issue whether catechetics should still be the foundation stone on which a Catholic school is constructed. As already noted, the isolationism too often implicit in the traditional idea of handing on the faith and avoiding contamination by the secular (or the Protestant or the Anglican) world must be viewed as outdated, especially in the light of the changed Catholic self-consciousness since Vatican II (*Gaudium et Spes*, para. 40ff.).[44]

Nichols' successor as national adviser, Patrick Purnell SJ, faced up more fully to the reality that more and more parents remain uncommitted; since 'many of them send their children to Catholic schools for non-religious reasons . . . faith-sharing is no longer possible'. In the Catholic school, 'dignity and freedom are threatened where pupils are told by an authority (which they are taught to accept and respect by the cultural context of their lives) what to believe. . . . Hence the classroom is not the right setting for deliberately evangelising pupils nor is it the place where catechesis occurs' (Purnell, 1985, pp. 73–5). His more liberal, implicit approach to religious education in schools encouraged respect for individual autonomy, knowledge and understanding of religious tradition and an appreciation of the experience of faith.

These issues were taken up by his successor as co-ordinator of the National Project of Catechesis and Religious Education, Jim Gallagher. In his 1986 *Guidelines: Living and Sharing our Faith*, he set out the bishops' priorities: to help adults mature in Christian faith; to create a greater partnership between home, parish and school in catechesis and religious education; and to clarify the roles of parents, teachers, priests, catechists and others (p. 7). He noted that RE, catechesis and evangelization were distinct (even if in practice they might overlap)[45] and that the emphasis had shifted from the exclusive view to a broader understanding of catechetics as a lifelong process of education in faith, involving the whole community (p. 17). In *Our Schools and Our Faith* (1988), Gallagher explained

[43]From the latter group, a major reason given was that the system of formal religious socialization is less important in an increasingly secular world, where religion is now considered by many to be mainly a private individual matter. Others went further, suggesting that the religious divisions perpetuated by separate Catholic education ought to be removed.

[44]The storm of protest which at Vatican I in 1870 greeted Bishop Strossmayer's declaration that there were Protestants who truly loved God would be unthinkable a century later.

[45]Cf. the Vatican document, *The Religious Dimension of Education in a Catholic School* (Sacred Congregation, 1988), para. 68.

we are concerned to justify the existence of our schools on sound pastoral and educational grounds. We wish to uphold their Catholic character in ways which enable us to offer a distinctive yet genuine form of education for all pupils who attend our schools and which respects the gifts of all members of staff.... (p. 10)

Religious education is not *primarily* concerned with maturing and developing Christian faith. Its aim is to help people to be aware of and appreciate the religious dimension of life and the way this has been expressed in religious traditions. It should at the same time encourage people to examine their own religious attitudes and to respect those of others. (pp. 12ff.)

To assist RE teachers, the project produced a 'basic framework' for RE (rather than a teaching programme), entitled *Weaving the Web* (Lohan and McClure, 1988) for 11–14-year-olds and *Here I Am* (Byrne and Malone, 1992) for primary children. Evaluation of *Weaving the Web* showed that, although its format and approach were widely welcomed by teachers and pupils,[46] since it met the needs of a wide range of pupils' ability and faith development, it tended to be misused by inexperienced teachers as a substitute scheme of work. The Vatican's Congregation of the Clergy endorsed the use of the '*Web*' in schools as part of 'a flexible framework for curriculum planning' and dioceses like Westminster recommended it, while complementing it with diocesan syllabuses and in-service training.

However, exercising their legitimate local episcopal authority, two dioceses (Birmingham and Salford) considered the programme 'defective' as an expression of Catholic doctrine, and advocated an alternative scheme (the 'New Christian Way', published by Veritas).[47] A storm of protests (especially in the *Catholic Herald* in the autumn of 1991) decried the lack of teaching of the Catholic faith in schools funded by the 'sacrifices of the faithful few', the confusion of 'religious tolerance with religious indifferentism', the watering down to the 'lowest common denominator' of what is distinctly Catholic, and religious sociology replacing teaching on Christ, the Church and sacraments. Pressure groups such as Pro Ecclesia et Pontifice lobbied bishops to re-examine their endorsement in the light of the new

---

[46]One head of RE praised 'the easy continuity between the experiential and more specifically theological material' (*Tablet*, 22 February 1992).

[47]See Mgr Daniel McHugh, Birmingham archdiocese's RE director, in *Catholic Herald*, 6 December 1991. Conservative criticism mounted when the '*Web*' was 'highly recommended' by the secular educational press: if it 'could just as well have emanated from a religiously neutral secular body ... it represents a capitulation to the canons of fashionable secular orthodoxy' (Kevin Preston, RE Adviser to the archdiocese of Birmingham, *Universe*, 2 February 1992). The Catholic novelist Piers Paul Read even accused it of portraying Jesus as a 'Che Guevara of the ancient world'.

Catechism. Fuelled by the parallel demands of the 'back to basics' campaigners for the National Curriculum and the increasingly vociferous 'parental complaints' lobby, the conservative groundswell was considerable. The theologian John Redford argued that Catholic schools are 'confessional', not 'denominational', in that they 'promote a specific belief system'; he asked the 'bishops to consider an appropriate syllabus in line with the new Catechism, since Catholic RE will . . . always be aiming to lead pupils to faith in Jesus Christ' (*Tablet*, 22 February 1992).

From the evidence we have considered, it seems clear that the current concerns among teachers and theologians about traditional catechesis in Catholic schools arise from more than one cause. All other curriculum subjects are taught in a style which encourages active participation by the pupils. The then director of the Catholic Education Service commented in 1992: 'the parents who expect RE to be taught in the way it was 20 years ago wouldn't expect that of science!' In part the doubts about catechesis spring from the plain fact that good Roman Catholic theology no longer makes such absolute assertions of the exclusive claims of the Roman Catholic Church to be the one ark of salvation; there is a more positive appreciation of authentic faith and love in other Christian bodies (1983 Code of Canon Law, canon 383.3), even if the spirit of conservative caution is far from exorcized. The modern concept of the Church as making an appeal to the conscience, and as being more witnessing than magisterial, is one that can easily be discerned in Roman Catholic writers of recent decades, such as Yves Congar.[48] Yet in part the hesitations also spring from the rising flood-waters of contemporary secularism, and from a loss of general confidence that the other-worldly message of the Church speaks to the condition of twentieth-century society. As the Westminster diocesan director, Kathleen O'Gorman, commented, the proper focus for conservative critics 'is the terrible, swamping pressure of a society which fastens on the functional and materialistic at the expense of the spiritual, moral and aesthetic. These pressures are no less strong within Catholic schools' (*Daily Telegraph*, 31 December 1991). Roman Catholics, as much as Anglicans, need to feel that Christianity is being taught in Church schools in a way that respects the conscience of the individual (both pupil and teacher), enhances its academic credibility and encourages young people to relate the challenge of the gospel to their own lives.

> With the emergence of a strong ecumenical movement, the Christian Church should be sufficiently at one to permit at least our educational efforts to be named by the generic term 'Christian religious education', which reminds us that we are all called to a universal Christian Church. In this a basic unity is both affirmed and proposed as a vision. (Groome, 1980, p. 24)

---

[48] For example *Priest and Layman* (1967), especially ch. 21 on pluralism.

5. CHRISTIAN ETHOS, VALUES AND CULTURE

The ethos of a school is so elusive a thing that it is tempting to suggest it is discernible only by some sort of intuition or hunch. One often hears people say 'I just feel the Christian atmosphere in the school'. Nevertheless the intuitive approach makes the task of appraisal or evaluation difficult: it may make it too easy to shy away from awkward questions such as 'What does the school believe it stands for?' It may prevent a school from responding promptly or positively to the changes in the surrounding community from which the children come. If the school is to anticipate the needs of society and to respond appropriately to its expectations, it has to develop its 'prophetic role', asking such questions as 'How does the school come to understand or question the values of society?' 'Does the school make a positive attempt to promote understanding of cultural/racial/national/ international dimensions?' Through this self-critical reflective approach, a Church school has the opportunity for self-renewal, rooted in the growth of the Christian community and responsive to the message of the gospel. The viewpoint of this chapter is that its ultimate allegiance should not induce a policy of defensive isolation from the outside world, but rather endorse an affirmative approach to the community around the school.

That Church schools exist to uphold Christian values may safely be regarded as non-controversial. There may be debate, however, if one asks to what extent parents look upon such schools as a welcome oasis in the arid desert of secularist values, dominated by market forces or by mere hedonism. Are parents expecting Church schools to provide a haven where right and wrong are rather more than hurrah or boo, a secure defence against a colder world which has become more impersonal, secular, and 'humanist' in the sense of rejecting the role of religion as a vehicle of morality and culture? (See O'Keeffe, 1986, p. 85.)

Secular institutions which include a wide diversity of opinion instinctively wish to treat all opinions, especially moral and religious opinions, as equally valid (or invalid): moral judgements quickly become matters to be relegated to the area of private decision by individuals. The term 'reasonable' is usually intended to mean that it will somehow be conducive to happiness, whether for the individual (i.e. eudaemonism) or for the greatest possible number in the community (i.e. utilitarianism).

Christian schools are faced with a problem of discernment here. To what extent can Christian values be assumed to be embedded in the moral values of contemporary society, and therefore implicit in the educational process? Or is it necessary for Christian schools to be more explicit in identifying and stressing Christian standards over against the values of the secular world? Christians are obviously not the only people to stand for the stability of the family or for honesty in commercial dealings, both being concerns of wide consequence for the quality of public life; but such concerns are certainly profoundly characteristic of Christian moral teaching. The anxiety expressed by parents and by government officials about declining moral standards or about the general ignorance of the Christian presuppositions underlying English culture (the kind of ignorance that makes much of Shakespeare and Milton remote and puzzling) suggests that a more explicit endorsement is needed.[49]

Pressure groups have been gathering momentum since the 1988 Education Reform Act to persuade the government to approve the establishment of more maintained schools for specific religious faiths and denominations. Like the Muslims, the Christian Schools' Movement has argued that central and local government, by blocking applications for aided status, were 'failing to honour the right of parents to have their children educated in harmony with religious and philosophical convictions as enshrined in the European Convention on Human Rights' (*Education*, 20 June 1990). This campaign, supported by representatives of all parties in the House of Lords, was further fuelled by the assumption that even Church schools were not sufficiently explicit in their endorsement of the values inherent in Christian faith, compromising their Christian character for state financial aid. The senior staff of one evangelical Christian school endorsed their school's all-pervasive ethos: 'We feel very strongly about discipline ... we're not an indoctrinating centre, but we allow no deviation from the rules' (*Daily Telegraph*, 4 March 1993). The 1993 legislation may facilitate the development of new independent Christian schools, but some opponents warn of the dangers of divisive sectarianism, that 'parental choice ... must be balanced with the needs of society and those real consumers, the children themselves' (Baroness Flather, *Hansard*, 4 March 1991, col. 1265). The Swann Report *Education for All* (1985) argued: 'It is essential ... to look ahead to educating all children, from whatever ethnic group, to an under-

[49]For example, the then Secretary of State for Education and Science, Kenneth Baker, commented in *The Times* on 1 February 1988: 'Children should be grounded in fundamental values like honesty, responsibility, self-respect and respect for others. . . . This government no less than the Churches wants to enhance the moral dimension of education.' The public outrage in February 1993 following the arrest for murder of two primary-age children stimulated the debate further. The then chairman of the National Curriculum Council, David Pascall, endorsed the role of the school in supporting parents 'by having a clear vision of the moral values which they and society hold to be important' (National Curriculum Council, 1992); see also *TES* leader of 26 February 1993, 'Stumbling out of a moral vacuum'. Baroness Cox has described the failure of schools to provide young people 'with an opportunity to become familiar with some of the most precious expressions of Christian faith which are part of this country's heritage' as a 'dreadful betrayal' (*Hansard*, 26 February 1988, cols 1454–5).

standing of the shared values of our society as a whole as well as to an appreciation of the diversity of lifestyles and cultural, religious, and linguistic backgrounds which make up this society and the wider world' (ch. 6, para. 14). The principle of 'diversity within unity' (ch. 1, para. 6) should reflect 'a genuinely pluralist society, as both socially cohesive and culturally diverse' (ch. 1, para. 5).[50]

More recently, anxiety has been expressed that the government is seeking to return to an assimilationist rather than a pluralist approach,[51] through its insistence on British ethnocentricity, for example in the National Curriculum Programmes of Study for history or English.

These tensions between diversity and unity have been explored by Edward Hulmes, among others.[52] The danger is that endorsing religious pluralism can risk a slide into mere relativism, which in turn can lead to greater demands for the recognition of sectional interests.

> In default of agreement about the limits of tolerance in a pluralist society, and about the role of education in helping to preserve a measure of social cohesion and integrity, it must be asked if unity, in all but a superficial sense, is possible. (Hulmes in Watson, 1992, p. 130)

[50]In spite of a dissenting minority of six of its members, the final report expressed 'misgivings about the implications and consequences of separate provision of any kind explicitly catering for ethnic minority group pupils', since this would undermine the principle that all pupils should 'share a common educational experience which prepares them for life in a truly pluralist society' (ch. 8, para. 2.11).

[51]The then Prime Minister Margaret Thatcher's negative attitude to religions outside the Judaeo-Christian tradition (lamenting their disregard for 'the worth of the individual', *TES*, 20 April 1990) reinforced this belief. A *TES* leader (8 June 1990) commented:

> The truth is that the Government, in its resistance to multicultural approaches, is simply demonstrating its suspicion of other cultures in general. . . . The aim presumably is that as many ethnic minority school-leavers as possible should pass Norman Tebbit's cricket test (i.e. which side they would support in a test match between e.g. England and Pakistan or the West Indies).

In January 1991 David Konstant, Roman Catholic Bishop of Leeds and chairman of the RC Bishops' Education Committee, spoke in support of extending voluntary-aided status to schools for Muslims and children of other minority faiths. In the magazine *Education* (December 1990) the chairman of the Church of England Board for Education, Bishop Michael Adie of Guildford, had already expressed similar views. Both bishops urged that such schools follow the National Curriculum and provide equal opportunities for girls and boys (report in *Church Times*, 11 January 1991).

[52]Hulmes (1989); also in Watson (1992), ch. 8 and McClelland (1988).

Hulmes considers that recognition of the creative value of diversity can contribute to a sense of unity. Are Anglican and Roman Catholic schools able to offer a coherent contribution to this debate? We have already noted the implications of, for example, divisive admission policies or 'ghetto mentality' Church schools. But where the distinctive Christian ethos encourages an holistic and integrative rather than segregated approach, the school may better prepare children to cope with the pressures of a secular society.[53] McClelland argues:

> The denominational school must be a community of love, not an inward-looking protective kind of love, but an out-going exhalation of love that reaches beyond the confines of the school into the family, the Church, the pluralistic community at large. (1988, p. 24)

If its 'mission' is one of creative growth, development or enrichment in a supportive and caring atmosphere rather than of 'spoon-feeding' in an authoritarian environment; if there is a transcendent perspective which unifies the curriculum; if spiritual values influence moral judgements and illuminate scientific and technological study; if Christian belief is appreciated in its cultural context yet seen to encourage a response to the needs of the local or wider community; then the coincidence of values between home, school and Church can provide a challenging springboard rather than a protective cocoon.

Anglicans

Within the Christian tradition, the strain of diversity within unity has often reached breaking point. It is not an easy message to sell in Ulster, for example, where those who speak of unity underlying the impassioned diversity are often regarded as traitors. Even within Anglicanism with its historic legacy of holding together a Catholicism without a Pope, an Erasmian liberalism, and a sharp-elbowed Protestantism,[54] the acceptance of diversity can be very reluctant indeed, producing organized party-groups in the General Synod, most recently over the ordination of women to the priesthood. Yet the 'broad' Church tradition characteristic of Anglicanism may have something to offer this debate.

Anglican schools that have tried to balance the twin aims of serving both Church and community are well used to the creative tensions:

---

[53] See also Hulmes (1992a), pp. 304ff.

[54] This diversity is admirably explored in Nichols (1993).

The ethos of the school will need to be developed through careful policy decisions regarding discipline in all its aspects, appointment of staff, admission of pupils, the pattern of worship and links with the wider community. But all these areas of concern need to reflect the Church's concern for the 'provision of general education in the neighbourhood' and must take into account the local community. (National Society, 1985, p. 45)

For Anglican schools, there are both opportunities and dangers in close affiliation with the values of their community. The residual respect for the Church of England in British society still leaves possibilities for the Church to present a challenge to the community to take the moral demands of the gospel seriously.

> Religion is still deeply woven into the fabric of cultural identity. The whole notion of belonging to the nation, of being English seems inseparable from a need to claim the title 'Christian' .... Most members of the population do not merely feel that they belong to the Church (which they rarely visit) but that the Church belongs to them. (Martin, 1981, p. 193)

Although, as we have noted, there may be mixed motives for parental choice, Anglican schools may welcome pupils whose family commitment to the Church is negligible but who profess to be wanting a 'good Christian education' for their children. 'Many of our families do not practise a faith, but all come to value the ethos of the school and the commitment of its staff and clergy and many are drawn to the faith', commented one headteacher in the 1989 Culham Report on Anglican primary schools in the London diocese (p. 12).[55]

Anglicans may actually find themselves appreciated for making explicit the principles and values on which they stand. *A Future in Partnership* (1984) warns those involved in Church schools:

> If relativising forces obfuscate traditional values and the Christian roots from which many of them have sprung, the Christian contribution to the debate may well be to work for the retention within publicly funded education of options based firmly on Christian values and truth. (National Society, 1984, p. 24)

These remarks may reflect a sensitivity to the exclusive intolerance of contemporary secularism which does not regard religious faith as an available option and resents any public support in the form of government funding

---

[55] However, Leslie Francis (1987a, p. 191) alerted such schools to the results of his research, which suggested that where the Church of England operated religiously distinctive neighbourhood schools and admitted children from non-'church-related' backgrounds, 'at best these schools are having no distinctive religious impact on the pupils when compared with county schools; at worst they are having a negative impact'.

for education with a religious ethos and commitment (whether Christian or Muslim or Jewish). Inter-faith dialogue is not merely about differences at a time when the great world religions share a common cause in the confrontation with radical atheism and secularism.

Nevertheless, within the Christian majority and the Muslim minority there are strident voices contending for monoculturalism, on the basis that Christians, Muslims and Jews believe different things and have different ways of worship, which are not amenable to a submerging of their characteristic identities. Ecumenism within the Christian tradition is inherently difficult; to transfer the methods and some of the presuppositions of the Christian ecumenical dialogue to multi-faith convergence is still more difficult. One Anglican headteacher in O'Keeffe's survey said:

> If multicultural education means Asian/West Indian awareness, it is a non-starter. When a person emigrates, he/she should adopt the customs and attitudes of the host country. This is not an arrogant statement, it is common sense. (1986, p. 132)

On the other hand, the Church of England's General Synod received a discussion paper in 1984 entitled *Schools and Multicultural Education*. This took up the question put by the National Society's *A Future in Partnership*: how can the Church, in preaching reconciliation, 'foster the processes that will reconcile alienated racial groups? Does the service to the nation need reinterpreting in a Britain that stands in some danger of racial disharmony?' These processes, it is urged, may include admitting to Church schools children of other faiths with a view not to assimilation or social integration, still less religious conversion, but to authentic dialogue which encourages not mere tolerance but open-hearted acceptance.

The difficulties experienced in defining multicultural education among secular educationists do not make it easier for Christian teachers to answer when the nature of the question is not yet clearly defined. Many may attempt to fall back on the view that they are there to teach Christianity, a response most likely in areas with few ethnic-minority children; others feel the need to prepare pupils to take their place in a multicultural society. Ball and Troyna (1987, p. 21) have observed: 'For teachers in voluntary schools faced with an unclear definition of multicultural education, Christianity becomes the vehicle on which the values of cultural diversity, tolerance, and harmony can apparently best be transmitted.' In the light of the 1988 Lambeth Conference where the bishops from the Third World formed so considerable a contingent, any suggestion that Anglican Christianity is monocultural would be ludicrously outdated. A school which calls itself Anglican ought to be aware of the massive diversity of racial and cultural traditions represented even within the Anglican Communion, of which only about 4 per cent would be Church of England. Since much of this diversity is also reflected among Anglicans living in Britain, particularly among the West Indian communities, Church schools have a responsibility not merely to enter into dialogue with other faiths, but also to be conscious of the different cultures within their own tradition.

A considered response along these lines is an important counter to critics who attack Church schools not only for perpetuating social inequality and economic disadvantage but for blithely taking no notice of the racism on their doorstep (e.g. S. Ball in O'Keeffe, 1988, p. 48). Ann Dummett has observed that in some areas 'West Indians are more likely to be practising Christians than local white people, and here Church schools can be seen to be doing something positive to overcome racism' (Dummett and McNeal, 1981, p. 17).[56] One headteacher questioned in the Runnymede survey suggested that the researcher ask a child in the playground 'Do you love Jesus?' The response from the white child was likely to be 'Wot, me?' The West Indian child's answer would be quite different: 'He knows what you're talking about' (ibid., p. 47). Dummett's research concluded with the remark that where there was a black Christian community, Christian preference for Church schools has 'the effect of creating multiracial institutions; where the black community was not Christian, it had the effect of preventing it' (ibid., p. 65). The challenge for Anglican schools must lie primarily in the latter area. Christians can sometimes have the illusion that religion is reconciling where race and class are dividing, whereas there is evidence that where the religion is different, it may be the most divisive force of all.

The government has claimed that Church schools are the kind of schools it wishes to encourage (see John Patten in *Church Times*, 30 October 1992). Increasingly researchers indicate that Anglican schools in particular perform well academically, maintain high standards of discipline and behaviour and are perceived as caring institutions which successfully encourage pupils in Christian values.[57] The London diocesan director, following the results of commissioned research, commented that there was a remarkable

---

[56]For further discussion see O'Keeffe (1986), pp. 108–9; Troyna and Carrington (1990), pp. 102–3; Tomlinson (1990), p. 16.

[57]For example Peter Mortimore, then deputy director of the London Institute of Education, considered Anglican-aided primary schools 'among the most effective in the country' (*Education*, 29 May 1992). Leslie Francis (1986a) noted that these schools might approach the secular curriculum and teaching methodology like county schools, but were distinctive in their Christian perspectives on RE, moral education, church links and assemblies and on pastoral issues such as parental and community liaison and a caring atmosphere. Indeed, one teacher went further: 'to withdraw a child from RE or assembly would be pointless because the Christian ethic permeates the whole life of the school' (O'Keeffe, 1986, p. 81).

consensus among his Anglican schools about the importance of their Christian ethos (often regarded as the most important item on governing body agendas): they had a distinctive contribution to make in this area to the public education system (*Church Times*, 5 July 1991).

It can therefore be seen that Anglican schools in general have a clear commitment to be both part of their local community and to offer a distinctive Christian presence in education. The pressures of grant-maintained status and flattery of parental oversubscription may encourage more emphasis on the latter role at the expense of the former. The Church of England's vision for its schools may need greater clarification[58] if their historic links with the local area are to be maintained, as well as those with parish and diocese.

Roman Catholics

Christ is the foundation of the whole educational enterprise. . . . In their individual ways all members of the school community share this Christian vision, and that is what makes the school Catholic. The specific mission of the school is a critical, systematic transmission of culture in the light of faith and the bringing forth of the power of Christian values by the integration of culture with faith and of faith with living. (Sacred Congregation, 1977, paras 34, 49)

In broad terms there is no special difficulty in discovering the central principle which makes a school Roman Catholic. In looking for signs of a Catholic ethos, some outward manifestations might be taken for granted: a crucifix in the entrance hall would not be distinctively Roman Catholic, but would certainly be characteristic. Once, however, one passes beyond either broad generalities or a few particular forms of devotion, it quickly becomes much harder to define the distinctive ethos or atmosphere by which a school can be identified as specifically Catholic. The document quoted above recognizes that the school community's vision is and will be interpreted in a variety of ways, and these ways can be in tension with one another if not directly contradictory.

The value system underlying and underpinning all aspects of relationships within the school provides a 'hidden curriculum', and could be a more important indicator of what makes a school Catholic than a well-developed catechetical programme. The variety of interpretation will also reflect the current debate within the Catholic community about questions of morality and even of faith (at least in the sense of theological understanding of the

---

[58] As recommended by *Schools and Church* (1991), a Culham survey of Anglican secondary schools in the London diocese.

tradition of doctrine). To the conservative Catholic, both developments in historical criticism of the Bible and in ecumenical outreach may appear threatening; there is discussion concerning the limits to which the Catholic is free to go in these and similar areas. Sexual morality also generates controversy and the very nature of the authority of the Pope and bishops to rule in this area can spark debate (see the media reports on the papal encyclical *Veritatis Splendor* in September 1993).

Tony Higgins, director of the Catholic schools' adaptation of the famous Humanities Project led by Stenhouse, reported back in 1979 that

> there is no consensus among those working in Catholic education about the distinguishing characteristics of a Catholic school.... . Conversations with teachers ... revealed a fair measure of agreement that a Catholic school should above all be a Christian community, but there was some divergence of view about the features which should characterise such a community—e.g. whether worship should be compulsory. Some saw its main characteristic as 'good discipline'. Others thought that the Catholic school was distinguished from other schools, not by the answers it gave but by the nature of the questions it chose to ask. (Higgins, 1979, p. 69)

These comments are not in such sharp tension as perhaps Tony Higgins implied, but his document as a whole attested to the widespread sense of questioning among Catholic teachers at a time when the supreme Catholic virtue had ceased to be acquiescence to whatever ecclesiastical authority decided.[59]

We have seen that Roman Catholic schools have been clear about their mission to nurture Catholics, but to assume that the effectiveness of the ethos of a school can be exclusively judged by subsequent Church affiliation would be altogether too narrow. It is often urged that a Catholic school's ethos is seen by the way in which such teachers live out their Christian commitment in their everyday lives and relations with pupils (cf. Sacred Congregation, 1982). As in Anglican schools, the qualities looked for by Catholic schools in appointing teaching staff are a combination of knowledge of their subject, ability to communicate such knowledge, and a sense of Christian purpose:

> A teacher who is full of Christian wisdom, well prepared in his own subjects, does more than convey the sense of what he is teaching to his pupils. Over and above what he says, he guides his pupils beyond his mere words to the heart of total Truth.... . This is what makes the differences between a school whose

[59]See Hornsby-Smith (1991, pp. 208–9): 'In practice, Pope John Paul II was seen as a "nice guy" but this had few implications in terms of obedience to his teaching. Most Catholics will in the last analysis make up their own minds on moral issues.'

education is permeated by the Christian spirit and one in which religion is only regarded as an academic subject like any other. (*Sacred Congregation*, 1977, paras 41, 43)

Catholic adolescents are no different from their non-Catholic contemporaries (religious and irreligious) in wanting to test for themselves what they have learnt. If the teacher is seen only as an authority figure who merely reiterates Catholic teaching each time a controversial question arises, then it is not wholly surprising that later adult appropriation of Christian values is not as profound as Roman Catholic educators would wish and hope. The teacher has to acquire some real personal understanding of the general principles and coherence of Christian faith in the Catholic tradition, being both a guide and fellow enquirer with the questioning pupil; the pupils 'are unlikely to be drawn into a deeper commitment in the following of Jesus Christ unless they see such a commitment reflected in the teacher's way of life' (Bishops' Conference, 1981, p. 104).

As in Anglican schools, governors appointing staff have to strike a delicate balance between the need for high-quality teachers and the need for practising Christians. Most Catholic schools advertising in the press place great weight on their senior staff and RE teachers being unreservedly committed Roman Catholics but, as we saw earlier, the figures show an increase in the proportion of non-Catholic teachers being employed in Catholic maintained schools.[60] At what point might a Roman Catholic school begin to feel that its identity was somehow being blurred by too many teachers who could not share in everything the Catholic tradition represented? No agreed answer has yet emerged.

Another focus for the values underpinning the Catholic school is commonly seen in liturgical celebrations. With the local priest or school chaplain leading teachers and pupils together in the offering of worship, these celebrations are an explicit manifestation of Christian faith and practice; in this respect Catholic, like Anglican, schools are marked out from their secular counterparts in the maintained sector. The 'message' the children receive will depend on a number of factors. Is the priest an effective communicator with young people? Are pupils subjected to regimentation in their attendance at mass? Are staff and pupils alike active participants (a participation which was more difficult for girls when the old ruling of the Roman Curia against their assistance round the altar was observed and

---

[60]The director of the Catholic Education Service in 1992 noted in a personal interview that, although RC primary schools had about 90 per cent RC staff, the figure was only 69 per cent in RC secondary schools. The revised code of canon law of 1983 (canon 804, 2) boldly asks for Catholic schools only to appoint teachers who are 'outstanding in true doctrine and uprightness of life ... and in their teaching ability'.

enforced)?[61] Is the service seen as a matter of priority in the day's events? The answers to such questions as these will indicate whether school worship is hardly more than a formalized ritual exercise, a training in correct responses, or a power-house of authentic religious experience.

In recent years, both Catholic and many Anglican schools and parishes have placed a special and singular emphasis on participation in eucharistic worship; this can bring difficulty in that it may involve a level of maturity and understanding not necessarily required in other forms of liturgical worship. To Catholics and Anglicans alike, a celebration of the eucharist requires a priest. However, it may also be important in a school to have services of worship to which an ordained priest is not indispensable, thereby allowing greater flexibility and an involvement by young people in which their role is not secondary.

In 1985, the national RE adviser to the Catholic Bishops' Conference of England and Wales, Patrick Purnell, expressed his reservations about compulsion for school eucharists:

> I find it extremely difficult to think of the eucharist ever being an appropriate act of compulsory worship, either for the school as a whole or for a class. . . . How can you impose worship on everybody? Worship is an act of devotion freely made by believers as a sign of their love and commitment. (1985, p. 132)

Many Church schools (like St Bede's, Redhill) offer their pupils religious services before class or during lunch hours. Such arrangements can testify to the importance of the school's Christian witness without the pressure of a compulsory requirement, and may correct the impression often retained by pupils that a free response is less significant than an act of duty. Support given to voluntary activities (such as discussion groups or retreat days) by staff and pupils can also help to assess the degree to which the Christian ethos of the school is 'permeated with the gospel spirit of freedom and love' (Sacred Congregation, 1977, para. 55).

Roman Catholic educationists have also argued that Christian values across the curriculum need more explicit focus. For example, science should encourage critical objectivity and intellectual challenge, without losing sight of a sense of wonder and contemplation at God's creation. In history, the period of the Tudors and Stuarts would be a useful study for Church schools, to enable pupils to have some understanding of the divisions of Western Christendom. Paddy Walsh considers it the responsibility of Christian schools to take a far stronger lead in developing courses on peace studies, the Third World, conservation, racial and sexual equality, 'because

---

[61]Though hard information is difficult to obtain, the ruling seemed to be observed more in the UK than in France or Germany: Roman Catholic parents at Redhill pressed Cardinal Hume critically on this ruling during his visit to St Bede's in March 1992.

these are areas in which learning relates directly to matters of justice and love' (O'Leary, 1983, p. 10).[62]

Roman Catholic schools situated in deprived city parishes may be able to demonstrate commitment to social justice by their very existence. In Britain, they have traditionally reflected considerable cultural diversity because of the substantial number of Irish, Italian, Polish and Hispanic families. Nationally the proportion of black families with a Roman Catholic allegiance is relatively small, and black pupils are often poorly represented in the schools. A 'divisive anomaly' can be created if Asian and Afro-Caribbean pupils predominate in secular schools, while Church schools remain almost exclusively white and ethnically European (cf. Catholic Commission for Racial Justice, 1984). At Vatican II, *Gaudium et Spes* observed that 'forms of social or cultural discrimination in basic social rights' are 'incompatible with God's design' (Flannery, 1981, p. 929, para. 29). Roman Catholics are not of course the only Christians who sense a mismatch between modern society's egalitarian values and their own practice, but the problem of equal opportunities seems especially acute for them in gender issues where female role-models have tended to be 'subservient'.[63]

Cardinal Basil Hume stated his view on the ethos and values of a Catholic school thus:

> If it is based on a true awareness of God, there should be an almost tangible atmosphere of freedom, welcome and warmth. Care, concern and respect for people as children of God should be demonstrated in the attitudes of staff to pupils and of pupils to each other. Individuals will be valued for themselves irrespective of ability and achievement. A noticeable sense of unity and family will affect the way that discipline is exercised without brutality or indifference ... young people will devote themselves generously and selflessly to those who suffer from any kind of distress ... the old and the handicapped in the area, the destitute in the Third World. There should be beauty, orderliness and an

---

[62]The Vatican acknowledged that 'since it is motivated by the Christian ideal, the Catholic school is particularly sensitive to the call from every part of the world for a more just society. ... It does not stop at the courageous teaching of the demands for justice even in the face of local opposition, but tries to put these demands into practice in its own community in the daily life of the school' (Sacred Congregation, 1977, para. 58). Such statements build on the texts of the Second Vatican Council, especially *Gaudium et Spes*, para. 29 (Hastings, 1969).

[63]'It seems to me that Catholics with their special devotion to Our Lady, their celibate religious, and their interpretation of the biblical predominance of man in prescriptive rather than culture-bound terms, are particularly prone to the ideology of the permanent maternal vocation' (Hornsby-Smith, 1978, p. 40).

absence of vandalism. Religious symbols should be well-chosen and their influence pervasive. . . . The quality of relationships . . . is decisive both for learning . . . and for growing in faith and commitment. (1988a, pp. 111–12)

The Church's mission and witness to the world should also be reflected in the school community. The Catholic school can now open its doors to non-Catholic pupils and staff (even if initially for pragmatic reasons, though this may also be seen as an opportunity); it can invite in visiting speakers with controversial opinions and can reach out to co-operate with the local community. This possibility, not everywhere perhaps, envisages a different model to that of the Catholic Church as a closed institution intent on preserving the flock from materialism, atheism and the 'apostasy' of Protestantism. The new model is prepared to challenge the world to take Christian values seriously, to liberate society from ignorance and prejudice through the power and light of the Holy Spirit, to point the finger at injustice and hypocrisy and to seek to take action to further the Kingdom of God. Such a challenge is addressed not only to the world; it also has to be faced within the Church and its schools.

6. CONCLUSION

Our survey has attempted to throw into sharp relief some of the problems confronting Christian schools in a Britain profoundly pluralist in faith and often detached from Christian tradition in morals. The Christian school exists to prepare its pupils for life in the contemporary world and is under pressure to achieve examination success and train young people for employment (or indeed unemployment); it also exists to retain and develop its distinctiveness as an institution of the people of God who are seeking to live out Christian faith and ethics. The double commitment, complemented by a profound sense of universal mission, is shared by both Roman Catholic and Anglican schools seeking to break down barriers and establish creative dialogue with Christian partners, and the question presses whether or not the time may soon come when those in authority can propose and foster a common educational policy of co-operation rather than rivalry.

The current revival of conservative evangelicalism in the Church of England is far from the only factor impelling Anglicans to think more of their Church schools as agencies of mission. There is a sense of reaction against surrender to scepticism and liberalizing relativism, which finds expression in the expectation that pupils attending Church schools will at least emerge at the end with a clear idea of the Christian faith. Nevertheless, a Christian school will be ineffective as a missionary agency (in the appropriately broad sense) unless the education provided is of high quality. And such an education is incompatible with a narrow and blinkered presentation of the relationship between faith and culture.

The Church of England approaches the task of mission through Church schools with a certain ambivalence. Those who desire simplistic answers to fundamental questions are likely to find themselves irritated and dissatisfied by the Anglicans' desire to 'have their cake and eat it'. Yet the responsibility for providing an education directed towards the community at large which is informed by a Christian ethos is a service to both nation and Church. If the education has ceased to be at any point visibly Christian, then the school's title as a Church school becomes questionable. If the school is primarily an evangelistic agency to which education of high quality is a secondary consideration, it must be reckoned a failure both as mission and as education.

The Roman Catholic Church faces difficulties closely analogous to those experienced in the Church of England; but because the Roman Catholic Church in England has no deep tradition of providing education for the community at large, but seeks rather to serve its own members in the first instance (usually making places for adherents of other Christian communions, or of other faiths, more to make up numbers than to foster ecumenical understanding), these problems may be less acutely felt, at least as yet. In 1993 the director of the Catholic Education Service commented that contemporary education debates have 'forced the whole Catholic community to analyse just what is special about our schools and what we want them to be' (*Tablet*, 13 February 1993). In this process, conscious that the grant-maintained option might lead to fragmentation or isolation, Catholic schools are being encouraged to see their mission in the context of the wider community.

It cannot be said, as we shall see in subsequent chapters, that joint Catholic/Anglican schools are something Roman Catholic authority necessarily wishes to encourage; rather they are to be tolerated *faute de mieux*, when the alternative is no Catholic education at all in a particular place.[64] Both traditions share the importance of Christian values over against those of secular humanism. But to carry this sharing into institutional reality with positive encouragement from authority requires a deepening of mutual trust and understanding, with agreement in principle

---

[64]In spite of the 1981 report to the Roman Catholic Bishops of England and Wales, *Signposts and Homecomings* (Bishops' Conference, 1981, pp. 150, 154) recommending that an ecumenical Christian college be established for training Christian teachers and shared schools should be developed. One diocese, whose joint school failed to compete for sufficient Catholic pupils with neighbouring single RC schools, announced in February 1993 that it was to withdraw, leaving the school to its Anglican foundation.

on how the Christian ethos of the schools is to be expressed, how 'the vision of Christ' is to work out in practice.

To say that the successful establishment of joint Catholic/Anglican schools has depended, among other things, on the (still controverted) acceptance by Roman Catholic authority of the view that a catechesis which is at once narrowly faith-oriented and closed to alternatives should not be the prime or distinctive element in the ethos of a Catholic education, may be interpreted by the conservative to mean that the openness to the world fostered by Vatican II involves some dilution of Catholic distinctiveness. It is a commonplace today that the degree of success that the Roman Catholic or Anglican Church can have in ecumenical dialogue is directly related to the degree to which it can contain diversity within its own unity. Today that Roman Catholic diversity is overtly much greater than it was before Vatican II, with no serious likelihood of turning the clock back. There are also many Anglicans (particularly High Church and evangelical) whose instinctive understanding of Christian faith and practice is altogether more conservative than that advocated by many progressive Roman Catholics; the Church of England in particular is not finding it easy to hold together its own historic 'fault-lines' following the vote on women's priesthood in November 1992.

There is probably a broad consensus among Roman Catholic and Anglican educationists that it is of the life of a Church school to be and to be seen to be Christian in its ethos and values. Science and technology have created a society 'characterised by depersonalisation and a mass production mentality' (*Sacred Congregation*, 1977, p. 31), and Christian schools need above all to retain the focus on the human being as an individual loved by God. Secularization and depersonalization are closely related. Roman Catholics and Anglicans agree on the proposition that in a depersonalizing world the Christian school has something crucially important to say to both Christians and non-Christians. To become 'the Christian leaven in the world', it is essential to point to 'the liberating power of grace' (ibid., p. 84), rather than to react defensively to either the contemporary modern world or the possibility of alliance with separated but 'sister Churches'.

Anglicans and Roman Catholics have much in common over against the predominant culture of liberal secular humanism in British society. Both share a sense of Christian mission which has the potential to transcend denominational boundaries. Yet for historical, theological and cultural reasons they have tended to emphasize their differences: Anglicans held to their Establishment position as providing schools for the nation, seeing themselves as primarily reflecting their own community and neighbourhood; Roman Catholics as a minority wished to remain separate in order to safeguard their own interests and maintain their wider universal perspective within the Church of Rome. Each group has much to learn from the other.[65] The increasingly secular nature of British society, the 'free-market' nature of government policy and the greater emphasis on parental choice in education in the last few years have encouraged Anglican schools to become more explicit about their distinctively Christian identity. At the same time, Roman Catholics have begun to face up to the greater openness towards society required by Vatican II, moving away from a too narrow catechetical model to embrace greater personal autonomy and freedom of conscience supported by the ethos of an explicitly Christian community. By identifying common aims in Christian education and elucidating distinctively denominational approaches, Christian schools, particularly those established as joint foundations, have allowed Anglicans and Roman Catholics to work together in educating young people in shared Christian values through formal ecumenical partnerships in schools. Their aim has been not uniformity, but 'diversity in unity', a mutual enrichment that draws on the gifts of each denominational tradition outlined in this chapter. The following chapter considers in detail how far this Christian unity has developed in practice over more than a decade in one joint Anglican and Roman Catholic secondary school.

[65]Bishop Alan Clark, the RC co-chairman of ARCIC 1, commended 'the riches of the Anglican spiritual heritage' expressed in 'its sense of the numinous, its sense of the liturgy, its care for all in the community. This sense of belonging to the country, to the region, to the village, is something very rich' (*Tablet*, 1 May 1993). Equally the Roman Catholics' greater sense of global responsibility, enhanced by liberation theology and the justice and peace movements, has much to teach a Church of England less conscious of its contribution to a worldwide Anglican communion (except perhaps through its support of missionary societies and charities, during Lambeth Conferences or when the courageous Archbishop Tutu appears on television).

St Bede's Joint Anglican/Roman Catholic School, Redhill

There can be no ecumenism worthy of the name without a change of heart. For it is from newness of attitudes, from self-denial and unstinted love, that yearnings for unity take their rise and grow toward maturity. (Second Vatican Council, *Decree on Ecumenism*, para. 7: Flannery, 1981)

CHRONOLOGY OF MAIN EVENTS

1974	Governors' formal proposal to establish a united CE/RC school
1975	Secretary of State gave approval
	Madge Hunt appointed as headteacher
1976	St Bede's School opened for pupils aged 12–18
1978	Phil Dineen appointed as headteacher
1982	'Parallel eucharists' developed
1985	Julian Marcus appointed as headteacher
1988	Visit of Dr Runcie, Archbishop of Canterbury
1990	Anglican and Roman Catholic bishops dedicated new building
1992	Governors considered proposal for Free Church involvement in the Foundation
	Visit of Cardinal Hume, Archbishop of Westminster

PREFACE

The first part of this chapter is based on my experience as head of religious education at St Bede's, Redhill up to August 1982. A casual staffroom conversation fortuitously revealed the existence of a file of muddled and incomplete papers concerning the school's foundation, which prompted my initial interest in research on ecumenical education. Returning to the school in 1992, I had expected primarily to review and update developments; however, my visits coincided with the school's fundamental reappraisal of its ecumenical foundation, which provided a fresh and exciting impetus to the story.

1. CREATING A JOINT SCHOOL 1972–82

Planning and consultation

LEGAL AND EDUCATIONAL CONSIDERATIONS

'It was just like getting married': so, quite independently in interviews in 1981, declared two members of the staff of the school, one Roman Catholic, the other Anglican, looking back on the amalgamation. And, like marriage, it was not without its strains.

The uniting of two Church schools of different denominations must in any circumstances be a process requiring sensitivity, with apprehensions and fears to be allayed. It is like two families, whose traditions are very different in some respects, coming together with their offspring to the matrimonial bond at the altar, nervous of the momentous decision about to be made, recognizing the risks involved in life together, yet prepared to face the difficulties with hopeful enthusiasm; aware that the marriage might well founder on the rocks of mutual incompatibility, yet prepared to make every effort to achieve success. In the case of two schools belonging to different Churches, the tensions are potentially much greater. Both parties to the union bring with them long memories of a past of which they may be only partly conscious.

The late 1960s were years of optimism and expansion. Money was readily available, and the comprehensive policy for education was increasingly credible and convincing. Surrey County Council, with its predominantly Conservative and middle-class catchment area, was reluctant to accelerate the reform of its educational system. But it gradually became apparent that change was inevitable. A three-tier system of first, middle and comprehensive schools feeding into sixth-form colleges was decided upon. But by the time Surrey LEA attempted to implement this policy in its south-east division, the mid-1970s were approaching, and the money supply was coming under greater pressure. It could be argued that had they implemented decisions more speedily, some of the subsequent problems might have been less acute.

The two denominational schools in the Redhill–Reigate area had developed very differently. The Roman Catholic school had begun as a fee-paying independent girls school in the diocese of Arundel and Brighton: in response to DES Circular 10/65, it changed its status in 1969 to become a Roman Catholic 'aided' coeducational school. This increased the number of school places available for less affluent Catholic families, but by the early 1970s the LEA's three-tier policy meant that the school was unlikely to receive support for a sixth form.

Meanwhile the Anglican girls secondary modern school had committed itself to sixth-form provision back in 1968 and was now determined to retain its curriculum beyond 16 despite the LEA's stated policy. This led to preliminary discussions with the Roman Catholic school about co-operation at sixth-form level. As one Roman Catholic priest later wrote in the Roman Catholic deanery *Newsletter* for November 1973:

> The idea that all children who wished to continue their formal education beyond the age of 16 would have no choice but to attend a County Sixth Form College seems to the [RC] Governors to be unacceptable; while the role of the Church Schools would in this situation be reduced to comparative insignificance.

County policy and increasing concern brought together the governing bodies of the two Church schools on 16 March 1972. They met to study the county plan, to suggest a possible alternative, and to decide on future policy if the scheme for a sixth-form college were adopted. As a result of this meeting, a working party was appointed to consider a paper prepared by the two headteachers, out of which there emerged two possible courses of action:

> (a) the building of a sixth-form centre to be run as a joint enterprise (thereby extending the cooperation at sixth-form level begun in September 1970 to retain minority A-level subjects in the curriculum);

> (b) the gradual merging of the two schools in a coeducational comprehensive school.

The second of these proposals, though more adventurous, came to seem more attractive:

> It was decided that Plan (b) merited serious consideration, and both sides

decided to call a special Governors' meeting to seek views on the possibility of a United School, and also to submit these views to the Diocesan Authorities. After careful consideration, the Diocesan Authorities gave their approval to the idea, and at a joint meeting of Governors on 7 November 1972, the two headteachers submitted a series of points later entitled the 'Manifesto', which they felt would be helpful to the Governors in their thinking together on the future of the two schools. (Unsigned paper on the history of St Joseph's School)

The headteachers' manifesto offered significant insight into both the theological and educational bases for ecumenical co-operation and marked out the areas where values were shared, responsibilities recognized and problems foreseen.

The Manifesto

1. The condition of society at present calls for a clear and convincing witness of Christian solidarity in face of the challenge from humanists, the general indifference towards moral issues, and the apathy of nominal Christians who are uncommitted to the Christian way of life.

2. Divisions among Christians are a scandal to the young people of today. Their reasoning is that if we are sincerely following Christ, minor differences become petty and irrelevant.

3. Not only is specifically Christian teaching in the form of school assemblies and religious education under fire but the Christian values of honesty and truth are also very much at risk. We believe they can only be taught in a convincing way in the Christian context. The children in our schools are just like all other children and we are dealing with young people who are at the mercy of the pressures from a sick society and the influence of the mass media. The difference in our schools is not in the fact that they are not tempted like others, and do not fail like others, but often lies in the action taken in consequence.

4. The all-round educational value of the larger school is probably already apparent, but perhaps it should be mentioned particularly because of the need to attract staff of the highest calibre.

5. To cater for all the needs of pupils, particularly at the top of the school, makes necessary a wide spread of options from the fourth year upwards. The advantages of the larger school can clearly be seen.

6. Between the ages of 14 and 16 young people go through a period of revolt against every established standard and authority. With the understanding and tactful handling of a community of faith, they come frequently in the

Sixth Form to see the values of what they have been tempted to reject. They are, at this stage, prepared to accept a more mature approach and a more personal commitment to the content of the whole Christian message.

7. If our convictions are sufficiently strong, in the light of the ultimate vision of a united Christian school serving the local community, they will carry us through all the difficulties and frustrations of the initial stages which are inevitable in any worthwhile and far reaching project.

8. One of the encouraging aspects of this whole idea is that the project of a united Christian school is unique in the whole of the country. It could well blaze a trail for further collaboration in other areas.[1]

The document was formally signed by Sr Mary Jerome, head of St Joseph's RC school and Miss Madge Hunt, head of Bishop Simpson CE school. Madge Hunt later recalled, 'A united school was a revolutionary idea at that time'. The 'Manifesto' may be seen to focus on three main issues:

(a) the increasing attraction of a larger school in its ability to offer a more interesting and viable curriculum for staff and pupils;

(b) the importance of a Christian school that could witness to Christian values and provide a Christian environment in which students might progress towards maturity;

(c) the vision of a united Christian school as an example to the local community, the nation, and even the universal Church.

During the summer of 1972 preliminary discussions began with Roman Catholic parents in the catchment area, and although support was far from unreserved, the governors felt confident enough by November 1972 to issue to parents a statement of their intentions, announcing the establishment of a working party to study the implications of forming a combined aided Church school for boys and girls aged 12–18.

The year of 1973 was spent in further meetings which concentrated on specific practical problems that would need to be resolved. The question of the size of the school occupied much of the discussion at the joint meeting of governors in February. The proposed ratio of 2:3 (Catholics:Anglicans), reflecting the Roman Catholic population in the catchment area, suggested a ten-form entry school, in order to accommodate the numbers of Anglican girls and allow a reasonable balance of boys in the new intake. However, the existing buildings could house at most a nine-form entry school; a ten-form entry school could be made possible only if the LEA and the dioceses agreed to finance additional accommodation. As it later turned out, the

---

[1]Cuthbert Mayne School in Torquay was yet to open as an ecumenical school in 1973.

ratio of 2:3 in an eight-form entry school (240 pupils in each year group) proved acceptable to all sides.

Another issue raised at this February meeting was the effect of the denominational imbalance in staff and pupil numbers. The Roman Catholic head explicitly voiced the fear felt among her staff: 'of being completely submerged—and the things they valued could very well be lost, or it would be such a struggle to maintain them that the material advantages would be of little or no consequence'. It was a natural enough fear on the Roman Catholic side that the school might be less decisively committed to a critical stance *vis-à-vis* the values of surrounding English society (e.g. on questions such as authority and conscience, birth control or abortion) than the more obviously uncompromising position publicly occupied by the official hierarchy of the Roman Catholic Church. The uncommitted Roman Catholic children might find, it was feared, that the ethos and assumptions of a predominantly Anglican establishment would draw them into a still less distinctively Roman Catholic attitude towards moral issues or sacramental practice. On the other hand, there were some among the Roman Catholics who suggested that the resulting situation might actually increase the sense of commitment. The Catholic head grasped a particularly awkward nettle by pointing out that the committee had still to face up to points of division which remained inescapable and insoluble, such as participation in mass (difficult enough to 'put over' to the children even within an exclusively Roman Catholic school), and questions such as the time that might properly be taken out of lessons for liturgical celebrations.

At this meeting considerable discussion also took place on the question of fund-raising. The Roman Catholics were accustomed to raising large sums through tombolas and raffles, and it would never cross their mind that these activities could raise ethical questions for some Anglican consciences. The Anglican representatives at the meeting felt it their duty to formulate the reservations likely to be held by some of their churches at this point:[2] 'Whilst the Anglicans would not object to receiving money raised in any way acceptable to the Catholics towards the new school, once the school was founded then they would not agree to money being raised by the joint school by means of gambling' (minutes of February 1973). Some Anglicans evidently did not feel confident that a clear distinction between a modest 'flutter' and excessive or compulsive gambling could be incisively and securely drawn, and feared that Anglican children might be corrupted by an altogether too complacent compromise with contemporary values, unless from the start they clearly asked for a rigorist position to be maintained in practice. The proposed union of the schools would thus bring together two

---

[2]The nearest Anglican church to the school had been 'planted' as a strong evangelical community earlier this century and preserved its thriving tradition.

contrasting moral traditions, one of which felt a centuries-old reserve towards 'amusements': what might be harmless enough for one person could (on the evidence of social facts) put another on the first step towards catastrophic corrosion of the character. Between the two moral traditions (present even within Anglicanism) there lies the divergence rooted in the Protestant tendency to individualism and the solitude of the soul in its moral struggle in this world, contrasted with the Catholic sense of the sacramental community protecting the individual from uncontrollable excess. Evidently the joint PTA would have to take into account the delicate sensitivities arising from this difference of moral tradition.[3]

Perhaps the most critical issue discussed at the governors' meeting in February was religious education and the desirability of an agreed syllabus. Should doctrinal teaching be sifted out from the academic study of the subject? Could Roman Catholics teach a 'shared' syllabus which might be so wide and comprehensive that the task of teaching it would impose excessive strain on the staff? The labour and technical difficulties of producing an agreed syllabus might become a source of 'constant staff irritation'. On doctrinal aims there appeared to be a mounting awareness of convergence and, at a level behind that of formulas, even agreement. But awareness of areas of disagreement (or at least hitherto unresolved matters of dogmatic significance) might be felt to necessitate a division for all religious education in the new school. Most governors on both sides regarded this situation as highly undesirable and one to be averted if possible. It was therefore concluded that the two schools should exchange copies of their RE syllabuses to ascertain the extent of common ground; that no child in the joint school would receive confessional teaching of the Church to which he/she did not belong; and that while morning assemblies would be held together, the eucharist would be celebrated separately. It was agreed that united services to mark the principal Christian festivals would be encouraged.[4] The meeting laid down that for denominational teaching, 'the RE on the Catholic side would always be in the hands of committed Catholics, and similarly on the Anglican side' (minutes of February 1973).

[3] A senior member of staff appointed about this time recalled that even her interview (with both headteachers together) principally focused on whether as an Anglican she could condone raffles. The teacher commented that 'it was interesting to find that our Christian ideals were common but our culture different'.

[4] The record here includes the at first sight surprising and bizarre qualification: 'but prayers would be to the Holy Trinity'. It seems more probable that this proviso was designed to safeguard the position of those Anglicans for whom the scriptural texts of the 'Hail Mary' would be perfectly acceptable as an acclamation but not as a prayer, rather than to reassure Roman Catholics that some possibly undogmatic Anglicans would begin to instil a liberalism indistinguishable from Unitarianism.

SCHOOLS OF RECONCILIATION

It will be seen that the discussion at this meeting focused on a series of deep issues, which have continued to be reviewed since 1973. They have also arisen in other ecumenical schools, such as Lagan College. The 'founders' of St Bede's rightly believed that for the maintaining of mutual confidence, possible sources of mutual abrasion needed to be vigilantly watched and not allowed to generate distrust and fear.

The joint meeting of governors in October 1973 reported that discussions between staff and parents had not proved discouraging; the desire to push ahead with the project was given impetus by the evidence of a willingness by the Anglican and Roman Catholic communities to find a way of growing closer together. The Anglican head commented that the proposal appeared to be the right one in the light of the future mission of the Church: a senior Roman Catholic agreed with her, saying that 'the starting-point had been an educational problem, but now the implications for the Church's mission were apparent'.

The spirit of rapprochement is equally apparent in this quotation from an article in the deanery *Newsletter* for November 1973 in which the secretary to the Roman Catholic Diocesan Schools Commission wrote:

> It is the belief of the governors that the time is ripe for an experiment of this kind; that its potential for promoting Christian unity—an aim urged upon us all by Vatican II and by our present Holy Father—is incalculable, and that without it the prospects for Catholic—and indeed Christian—education in the area are far from bright.
>
> Whether or not this experiment can be put into effect depends upon two factors: first, it must have local support—from clergy and people, as well as from the LEA; secondly it must be approved by the Department of Education and Science, as fitting in with the general scheme of reorganisation in the area which meets the requirements of the Minister. Of these two factors the overriding one is the former, and it is to be hoped that in all parishes in the deanery there will be full and open-minded discussion of the issues at stake, with all eyes on the future rather than the past.

By July 1974 the two diocesan authorities had endorsed the governors' proposal and the Section 13 notices (officially changing or closing a school) had been issued: the ecumenical coeducational school would cater for the 12–18 age group, and the amalgamation would come about by closing the two existing schools and establishing the new school on the old premises. The governors were fired by an exciting vision of what might be achieved.

THEOLOGICAL AND ECCLESIOLOGICAL CONSIDERATIONS: THE BRAMLEY SEMINAR, NOVEMBER 1974

The legal decisions were now in the hands of the Secretary of State, and attention turned to the weighty practical and theological questions involved in establishing an 'Ecumenical Secondary School'. In November 1974 a distinguished group of seventeen national, diocesan and local representatives including members of the hierarchy, clergy, educationists, advisers and senior teaching staff involved in the project, were invited to a three-day seminar at Bramley in Surrey under the auspices of the Catholic Education Council in 'an atmosphere of friendliness and charity'. The Catholic secondary schools adviser suggested that his aims in convening the seminar were twofold:

(a) to help the interested parties ... to come together to assess the problems and to arrive at solutions which were theirs and not mine;

(b) to try to establish useful hints and advice which might be helpful at a national level.

The conference was first presented with a paper on 'Christian Schooling' produced by the Roman Catholic Ecumenical Commission. It struck a cautious note: multi-Church schools could not of themselves be the panacea for all religious divisions; indeed, if such a school were to be established within a community sharply divided on religious issues, the school would be more likely to foster divisions and delay rather than promote unity (an interesting comment in the light of future developments in Northern Ireland at Lagan College).

Many feel that, at the moment, it is only in 'ecumenically advanced' areas that we should even consider the possibility of some experiment in this field.

The next observations throw significant light on the way in which ecumenical opinion was developing:

All progress towards unity presupposes a solid grounding in a real appreciation of one's own tradition. The true value of ecumenical action is to be found in the coming together of traditions rather than in the elimination of differences.

This must be true, it was urged, not only so that the pupils may be educated as members of their respective churches, but also so that the teachers are ecumenically 'aware' and in no way anxious that they will be asked to compromise their personal integrity by doing something they cannot honestly accept. The parents, for their part, would need to be educated in the new approaches to catechetical teaching because a lack of understanding on their part might lead to polarization rather than ecumenical growth. These observations were to be prophetic of events as the joint Church school came into being.

The paper also outlined the main advantages and disadvantages of 'multi-Church' schools, again highlighting issues that became important in subsequent discussions. The advantages were listed as follows:

(a) The general ethos of such schools could provide as Christian a life-style as does the ethos of a one-Church school.

(b) The 'ecumenical education' involved, however informally, would match the ecumenical experience and situation of the churches in the area.

(c) It can be hoped that such a school, calling as it does for increased co-operation from parents and others, would stimulate further growth in the area.

(d) Such a school would itself be a witness to others of the degree of unity already experienced by Christians in the area.

(e) On general educational (and economic) grounds such a school might ensure a fuller general education for all concerned.

(f) In any number, such schools could eventually play a valuable part in preserving the truly Christian character in British education as a whole.

These six points were balanced by an equally significant statement of the possible disadvantages:

(a) The very concept of such a school and the ensuring of a proper ethos would call for real 'ecumenicity' on the part of the teachers: they would need to be a united team and perhaps be prepared to forgo transfer for promotion in the interest of the school's stability. Can this be sufficiently guaranteed? An 'indifferent' staff could do more harm than good.

(b) Would 'training in unity' lead to a degree of indifference even to the real grounds of our present division?

(c) While our large areas of doctrinal accord would be better appreciated, difficulties affecting practice would remain. What effect would these have on the life of the school?

(d) The support of Catholic parents for such a school would be essential. In most areas has the ecumenical education of the Catholic *community* (as opposed to a number of individuals) gone far enough to ensure this?

(e) Might a multi-Church school end up by being too inward looking and 'exclusivist' (a charge that is sometimes levelled at one-Church schools)?

(f) There are obvious problems about religious education and school worship.

The second list suggests the strong misgivings that were still felt in some Roman Catholic quarters, perhaps especially on the part of those representing the hierarchy and further from the educational situation 'on the ground'.

The paper of the Ecumenical Commission expressed particular fear that doctrinal divisions might be dismissed as if they were negligible. Loyal Roman Catholics might often desire to stress just those elements most distinctive of their position: in regard to the eucharist, penance, confirmation; devotion to Mary; Church attitudes on such questions as authority and the special loyalty to the Holy Father. The Ecumenical Commission felt confident that there would be no special difficulty about the great social virtues such as Christian action for peace and social justice, or about matters of personal morality such as honesty and truth-telling. But, again, would a united school be able to witness with an uncompromising voice on contemporary issues of sexual morality such as birth control and abortion? Almost all Anglicans, admittedly, regard abortion as morally justified only in rare and highly exceptional circumstances; the majority feel contraception is a matter that has to be left to the individual conscience judging in the light of Christian principles. Roman Catholics, by contrast, fear virtually any concession that there can be even very unusual circumstances in which abortion may be justified and, at the official as opposed to the individual level, feel bound to stand by Paul VI's encyclical *Humanae Vitae* (1968). Catholic individuals may in practice act in ways indistinguishable from their Anglican counterparts, but they nevertheless are normally much readier to acknowledge the teaching and legislative authority of the Church.

It could be argued that a large number of children in Roman Catholic families no longer find it in the least easy to accept ethical norms presented even by the most gifted teachers, and find themselves instinctively and intuitively thinking of ethical norms as emerging from the moral judgements of their own reason and conscience; this carries the uncomfortable consequence that the immediate presence of numerous Anglicans can be felt to be a threat. In some sense the characteristic attitude of many Anglicans—that the Church is there to form and guide the individual conscience, but in a supporting rather than autocratic role—may easily seem to encourage in the Roman Catholic children at the same school precisely those attitudes which Roman Catholic authority has wished to discourage. The Roman Catholic Ecumenical Commission's paper articulated these anxieties: in the joint school Catholic children might not have their consciences formed in accordance with the Church's teachings, but would be left to splash about in a confused sea of open-ended discussion without norms or standards.

The paper spoke finally of the difficulties likely to arise with worship in a joint school. These would hardly exist in the case of assembly or 'paraliturgical services', but would become acute with the celebration of the eucharist. Roman Catholic authority was then, as it remains according to the new Ecumenical Directory (Pontifical Council, 1993, p. 130), strongly opposed to indiscriminate and unauthorized intercommunion. Underlying this opposition is a view of the nature of the Church according to which intercommunion presupposes the resolution of division.

The Second Vatican Council's decree on Ecumenism, subsequently rein-forced by repeated papal statements culminating in Pope Paul VI's insis-tence in 1970 that the Anglican Communion is to be treated by Rome as a 'sister', made it an obvious impossibility for the Roman Catholic Ecumeni-cal Commission to adopt a public stance of disapproval towards the pro-posal for a joint school in which ecumenism might, of necessity, be forced to move beyond the stage of mere talk. Nevertheless the Commission remained tied down by the official inability of the Roman Catholic Church to acknowledge sacramental authenticity in an Anglican eucharist.[5] Fear was articulated that at Redhill ecumenism might become 'indifferentism', in consequence of which distinctive themes of Catholic dogma and devotional practice might easily become submerged.

In his conclusions to the seminar report, the national Catholic secondary schools adviser wrote:

> I do plead that people do not rush into this kind of venture—it requires years of discussion and consultation if one is to receive the fullest support which is so essential to the success of this experiment.

This comment came too late in the day. Perhaps it might be read as express-ing anxiety at the fact that the prime motive and driving force which had originally impelled Roman Catholics at Redhill to co-operate in the pro-posal for a joint school had been much more educational and pragmatic than ecumenical. Without the joint school a substantial group of Catholic children in the area would be left without effective provision in religious education. For some of them, therefore, the proposal represented not an instrument for the realization of an ecclesial ideal of Christian reconcili-ation but, *faute de mieux*, a school which at least claimed to provide a Christian education. If the joint school had to be accepted as an educational necessity, it was important to voice loud and clear the reservations that more conservative Roman Catholic minds would have on some central religious issues.

Nevertheless, those fearful of the new venture were not the majority. That consultation procedures concerning the very viability of the scheme should be continuing after the Secretary of State had already formally received the proposals was somewhat bizarre and was immediately ques-tioned by several Roman Catholics among those present at the seminar. That misgiving was shared by the Anglican headteacher, who also expressed the fear that the seminar, while ostensibly purporting to be 'an

---

[5]It is probably of some significance for the state of mind underlying the Commission's statement that no reference was then made to the recent Agreed Statement on the Eucharist issued by the Anglican/Roman Catholic International Commission meeting at Windsor in 1971 (McAdoo and Clark, 1972).

exploratory exercise', was in reality attempting to lay down too definite and limiting a programme of action.

Confidential documents from the meeting show quite a number of the participants shivering on the brink, but there were two important positive outcomes: the establishment of a Working Party on Religious Education and the impetus for a public relations exercise to develop enthusiasm for the scheme and particularly to encourage fund-raising (itself a useful criterion of the degree of enthusiasm and support). The goodwill of the community in Redhill was seen to be vital.

In order that the necessary arrangements for staffing and curriculum could be completed in time, fast and effective planning was needed. The new school, to open in September 1976, was to have eighteen governors, six representing the Anglican diocese, six the Roman Catholic diocese and six the LEA, each appointed by their respective bodies. Building considerations were also a high priority, especially facilities for the new influx of boys, such as cloakrooms and craft workshops (even in 1975 seen as a boys curriculum area). The 'pioneer status' of the joint Church school placed extra demands on material and staff resources but there was little or no external support for ameliorating the problems associated with operating a split-site school.

In any closure or amalgamation of a school it is the teaching staff who usually need the greatest reassurance that, under the new regime, their jobs and status will be safeguarded and their career prospects unaffected. Once the headteacher of the Anglican school had been appointed as head of the new school and the Roman Catholic headteacher as her deputy, attention could turn towards the more delicate operation of ensuring the best possible allocation of staff posts and also of allaying staff apprehensions about the consequences of the amalgamation. The LEA's general inspector interviewed all staff to ascertain their wishes. Sideways movement to other schools in the area was highly unlikely since they too were in the process of undergoing major reorganization in 1976. Staff claimed that there was never the least touch of animosity between individual staff on a personal level, but they would hardly have been human if there had not been some tensions over status. Interestingly, when the inspectors and governors of the joint school came to appoint the 'best' heads of department, all but one were Anglicans, an imbalance largely corrected by 1983. Some were not unnaturally resentful of this, and even attributed to the Anglican headteacher the motive of ensuring that the graduate Anglicans had the academic predominance when the new school came into being, while the Roman Catholic teachers were appointed to the main pastoral jobs (such as head of year). Others felt that the county should have removed both heads into advisory posts and then appointed new top personnel brought in from elsewhere, who would have no 'axes to grind' and no concern to continue policies inherited from the recent past. One comment was that 'no one really got what they wanted'. Several, who perhaps hoped that in the new school they would have wider scope or greater opportunities, felt resentful and disappointed at the new arrangements. One commented with some asperity that the amalgamation had been skilfully 'sold' to the staff.

The two headteachers, who had been prime movers in the entire exercise, took considerable trouble to try to allay the fears of individual members of staff by jointly interviewing all of them and introducing them to the head of the sister school with whom they would have to work. The Roman Catholic head, not unaware of the staff apprehensions, felt profoundly encouraged by the results of these conversations: 'Throughout these interviews and indeed throughout all the negotiations, a marked goodwill and spirit of charity was tangibly present, confirming the fact that the Holy Spirit himself was the originator of the enterprise' (private letter, 1976). The difference between this perception and that of some staff is perhaps not surprising in the circumstances. 'Birth inevitably involves pain', recalled the Anglican head in 1992.

As is the general pattern with amalgamations, it seemed necessary to maintain staff in their existing status, and this led to a situation with too many 'chiefs'. Some felt that the management would have produced a more efficient arrangement if they had been rather tougher with individuals, that 'they failed to grasp the bull by the horns', as one teacher put it, and did not sufficiently clarify job descriptions for senior staff from the two schools. In some cases potential was left untapped, while others had greater responsibility put on their shoulders in the larger school, and this was to prove excessive. Some teachers felt 'pushed out'; others nursed doubts that either of the two heads really possessed the practical administrative ability necessary for the complex operation of running a split-site school for the large number of 1,140 pupils.

An outside observer might expect that staff attitudes would have been significantly pushed in the direction of distrust by the religious and denominational differences between the two communities. In fact it was not so. The evidence of investigations and oral evidence from staff showed that, if anything, religion was the principal factor that made for the overcoming of tensions. The feeling 'we are all Christians together' enabled them to survive the most difficult period. This religious sense of commitment may have been reflected in the staff attendance at meetings for prayer on Friday afternoons after school, which continued for two years after amalgamation.

The Roman Catholic school was smaller than the Anglican, and for that reason alone it was inevitable that it should feel defensive. An almost trivial indication of this was that the Roman Catholic children would make the sign of the cross if a Roman Catholic priest were taking morning assembly, but otherwise tended not to do so. Certainly the Catholic school appeared to have lost more in the amalgamation: its premises, its head, its close parochial identity. Tensions caused by the amalgamation of two sets of fourth- and fifth-year pupils midway through their education were predictable but, as one Catholic teacher commented, the Anglicans may well have felt that 'it was an invasion', an influx of working-class Catholic boys into a predominantly middle-class Anglican girls school.[6]

On the other hand, the united school appeared in a number of ways to be more Christian in spirit than either of the two schools had been before. An Anglican colleague reflected that the Catholics brought with them a greater sense of spirituality, and that the Catholic staff were certainly more explicitly committed to the Church than several of the Anglicans. Some Anglicans were favourably impressed by the open attitude of many of the Roman Catholic staff when discussing controversial issues; they did not retreat behind the authoritative decisions of the Church or avoid debate. Many felt that the united staff showed a deeper concern and commitment to each other, to the children and to the community than they had seen before. 'I have never met so much goodwill in any staff', commented one teacher in 1981; 'the emphasis is on resolving problems—there are no factions, and things here do not get out of proportion.'

Some of this goodwill was due to an amount of inter-staff practical co-operation encouraged by the head. Even before St Bede's opened, it was pointed out at the first joint staff meeting, back in June 1975, that 'we are blazing a trail for Christian unity'. Departments were asked to prepare reports for discussion, including the justification of their subject's place in the curriculum, an analysis of traditional areas to identify irrelevant concepts, and a report on where their subject overlapped others in the curriculum. Working parties were set up to consider issues such as uniform, discipline and school rules, social education and training, the sixth form, guidance counselling and school assemblies. It was clear that such detailed and extensive discussions between staff, even before amalgamation came about, created an open climate for the effective establishment of the joint school.

On 22 October 1975 the governors of the new school met to appoint their first chairman, Canon John Montague. He later described his onerous responsibilities as 'the most creative activity in which I have engaged in over 40 years'. A statement of intent was made as follows:

> As the promoters of the United School we would like on behalf of our Diocesan Schools Authorities to put on record our profound gratitude to Almighty God

---

[6]By 1976 St Joseph's had changed markedly from its status eight years earlier: middle-class Catholic parents now sent academically able boys to Reigate Grammar or independent schools while St Joseph's attracted more working-class children from Irish and Italian families recently settled in Redhill.

for the imagination, tenacity and courage of those who have taken the initiative in bringing this new United Anglican/Roman Catholic School to this point of its inauguration. In particular, we would like to record the key part played in all the negotiations by Sr Jerome and Miss Hunt. Their friendship and mutual understanding and appreciation of each other's deep commitment to Christian Education have been of immense importance in the long journey to the establishment of the United School. Coupled with this tribute to them, we would like to record our appreciation of the very important and positive part played by the two Governing Bodies.

We would also like to record at the outset our hope that all will work consistently together both for the educational good of the school and for the deepening understanding of the two traditions of Christian Faith. It is agreed between the promoters of the school that every attempt shall be made to see that both Christian Churches will be fairly represented in appointments and positions of responsibility. However, since Church allegiance can never guarantee that a person has the particular skills needed for a particular job, we do not expect or think it right that there shall be a rigid commitment to alternating Catholics and Anglicans in particular posts. We hope that the person best qualified for each post will be chosen, so long as overall there is a reasonably fair balance between the representatives of the two Churches.

We recognise that in Worship and in Religious Education there is much that at the present time must take place separately, for conscience's sake, and because of church discipline. It is our hope, however, that at least some worship and religious education can take place together, and that this area of what can be done together will be allowed to increase and expand naturally as the staff feel it right.

Between 1972 and 1976, substantial progress had been made: the principles of the new school had been agreed, the legal requirements of government met, the staff brought into sufficient agreement, and the support of the diocesan authorities secured. The possibilities for the future were challenging as practical ecumenism took a step forward on 6 September 1976 when the new St Bede's School opened its doors.

Establishing ecumenical religious education

It may seem surprising that so much attention was focused by diocesan and educational bodies on one subject in the curriculum. However, the previous pages indicate the high level of interest in the area of religious education and the realization that this issue was one on which the ecumenical experiment could easily founder. If assurance was not given that both denominational interests could be safeguarded, St Bede's would not succeed. If the respective Churches, at both parish and diocesan level, could not be confident, the school's position would be undermined.

Similar assurances were to be needed in Northern Ireland: Lagan College was to adopt the St Bede's model of common 'general RE' for all pupils, complemented by denominationally specific teaching. Its founders would also have to provide support for Roman Catholic parents anxious about their children's religious formation outside their local parish network. The groundwork for both schools, it might be said, was done by the working party in Redhill back in the 1970s. We must now consider in detail the work of this group and its outcomes.

THE WORKING PARTY, 1975–77

The Religious Education Working Party (established in response to the seminar at Bramley in November 1974) held its first meetings in March and April 1975. It included the two headteachers, the two heads of religious education, diocesan religious education advisers and representatives of the hierarchies. Its aim over several months was to produce a framework within which the teaching staff could produce a syllabus. It had been set up by the bishops of the two dioceses, with a view to reassuring clergy and parents that a body of experts was dealing with the question of religious education, which in the minds of some was a prime cause for misgiving. It was urgent to allay doubts.

The early meetings seemed rather idealistic. The minutes of the first two suggest a lack of firm steering or direction towards the issues most likely to need a solid basis for mutual understanding and confidence. There may well have been an underlying dread that the idealistic atmosphere in which everything had been discussed hitherto might be quickly shattered if the more obvious sources of mutual discomfort were dealt with. Some of the distinguished national figures serving on the working party acknowledged at interview that they felt the initial sessions were unstructured and desultory, and that no great progress would be made until the group got to work in a more systematic and businesslike way. There seemed to be a fatal propensity to take off into abstract discussions of religious education and the theoretical principles and theology underlying it. What was vitally needed was the provision of some down-to-earth guidelines which would help those responsible for teaching the 'flesh and blood children arriving at the front door fifteen months later'.

Some members of the working party seem not to have been clear about their objectives. This is suggested, for instance, in the following excerpt from the minutes of the meeting in March 1975:

The school's expectations of the end product are important. Are we prepared to let them find their own way forward or do we instruct the pupils only in the one

Church? It must be remembered that we are thinking of one Church, one school, and things are being done more together now. Again, the parents come in here, so we have to tread carefully. We should perhaps work out the school's function, well reasoned and expressing what it hopes to achieve and its limitations. This way, people will understand that it cannot do everything. One of the positive sides of these expectations is that education is different from indoctrination.

It may, of course, be unfair to judge the degree of clear thinking in the working party from a faintly incoherent paragraph in which a generous secretary tried to summarize the wandering thoughts of some participant in the debate. Nevertheless, an incisive view of the problems needing to be tackled did not yet seem to have emerged.

The Anglican and Roman Catholic views on the objectives to be achieved by religious education had by long tradition looked somewhat different. No one in 1975 seems to have ventured to articulate this difference. There was therefore a danger not only that the guidelines, once agreed, would be interpreted in divergent ways by the diocesan representatives of the two communions, but also that the teachers themselves would in practice understand them in hardly compatible ways. At Redhill the working party certainly sensed that considerable time and effort would be required by all sides if the distinct and complementary tasks of school and parish church were to be sufficiently appreciated, and if it were to be realized that a greater weight in respect of catechetical instruction and religious formation ought to be carried by the Church than by the school. Moreover, parishes vary. Active parish churches would be keen to take their responsibilities seriously, but inevitably others would have neither the material resources nor the personalities to respond effectively. Communicating with young people over the age of 13 is a daunting task for a large number of parish clergy (and for some teachers too). The Roman Catholic representatives on the working party did not really want the school to contract out of catechetical instruction altogether. They wanted guidelines which would allay the fears of their constituents, but that would be possible only if arrangements were made to 'ensure that no one is the loser, faith-wise, by this merger' (private letter of one participant, 16 June 1975). Religious education divorced from the Roman Catholic context in which such instruction was customarily given seemed a threat, principally for the reason that it would not necessarily begin from the authoritatively defined doctrines in faith and morals laid upon the hearts and consciences of the faithful by popes and councils.

Later there was discussion of confessional versus non-confessional approaches to religious education. One Anglican said: 'The Christian life is an interaction between tradition and the experience of the individual. The individual then arrives at his own personal faith. The school can at best put them on the right path on which they will, hopefully, continue and grow' (minutes of 1 July 1975). The Roman Catholics did not think of the sacred tradition as something that would somehow assist individuals in working things out for themselves in the idiom that they happened to find most helpful: that would have seemed a replacing of 'I believe' by 'One does feel'. The Anglicans had not said that, but could have been so understood.

At the same meeting a Christian educationist drew attention to the problem of objectivity and neutrality in the classroom; teaching a faith is different from teaching about a faith: 'A teacher must control his own commitments so that he is dealing with the material and treating the children in a non-partisan way.' However, it is more difficult to talk in terms of objectivity or neutrality when one is dealing with subjects with a profound moral engagement. Obviously instruction should and can be non-partisan and fair-minded, objective in considering the facts. But RE teachers can hardly introduce their pupils to fundamental questions of religion and ethics in exactly the same spirit as if they were explaining rows of beetles in a glass case. The Roman Catholics were anxious at any suggestion that such questions should be put before the children as if they were entirely open for detached debate when, in central issues, the teaching authority of the Church had already laid down the answer. Among the Anglicans some talked as if the notion of a teaching Church was not part of their vocabulary. At a meeting on 19 September the Catholic headteacher commented that 'the Catholic school exists for the purpose of teaching religious doctrine—our concepts of the Church school are totally different'. A gulf seemed to be emerging between the Roman Catholic and Anglican understandings of the role of Church authority in defining Christian truth, which had direct educational consequences for the way in which the Church school was expected to operate. Eventually the will to stay together proved stronger than the capacity to solve the theological and educational issue, and the September discussion was finally summarized in a manner which (no doubt pardonably) left the principal nettle ungrasped: 'There seems no reason why a predominantly Christian emphasis should not be educational, providing it is ecumenical . . . and open to the twentieth century.' A possible interpretation of these minutes could be that the Roman Catholics were in effect recognizing

(a) that in the contemporary world, religious education could not effectively be taught in a way and with presuppositions which wholly differed from those governing other subjects in the curriculum;

(b) that elements in the Roman Catholic dogmatic tradition not shared in the same way by the Anglicans, such as the Marian dogmas, could not be thrust forward in a militant manner;

(c) that Christian instruction would not be given as if it were a 'closed' system impenetrable to the moving progress of knowledge in the sciences.

If that is a reasonably correct approximation to the sense of the agreement reached, it seems both that the Roman Catholics had not 'given away' anything crucial to their faith, and that they were willing to modify their own attitude towards the issues in the light of discussion with the Anglicans.

It was one thing for the participants in the working party to wrestle through to a position of mutual understanding, quite another for them to be sure of having teachers to implement the policy, and quite a third thing for them to be confident of pacifying anxious parents and clergy. That a shift of position was acknowledged at the meeting appears in a sentence in the record: 'If we take too much notice of parents and the clergy, we are going to run into a lot of trouble.' It is interesting to note the contrast with Lagan College, where it was parents who took the lead in the move to integrated education.

A measure of the underlying feeling that the working party had been in a potential minefield may be seen by the fact that an influential Roman Catholic participant produced a short paper outlining a position on the main points of issue discussed on the previous day. This suggests some lack of confidence that the minutes of the meeting would make his points sufficiently clearly. At the same time the paper is remarkable for the hope and aspiration it expresses, reflecting a belief that some of the thorny problems the working party had not at that stage solved were in principle soluble and would in time come to be looked at in a different perspective. The document marks an important stage in the group's thinking, and deserves to be set out in full:

1. The extent of common faith between our two Churches is much wider than very many people yet appreciate. It is this that is the basis that makes possible a joint Church school, and makes desirable the *ultimate* ideal of a joint syllabus taught in common.

2. But there are substantial matters of division between our Churches. It is our duty to our respective constituencies to ensure that these matters on which we differ are treated neither as unimportant and irrelevant appendices *nor* in such a way as to make them 'flashpoints' (we do not wish to re-awaken the 16th century). For, in hard fact, these matters on which we differ do affect our whole presentation of religious truth to those we are instructing.

3. It is now less than twelve months before the joint school opens, and before very long the staff responsible, the governors, local clergy, etc. will need to have some practical details that will enable them to plan ahead and also to offer advice/reassurance to interested (or worried) parents. It

seems preferable, therefore, that from the start of the school the Catholic and the Anglican children should receive religious education *separately*. Separation need not mean isolation: this should be possible if care is taken to ensure—

(i)   that the overall aims of religious education are commonly expressed and accepted (cf. discussion of paper on 19 September);

(ii) that the syllabuses are so arranged that, where possible, both deal with similar or common matter at the same time (e.g. the life of Our Lord; the sacrament of Baptism; basic moral issues). Within the course(s) in each year there should be quite a number of occasions when both are covering the same ground ('points of contact');

(iii) that these 'points of contact' are used by the staff responsible not only for consultation and cooperation at staff level, but to promote exchange and interchange between the children. This would be important at any level, but vital in the senior classes; it could lead all to a maturing in faith by dialogue which, ideally, can 'invite all to a deeper realisation and a clearer expression of the unfathomable riches of Christ' (cf. Vatican II, *Decree on Ecumenism*, art. 11);

Treated in this way, divided teaching need not be divisive, but could lead to a true maturing in the faith. At the same time it would make clear that no child, Anglican or Catholic, is being offered a 'watered down' version of his faith.

4.   The sort of exchange and interchange just mentioned would in part depend on and in part contribute to the whole Christian context or ethos of the school. (As yet we have spoken about this ethos, but have not really defined it; we must beware of taking the idea for granted in perhaps too general a way ...)

5.   This in turn is closely related to the expression of the school's Christian and Two-Church character in its worship. It looks as though Assemblies and 'special services' need present no problem. But questions about the Eucharist are sure to arise (and our Churches differ on the age of admission to Communion). Related to this are our respective attitudes (as yet undiscussed) to school chaplains, and to pastoral visits by other clergy from whose parishes some of the children come, not to mention 'class Masses', etc.

6.   My purely personal point of view is that if we can reach sufficient agreement on the matters outlined in 3 above, many of the practical points alluded to in 4 and 5 should be patent of an initial solution: initial, since so much will develop with the developing life of the school as a whole.

Despite the expressions of hope and confidence in future development, the document at crucial points reflects a position which may fairly be called defensive in laying down a strong preference for separating Anglican from Roman Catholic pupils for RE from the beginning of the new school. The reasons given are that the differences between Anglicans and Catholics affect the whole way in which RE is conducted and the fear that parents could otherwise feel that their child was being offered no more than a 'watered down' version of the faith. Yet as far back as February 1973 the governors had thought separation for general RE highly undesirable. The document reflects a conservatism which regards a common ecumenical and educational strategy as being still out of reach. Nevertheless, it is capable of a more cheerful exegesis, namely that its author thought the attainment of the ultimate goal, towards which he is wholly positive, likely to be prejudiced if the stages of movement towards it were taken too quickly; in other words, if the joint school moved very far ahead of the two participating Churches. This would mean that the defensiveness is more tactical than strategic.

The document states well the aspiration for a common syllabus simultaneously covering similar topics in Anglican or Catholic groups, to provide 'points of contact'. The argument shows an important intention to reduce division, which might otherwise seem to be advocated, to the minimum. The eventual decision to supplement periods of general RE taught to Anglicans and Roman Catholics together with one 'denominational' period taught to separated groups (agreed by January 1976) ignored this valid and useful point. As late as 1979 the two 'sides' were still teaching denominational RE in accordance with independently constructed syllabuses that bore little or no relation to each other.

On one further point, the document sowed a seed which bore fruit. The idea that dialogue, especially for senior pupils, would lead to a maturing in faith was later taken up, though probably not in just the way expected in 1975. For, in September 1979, the separate 'denominational' teaching was integrated into examination courses for fourth- and fifth-year students. We shall see that this represented a sea-change in policy, and had the effect of encouraging the students' understanding both of their personal faith and of that of their communion, and their appreciation of ecumenical developments.

The document of 20 September 1975 indicated ecclesiastical and pastoral concerns and anxieties as much as educational considerations. The latter were brought to the fore in a paper prepared for the next meeting of the working party in October by Mgr Kevin Nichols, national catechetical adviser, reflecting experience of the classroom and awareness that religious education and catechesis are distinct, even when there may be some overlap in content. This very different document also merits quotation:

1. One definition of 'catechesis' (as opposed to religious education) is that it is a dialogue between believers. Evangelisation presupposes non-believers, and its aim is to convert them. Religious education does not necessarily presuppose either belief or non-belief. It aims to make a particular educational contribution to religious life.

2. In a Church school, the assumption is that a fair number of the children come from believing families and are themselves believers. There seems therefore to be a justification for both catechetical and educational elements in the curriculum.

3. Moreover, in a Church school, there will be a general context of Christian life. So, the education will be closely connected with worship and with the kind of community a school is.

4. The general approach to religious education in a Church school might be expressed as follows:
    (a) 'Being educated in religion' does not focus on commitment to one's own beliefs.
    (b) It does 'home in' on one's own beliefs and this involves:
        (i)   seeing how they differ from other beliefs
        (ii) understanding how one's own faith stands in the world of religion
        (iii) understanding how it relates to contemporary life
        (iv) consequently, being in a better position to 'adhere to God in a free act of faith'.

5. RE will in no way 'water down' the Christian (or the Anglican or the Catholic) faith. The full teaching, practice and tradition of the Church will be reflected in the curriculum. But this will be done in an educational way—aimed at better, deeper, and wider understanding and freer choice.

6. The balance between catechetical and educational elements may require separate optional courses.

7. A possible summary of aims might be this:—

    (a) An understanding of the teaching and practice of the Christian church and especially of the Anglican and Catholic Churches.
    (b) An understanding of the world of religion and the distinctive place of Christianity in it.
    (c) An understanding of the contemporary world and the place and problems of religion in it.
    (d) A deeper understanding of the children's own experience and the way in which religious belief fits into this.
    (e) Consequently, a freer and more informed faith which extends more effectively into life.

81

This paper starts from the essential distinction that 'education in religion' is not focused on and directed towards commitment but on a greater understanding of the way in which one's personal beliefs relate to the world. Making this distinction enabled considerable progress in the thinking of the working party. Admittedly there was further argument over the ideal of 'rational autonomy' as being 'the goal of the educational enterprise'. However, by the end of that meeting there had been sufficient progress to make it feasible to ask the teachers to prepare a possible joint syllabus for presentation at the next meetings in November and January. The time constraints made this urgent.

By January 1976, the last meeting of the working party, the heads of religious education from the two merging schools had been given the go-ahead for three RE lessons a week, two periods with all pupils together and one period for denominational groups. The general syllabus covered five areas over a five-year course: (1) creation; (2) sacramentality; (3) incarnation; (4) redemption and freedom; (5) the theology of work. The value of examination work for older pupils was discussed, and the advisers emphasized the importance of external examinations.

The governors of St Bede's received the working party's report at their meeting in June 1976, only two months before the start of the first term. The group had met on seven occasions, and for the last three of its meetings had been joined by the RE specialists from the two schools. They had not succeeded in eliminating all possible sources of difficulty, but they had made real advances in thinking through some of the educational and practical issues. Two sample excerpts may be quoted from their report:

> It is important to hold together both sound educational principle and theological integrity. Attention must be paid to the development of the children as well as to the content of the teaching; and the teachers must be able to feel that the syllabus is acceptable in terms of educational standards to their colleagues in the profession. The prime objective must be to develop understanding, and in the learning process controversy and argument have a significant part to play. But the school is committed to the faith that Jesus Christ is the Truth, as well as the Way and the Life. The Christian tradition will, therefore, be presented for explanation and understanding by the pupils, against the background of the firm conviction of the teachers that Jesus and the Truth are one. (item 4)

> While the school is committed to the presentation and commendation of the Christian religion, clergy and parents must realise that they cannot devolve all responsibility for the Christian education of the young people onto the School. The Churches themselves and parents must share in the task of nurturing the Christian faith of the young people. In particular, the Churches have an important role to play in encouraging commitment and movement towards church membership. The school, on the other hand, while accepting a share in fostering

Christian commitment, must encourage the exploration of Christian beliefs and practices critically and openly (an openness which must include an awareness of other religions) and in ways suitable to the pupil's personal development. (item 9)

Probably this was as far as anyone could have been expected to go in bringing together two traditions in Christian education before actual interaction in the classroom was experienced.

ECUMENICAL RELIGIOUS EDUCATION IN PRACTICE

One year after the ecumenical school opened its doors, four members of the RE working party returned, in September 1977, to evaluate the practical consequences of its recommendations. They expressed 'delight' at the team spirit which, they felt, had contributed to a 'remarkable unity of thought and purpose', and congratulated the department on the way they had been coping with the novel and potentially difficult situation. The balance of general and denominational periods appeared satisfactory, and the syllabus was evolving well. However, problems were occurring in the fourth and fifth years (in common with many senior schools), where pupil resistance to RE, even from those who came from Christian homes, was considerable. The RE department requested support from the working party committee for introducing examination courses in religious studies, a request which was fully endorsed as being likely to encourage pupils to treat the subject more seriously and so to increase their motivation.

Another area of concern to the evaluating committee was co-operation between the staff. The committee suggested that the Anglicans and Roman Catholics should give time to a sympathetic exploration of each other's beliefs, and even that each individual teacher should be willing to undertake a radical reassessment of his or her own beliefs; this would lead to a situation where the thinking of staff and pupils might forge ahead of that of the parishes and parents, immobilized in the age-long tradition of group rivalry. The need for adult education to reach out to the parents and clergy was to become increasingly important as the experience of teaching RE in an ecumenical school encouraged new initiatives.

The sun did not shine all the time. Within the first three years of the new school, the RE department, which was inevitably the most sensitive area of the school's work in relation to its constituencies, suffered a series of setbacks. At the initial planning stage the hope had been expressed that the school would retain staff with the vision to see the school's task as a service to the Church; in practice, it was hardly practicable to ask individual teachers to forgo opportunities for promotion which would affect the provision they could make for their dependants. The change-over of staff within the department caused tensions and upheavals. At amalgamation the Anglican head of department had been designated 'head of faculty': he left for promotion elsewhere in early 1978, and the advertisement for his replacement described the post as 'head of religious education'. Not unnaturally there was considerable confusion in the mind of the staff about the position of the surviving Roman Catholic head of department, who perhaps very reasonably expected the reversion of the post with responsibility for the department. The person appointed under the terms of the advertisement was an Anglican woman who took over in April 1978 but quickly found herself in an embarrassing and untenable position and resigned at the end of the summer term, leaving the Roman Catholic sister in charge of the department. When the sister too moved on to another school at Christmas 1978, various supply teachers were appointed as stop-gaps. In practice, they fulfilled a role far beyond that of merely temporary teachers: such was their personal quality that each contributed very effectively to the team spirit of the RE staff over the next year. Nevertheless, the situation could hardly be anything but delicate.

In April 1979, I was appointed as 'head of religious education'. At the interview vague hints had been made that all had not been well in the department, and that there was an urgent need for effective control to be established. Even so it cannot have been easy to envisage the extent of the restructuring required. So much ground had been lost that it was necessary to return to the foundations and to build up the teaching of RE almost from scratch. The general syllabus needed modification to give it a reasonably coherent pattern. The previous plan had been more pastoral than academic in character and, while the intention was laudable enough, it resulted in few of the pupils taking the subject very seriously. Some tact was needed to make the syllabus rather more academic without undermining or jettisoning the valuable pastoral tradition and experience already built up.

In the fourth and fifth years the situation had become particularly disordered. By April 1979 the single weekly denominational period was being timetabled as a double period each fortnight because of the constraints of a split-site school. The pupils were divided into Anglicans and Roman Catholics for this one occasion and were being taught by teachers who normally only saw them once a fortnight. It was immediately apparent that this made no educational sense. In addition, the published denominational syllabuses bore little relation to each other or to the general syllabus, while actually the Anglicans in particular had to all intents and purposes abandoned any pretence of doing specifically Anglican teaching and were using the time to continue with CSE work on St Luke's Gospel. Moreover, the 'denominational' issues related to moral and social education which their Roman Catholic counterparts were covering were all ones that the Anglicans would have found equally appropriate. Besides the denominational teaching, those who had chosen to do examination work for O level were doing four lessons of O-level work, two lessons of general CSE work, and one lesson of denominational RE, amounting to more than a fifth of their curriculum time. Overkill on this scale required urgent reassessment.

At this time the denominational teaching was not working effectively either, but a solution to the problem seemed related to several other difficulties. If a major shift in school policy regarding RE could be carried through, perhaps all or most of the problems could be resolved in a single overall plan. Such a change of policy required the confidence and assent of the governors, so a proposal was submitted to the school governing body as follows: if the denominational RE (DRE) could be integrated into the examination courses for the fourth and fifth years (so that, for example, the sacramental aspects of Christian marriage could be taught within the syllabus section about Jesus' teaching on marriage and the family), then the pupils would not only learn more but would relate the academic knowledge to their own spiritual development, while at the same time they could amicably discuss with each other differences in the approach of Anglicans and Roman Catholics.

There were, however, to be three important safeguards. First, the two chaplains were to be invited in to discuss these issues of difference with the mixed groups of pupils, while they were also available for private consultation with individuals if further information or counselling were required. Secondly, if Anglican teachers were to be discussing specifically Roman Catholic positions and Roman Catholic teachers explaining what they understood to be distinctively Anglican, then it was essential that the staff meet regularly to exchange ideas. This was the start of the seminar groups run by the two chaplains to provide a vital underpinning on controversial matters for the teaching staff; in addition, these seminars enabled prejudices to be aired and clouds of misunderstanding to be cleared away. One Anglican RE teacher reflected: 'I learned an enormous amount about Roman Catholicism, which was very helpful when we came to teach a GCSE syllabus on Christian denominations.' Thirdly, there was a feeling that specific denominational teaching at a senior level was more effectively done outside the classroom—for instance on 'awaydays' out of school with staff and chaplains, to enable pupils to talk more openly and to share their personal feelings about religious questions in less formal circumstances. 'Awaydays', at which the pupils would go together with staff to visit some place of religious significance, were to develop into an important feature of the RE department.

After considerable discussion, the governors finally endorsed the proposals and consented to a two-year experimental period for their implementation. Denominational teaching would now be timetabled separately only during the first two years of the pupils' time at the school.

An immediate consequence of this was the need to determine the essential elements covered by the DRE syllabus while the pupils were still in segregated Anglican and Roman Catholic groups during their first two years. It was desirable that, so far as possible, the denominational syllabus should be common to the two groups—a suggestion closely akin to that put to the working party in the document of 20 September 1975, but not implemented hitherto. For example, baptism and Church membership constituted a shared experience for most of the children: there seemed everything to be said in favour of arranging that Roman Catholics and Anglicans should discuss this at the same time; they could then talk it over with each other. Careful thought was required to define the main areas of denominational concern, especially areas in which there was a history of past controversy. On the significance of baptism there ought not to be disagreement between Roman Catholic and Anglican, nor concerning the pastoral significance of the sacramental act of confirmation by the bishop. But there would be diversity of liturgical custom, whether confirmation be by laying on of hands with prayer or by chrismation with consecrated oil, and also a traditional difference not in doctrine but in practice about the age of confirmation and admission to communion. The Council of Trent recommended that confirmation occur between the ages of 7 and 12, normal Roman Catholic practice, while a later age was common among Anglicans, although the local Roman Catholic diocese was moving to confirmation at 13, a recommendation endorsed by the National Pastoral Congress at Liverpool in 1980.

There would again be scope for some differences in style, if not in fundamental approach, between Anglican and Roman Catholic in their way of thinking and speaking about biblical authority and the role of tradition. In regard to the central question of the eucharist, the rapprochement achieved by the theologians in ARCIC was only slowly percolating through to the consciousness of the Churches at the grassroots level. One Anglican priest in a parish near St Bede's commented that such ARCIC agreements provided a valuable stimulus to ecumenical co-operation in the area. On questions of reconciliation, the traditional divergence between the Roman Catholic 'you must' and the Anglican 'you may' in regard to sacramental confession and absolution reflects variant conceptions of the necessary role of the priest. While both communions share an episcopally ordered ministry and set high value on the continuity and unity of which the bishop is intended to be sign and instrument, there is an obvious history of long disagreement between Roman Catholics and Anglicans about the conditions for the possession of valid ministry and an authentic eucharist. Nevertheless, even in these areas the amount of common ground greatly exceeds that of disagreement and divergence. By every educational criterion it was highly desirable to formulate a shared syllabus of topics for the segregated periods of instruction; and with so much common ground this would not be too difficult to achieve.

The new proposal did not come into being without some anxiety being expressed. There was bound to be fear that the specific was being pushed out in favour of something more general and therefore vaguer; perhaps just that kind of common Christianity which hopes to find unity in 'fundamentals', defined as those doctrines on which no important disagreements seem to emerge between groups who in fact disagree on many issues that are certainly not felt to be optional extras by those who consider them seriously. A Roman Catholic diocesan team which visited the school in February 1981 commented that 'it will be necessary to reflect continually on the denominational aspect of the syllabus in order to ensure full integration of different parts of the programme in the second and third years'.

The extension of integrated denominational teaching to the lower school could not be pressed without running up against the anxieties of the parents and clergy. The less they knew about the school, the more anxious they felt. This was especially evident among the Roman Catholic parents who, like others even in single-denominational schools, were finding it difficult to understand how religious education had shifted away from the catechetics of their own schooldays. They proved very ready to express their sense of alarm to their parish priest, and to put the blame on the school if a son or daughter were to begin to ask awkward questions or even to cease to practise the Christian faith. The lack of independent denominational instruction throughout the school was an inviting scapegoat for their apprehensions. The point again brings out the difficulty that the ecumenical school may tend to push ahead of the uniting churches that have come together to form it, and underlines the essential importance of educating and keeping the confidence of the community beyond the school gates, a role the second headteacher, Dr Phil Dineen, took very seriously. She recalled: 'I was pleased to have got the RE right at the right time.'

In the autumn of 1982, two open evenings were held for all parents and clergy who wished to find out more and to discuss the nexus between the school, the home and the parish. These useful sessions were later extended to new parents in the July prior to the admission of their child; they not only provided information and clarified the RE programme, but also gave parents the direct opportunity to express their fears to the teachers. The parents not unnaturally tended to rely more on their feelings and apprehensions as to what might happen than on actual knowledge of what was really going on. Conditioned by upbringing and centuries of traditional rivalry, it might be expected that they would approach the question of an ecumenical school with some prejudice and inaccurate information. If an ecumenical school is to be successful, it needs to enhance the understanding of Christian faith within the surrounding community.

The search for suitable resources to use in the classroom is difficult enough for the RE teacher in a state or denominational school. How much more problematic for a school that has to give a balanced picture of two denominational traditions while retaining academic respectability for the subject and the interest of the pupils. Textbooks for the general religious education course were easily obtainable: the traditional academic syllabus of introduction to the Old and New Testaments (including the life of Christ), world religions and moral and social issues has always been well resourced by the publishers of RE materials. The denominational elements on the other hand required further research. The main Anglican contributions to this area attempted to present materials of contemporary interest but their layout and approach were unimaginative.[7] On the Roman Catholic side a more determined effort had been made to produce resources and syllabuses that followed pupils' own concerns as well as providing them with the necessary knowledge and understanding to encourage informed discussion.

Two publications proved useful for DRE. An attractive and contemporary syllabus entitled 'In Christ' had been produced by the Roman Catholic diocese of Birmingham in 1979. While covering the essential denominational elements of the sacramental teaching of the Church (e.g. baptism, reconciliation, eucharist, priesthood), it presented its ideas in a way which stimulated the interest of secondary pupils. The other publication, the 'Veritas' scheme, had been introduced successfully into primary/middle schools during the late 1970s and was beginning to have an impact at secondary level. This too presented catechetical ideas in a contemporary context, like *Weaving the Web* (Lohan and McClure, 1988), involving the pupils rather than instructing them as had been the tendency in much previous Roman Catholic classroom material. Such resources were helpful in producing a viable denominational course, particularly for the second- and third-year pupils. Both Anglicans and Roman Catholics could follow a common syllabus while emphasizing their distinctive traditions and producing work that reflected pupil interests.

RELIGIOUS EDUCATION BEYOND THE CLASSROOM
In a Church school, above all, a balance needs to be sought between the academic and the pastoral dimensions of religious education; either one without the other renders the enterprise invalid. Children must relate their understanding of religious ideas to the local community and to the world. The three-way relationship between school, home and parish has to be seen

[7] A leading Anglican spokesman on RE commented in 1992 that, since Anglicans tend to see themselves as 'the Church of the nation', there seems some hesitation in producing denominational materials for specific use in Church schools rather than county schools, particularly in the secondary sector.

and felt by the child to be effective. But in practice this relationship is not always easy to maintain.

At St Bede's it became apparent by the summer of 1979 that parish involvement in the school was, to say the least, haphazard. Some clergy might come to take an assembly; others might attend the wine and cheese evening each autumn. But there was still a number whose contact with the school and, more importantly, with the pupils from their own parish, was minimal or even non-existent. To attempt to rectify this became a major logistical exercise, for the school was attracting students from over 50 parishes across two dioceses. The RE department decided to organize a day in their own parish for all 240 12-year-old pupils (the new intake year), so that in the first term of their secondary education they might realize that a Church school had something to do with the Church, and therefore had a dimension additional to that of a county school. Their Church school was not only a place for the pursuit of academic excellence and a house of pastoral concern, but was also linked with a wider believing community which expressed its Christian faith in everyday life from cradle to grave.

The majority of the parish clergy responded favourably to the idea, and the second Monday in November was set aside for the first of what were to become annual parish days. It was not expected that any specific catechetical activity should be included, since the day was compulsory for all the pupils. However, it provided an invaluable opportunity for both 'sides' to explore the link between the Church and the school. Above all, it introduced the local priest to his flock, some of whom he would know well, others hardly at all.

An interesting further development was initiated by the clergy themselves in 1980. Where small numbers of pupils were involved, it seemed sensible for parishes of different denominations to combine their efforts and, by sharing resources, give the day an ecumenical flavour. These programmes proved extremely successful and by 1981 were extended to include the Protestant Free Churches as well as Anglican and Roman Catholic parishes. The personal commitment to these days by the clergy was impressive and, as the school chaplains were able to take increasing responsibility for the organization at the school end, the links between the Christian community within the school and the parishes were substantially strengthened. They also illustrated how the joint school could take on a 'prophetic' role in enhancing local ecumenical co-operation.

Apart from these parish days, extra-curricular 'awaydays' were developed for more senior year groups. Third-year pupils, making decisions about their public examination courses and possible future careers, and fourth-year pupils, coping with the heavy pressure of examination work, were offered residential experiences with the aim of challenging them to think through the material and spiritual values underpinning their decisions and relationships. This process of self-analysis demanded considerable maturity and the support of RE staff, pastoral teams and chaplains. In the fifth and sixth forms, residential opportunities, including a pilgrimage to Lourdes or a weekend in the soup-kitchen of St Martin-in-the-Fields, allowed older students to appreciate the importance of the spiritual and personal alongside their academic development.

What then, were the essential perceptions of the RE task in a joint Church school that developed at St Bede's in those early years? To summarize:

- If religious education in a Church school, and especially an ecumenical one, was to be effective, it had to succeed in the classroom by producing high standards of work and by being accepted by the students as a serious academic subject.

- At the same time, it had to look at the whole person and contribute to the student's spiritual development which generally took place beyond the classroom.

- This wide-ranging responsibility required a dedicated team of teachers who not only had good academic qualifications, but also related easily to young people.

- Alongside these requirements, such teachers evidently needed to have a mature understanding of their own faith and a commitment to ecumenism that went far beyond merely working alongside each other.

- Naturally such maturity and commitment were a matter of dynamic growth rather than static possession, and could be born and fostered in the experience of teaching at an ecumenical school, provided that the person concerned was seriously willing to listen to what 'separated' Christians had to say.

- Finally, the ecumenical task is one of great difficulty, requiring sensitivity and hard work, a resolution to remain undiscouraged by the virtually inevitable setbacks, and a vision that the ultimate end of Christian unity is possible.

School chaplaincy and ethos

THE CHAPLAINCY ROLE, WORSHIP AND COMMUNITY LIAISON

'Wasting time usefully' was how one chaplain described his job when interviewed in 1981. Great discipline was required to ensure that he was not doing something all the time and really was available to staff or students. Without the detailed timetable that other members of staff had, the chaplains felt their role was to be at the service of all in the school community whenever they were needed. This availability was cardinal to the success of their task.

A national *Memorandum on School Chaplains* by the Education Commission of the Bishops' Conference, circulated in February 1979, spelt out the chaplain's role as one of service:

(i) to be an evangelist and an example of Christian living;

(ii) to encourage and stimulate the individual and group to live a Christian life of prayer and action;

(iii) to be adviser and counsellor to the individual pupil or member of staff on matters of faith and Christian living;

(iv) to be a reconciler in a community within which, because of its size and artificial nature, communication at all levels is frequently very difficult;

(v) to be a bridge between school and home and between school and the parish. It is particularly important to help pupils become properly integrated into their own parish life, particularly at the time of leaving school.

In essence, his role is to assist in the building up of the school as a worshipping community in which the celebration of the Eucharist is a genuine expression of the faith of the school.

This document highlighted several of the opportunities and difficulties that a chaplain in any Church school was likely to encounter and which in an ecumenical community required additional sensitivity.

From the beginning of the joint Church school, two chaplains were appointed. The head, Madge Hunt, in a paper on the role of the chaplains, emphasized the importance of links with the clergy, involvement in denominational religious education, more general areas like community service, and availability for spiritual advice and counselling. She pointed out that the role could not be precisely defined, for it depended greatly on the personal gifts and inclinations of the individual. By 1980 the headteacher, Phil Dineen, was able to report to governors: 'We are conscious of the heavy demands we make on our present chaplains and of how fortunate we are to have within our school community two such able, popular, and dedicated pastors.' There can be little doubt that without them and the way in which they approached their work, innumerable problems would have arisen.

The qualities required of a school chaplain were formidable:

He must want to be with young people and willing to learn about their environment. He must be able to accept them as they are and listen to them sympathetically and with understanding. He should be a man in whom dignity and humility meet and whose authority derives from his closeness to God. He must be willing to be subject to the proper authority of the Headteacher and ready to work with him for the Church in the school community. (Memorandum of February 1979)

Such qualities were not found in all priests. Particularly in the ecumenical context, the Christian community of the school could suffer serious damage if an ineffective appointment was made. Phil Dineen, interviewed in 1993, recalled that the Roman Catholic diocese did not always offer its best clergy to St Bede's; they seemed 'totally untrained' and often immature in their faith as well as socially; 'when we had the right people, it worked superbly'. The need for a breadth of vision and sense of initiative could not be over-emphasized, for the students quickly responded to the inner strength such qualities reflected.

One chaplain, when asked in 1982 how he saw his role in the school, replied in the following terms:

As a chaplain you haven't got a niche. You're everything or nothing. At the end of the day, how do you measure what you have achieved? Teachers can aim for examinations and measure themselves by results. A chaplain cannot measure what he does so easily. My aim is just to be alongside, to pray with people and for people, but one's effectiveness cannot be measured.

Before 1981 the chaplains in the joint school had no base in the building from which to work, which considerably exacerbated the problem of having no 'niche'—there was not even a perch. Discussing personal concerns with individuals in a corner of the cloakroom or after displacing the deputy head from his office underlined the unsatisfactoriness of the position. By the end of 1981 cloakroom space had been reallocated as a chaplain's room, and pastoral counselling was able to develop more effectively and with greater respect for the feelings of the counselled.

Inescapably, the problem of confidentiality and liaison with the pastoral heads of year or form tutors became a cause of difficulty. Should the chaplains pass on information to a head of year about glue-sniffing among those whom they were counselling? What was the relation between chaplain and teacher when confidences about pregnancy or truancy were entrusted to the priest's ear? One of the Roman Catholic heads of year in 1981 unhesitantly considered that chaplains should always be seen to be separate from the year system. If the pupil confided in the chaplain as a priest and the confidence was given in the form of sacramental confession and reconciliation, then it could not be passed on. And it was not only when the confidence was in this context that the priest was bound to keep silence; the chaplains had to use their discretion and do what they believed to be best, but 'it only takes one child to feel betrayed . . .' (as one chaplain put it) and, in delicate cases it was thought wisest for the chaplain not to involve the school authorities. The chaplains' responsibilities extended into the staffroom. New teachers often needed and responded to the support shown to them. A helping hand and encouraging comment were sometimes even more welcome from someone not involved in assessing one's success as a probationary teacher. Chaplains worked alongside staff in a variety of ways: sometimes standing in for an absent teacher when the pressure was severe; participating in 'awayday' excursions and camping weekends; or team teaching especially in the denominational RE (by now called DRE) lessons. Staff goodwill was important if there was to be a sympathetic response to the disruptions caused by religious services and, if the chaplains were seen to be involved in the demanding tasks of teaching and counselling, then staff would respond positively and welcome the additional support.

Apart from these qualities, the chaplain's practical tasks included responsibility for *worship*. Celebrating the eucharist is the focal point of the community of faith. However, in an ecumenical context, it is not enough for the Anglicans to see ministry in terms of Anglicans only, nor for the Roman Catholics in terms of their own flock. In an ecumenical school both have to be able to see beyond their own traditions to the Church united in Christ, even if the road towards such unity seems hard and long. A policy of caring only for those of one's own denomination may underline and entrench division.

At St Bede's the two main denominations at first came to celebrate the eucharist separately at the beginning and end of every term as well as on days of obligation, and these services were compulsory, leading to an atmosphere of pupil hostility and staff resentment. 'It was like sitting on top of an active volcano', said one Anglican teacher required to supervise pupils of 'all denominations' other than Roman Catholic at the Anglican eucharists in 1980. Catholic staff used to take it in turns to supervise pupils in the mass because 'the children were so awful'. Some priests found it difficult to make services relevant to young people and the subsequent disciplinary problems were hard to manage. The introduction of a *voluntary* eucharistic celebration in 1981, however, was perceived to encourage large numbers of pupils to take a more active part in the liturgy, creating an atmosphere of prayerful worship rather than one of tension. In addition, weekly celebrations were held before school for smaller groups of students whose commitment and enjoyment acted as a magnet to others.

It is striking that regular church attendance on Sundays was no guarantee of involvement in school worship. Approximately half of the pupils who came to the school eucharists in the 1980s did not attend a church regularly, perhaps feeling that, if they participated at school, it would be overdoing it to go to church as well. Others who were regular church attenders might not necessarily come to school celebrations, because they preferred to see worship in the context of the family rather than as something shared with their friends and school contemporaries.

When the two eucharists for the whole school were made voluntary, they were timed to fit into an extended morning break to lessen the amount of supervision required for the non-attenders. This meant competing (in many cases unsuccessfully) with the iced buns on sale in the canteen. The services were subsequently moved into the place of assembly or form time during the first session in the morning. This ensured that the service was seen more as an official activity of the school, while retaining its voluntary character, thereby encouraging more active support from the pupils. The Roman Catholic chaplain also pioneered joint services of reconciliation, especially during Lent, which, though non-eucharistic, enabled students to contribute readings and music in an atmosphere free of tension. These were most successful, attracting over a hundred pupils to celebrations of Christian fellowship in 1982.

Several times in the early history of St Bede's the staff (sometimes together with the sixth form) attended their own celebrations of the euch-arist at which great efforts were made to do everything together which could be done without offending consciences and the rules that restrict intercom-munion. These services were held especially to mark significant occasions such as the Week of Prayer for Christian Unity. Initial attempts at such joint celebrations in 1980 were markedly unsuccessful. At first the ministry of the Word was celebrated with everyone, Anglicans and Roman Catholics together, and the hope for unity was pledged in the kiss of peace (this being transferred to its normal Anglican position before the offertory rather than kept in its normal Roman Catholic position between consecration and com-munion). But then the two groups turned their backs on one another, facing in opposite directions towards their respective celebrating priests. The experience was one of sharp pain and not a few tears. A new Anglican chaplain was appointed in 1980 and a year later a new Roman Catholic: both were able priests who together felt these liturgical arrangements were wholly unsatisfactory. After respective consultations, they produced a form of service for a 'parallel eucharist', in which both traditions could be respec-ted yet common liturgy said together. The two altars were narrowly separ-ated, the celebrants used their respective liturgical forms alongside each other and communicants received from their respective priests without embarrassment. By 1982 the sensitivity and experience of the two chaplains made it possible for things to be done in such a way that the worshippers came away inspired to hope and pray for unity instead of feeling that their highest aspirations had been disregarded. Phil Dineen described it as 'the most poignant statement of ecumenism and its limitations; a moving and thought-provoking experience'. Such services were also opportunities for local parish clergy to come into the school to share in the community act of worship. Once staff and other adults felt comfortable with the appropriateness of these services held on special occasions about three times a year, it was decided to open them to sixth-formers. This again worked well since these older students respected the denominational 'boundaries', yet appreciated the significance of the joint service.

In addition to the chaplain's role in leading worship and presiding over the eucharistic celebrations, there was the responsibility for *liaison with the Christian community* beyond the school walls. In 1981 pupils came from 42 Anglican parishes, 13 Roman Catholic parishes and 19 Protestant Nonconformist congregations. Communication between the school and the local clergy could hardly be anything but an administrative and pastoral nightmare.

In 1982 the Anglican chaplain, combining his work in the school with part-time responsibilities as a local curate, made a point of visiting as many Anglican churches as possible to preach or assist with services. Local deanery meetings also provided a useful forum for discussion of the development of St Bede's and a chance for the chaplain to pick up any cause for concern that needed to be communicated to the head for the sake of the pupils. Meanwhile the Roman Catholic chaplain, working part-time at the diocesan religious education centre, also proved his sterling worth in the field of public relations. From her point of view, Phil Dineen recalled: 'As head of a joint school, I had to spend more time with Catholic clergy than I would have as head of a single Catholic school; they needed so much reassurance.'

Both chaplains saw it as part of their work to forge links with the first and middle schools, which not only broadened their contact with the children in the parishes, but also proved invaluable when helping the new second-year pupils at St Bede's to settle into secondary school; it was reassuring for the 12-year-olds to see a familiar face on the first day inside a new institution where everything else was strange. The chaplain's role in coordinating the parish day has already been noted for its effectiveness in linking all the parishes with the school and encouraging new ecumenical partnerships.

It became self-evident that the chaplains in a joint Church school had a key role. According to the Roman Catholic Ecumenical Commission's Working Party on Joint Schools (1978):

He is not teacher nor administrator but priest. His first task is to celebrate. His celebration of the liturgy must tap all the riches of his own communion. Yet he also has a pastoral role. He knows himself to be a Minister of a particular Church, and his first responsibility is to his fellow-members. But he has a responsibility for all those in the school. Especially he must relate to the head and the staff, trying to discern prophetically the call of God in policies and problems. He also has a crucial role in relation to the local clergy. It is to help them to understand what is going on in the school; to involve them in the pastoral care of the young people who are students there.

The essential qualities required in a chaplain have not changed. Yet effective communication with young people and a prophetic grasp of the opportunities for ecumenical co-operation have not been seen as characteristic of all St Bede's chaplains. Experience has suggested that when the bishops have appointed 'good' chaplains, their prophetic insight has taken the whole enterprise forward in its exploration of paths to unity in truth. 'Poor' appointments not only stalled but put back the process.

SCHOOL ETHOS: SHARED CHRISTIAN VALUES

Parents turn towards Church schools for the education of their young because they set a high price on the values that will be emphasized in such schools. Some react with apprehension as they contemplate the secular comprehensive school because it seems so large as to be impersonal, almost a kind of knowledge factory or bazaar of training in diverse skills, but without itself having an allegiance to an overt, coherent moral ideal. They further react with fear of the laxities of the 'permissive society' in which sexual mores are treated as each individual's purely private affair into which society may not without impertinence poke its inquisitive and censorious nose. Some parents speak with a genuine concern that formal religious education should be sympathetically timetabled and treated with respect as a discipline, and above all that the whole life or 'ethos' of the school should reflect those Christian values that the parents are seeking to foster at home.[8]

A letter written by one parent to the head of St Bede's in 1980 contained a passage which crystallized the attitude in direct terms:

> We need a school where our children can receive a total education. We ask for them more than training in academic, social and physical knowledge and skills (though we demand the highest standards in these as well); we require a school environment where Christian values are upheld, where the moral and spiritual lives of children are not only acknowledged, but nurtured and developed, where by constant example they can grow up as part of a caring community. We do not believe that 'religious education lessons' provide all our children need in the way of religious education, but that the latter goes on all the time, at home and at school, in every subject on the curriculum, in the corridors and in the dining hall. We want teachers who are not afraid to take a stand and speak out against society's evils, prejudice, materialism, intolerance, racism, whatever they may be.

[8]Similar views are discussed in Cardinal Hume's speech to the first National Conference on Catholic Education (July 1992) and in *A Shared Vision: Education in Church Schools* by David Lankshear (1992a), p. 25.

In a *Memorandum on Christian Schooling* of January 1974 the Roman Catholic Ecumenical Commission for England and Wales wrote as follows:

The whole life of a school is part of the educational process, and the Christian must value the educative effect of a community atmosphere that springs from Christian commitment, difficult though this ethos may be to define in set terms.

The question is in what ways Christian faith and practice can be discerned to be constitutive of the prevalent tone, atmosphere and assumptions of the community in a Church school. In a paper produced by the Roman Catholic Ecumenical Commission's Working Party on Joint Schools in 1978, Mgr Kevin Nichols wrote:

Christian values have to be translated into the school's community life. They should affect—indeed create—its ethos or atmosphere: that reality which is hard to put a finger on, but which is of such great importance. A school, like any other community is a network of human *relationships*. The quality of those relationships as a whole is a major factor in building a school's ethos. (Ecumenical Commission, 1978)

The Anglican diocese of Southwark in 1983 also endeavoured to formulate what it understood by the ethos of a Church school:

In a school, ethos is created and influenced by factors from both within and without the school community. As these factors are in a state of movement, it follows that the ethos of a school must itself be dynamic and therefore open to review and appraisal . . . Attempts to restrict the nature of ethos by hard and fast rules can curtail the evolutionary process of this very elusive and yet fundamental concept. . . .

Through its legal right to appoint staff, select Governors, control RE, and in the secondary school to be responsible for the whole curriculum, it (i.e. the Church) may create an institution in which the Christian faith is manifest through every aspect of the school's individual and corporate life. (Green, 1983)

Anglican and Roman Catholic educationists agree that the ethos of a Church school is critical to its Christian success. For an ecumenical school this ethos must reflect the richness of both traditions yet encourage mutual respect and understanding. How well was this achieved in the early years of St Bede's?

The headteacher, Phil Dineen, herself 'absolutely committed to ecumenism', realized that the school's key appointments had to be equally committed—not only members of senior management or the head of RE, but also the school secretary, whose communication skills and use of the 'right terminology' in responding to enquiries were critical to good community relations. Reassuring local clergy, Catholics apprehensive that Catholic education was being diluted, Anglicans fearful of catechetical indoctrination, took considerable time and effort. Dineen explained her dilemma:

> Different Christian denominations use language which is culturally distinctive. I found that my efforts to use inclusive Christian terminology, which avoided offence to either party, would upset traditional Catholics who looked for familiar language and symbols to reassure them that St Bede's had the ethos of a Catholic school. Far from being obstructive, their real fears resulted from ignorance of Anglicanism. Anglicans too were watching us but were generally less defensive.

By contrast, staff found the Christian ethos of an ecumenical school more rather than less explicit. Dineen felt that some not particularly committed Roman Catholics, who might have been used to remaining on the sidelines in a Catholic school, could not do so in a joint school where the Christian ethos was under the spotlight. Ironically, more attention might have been paid to RE and Roman Catholic teaching at St Bede's than in some Catholic schools, she suggested.

One Roman Catholic teacher, new to the joint school in 1981, said: 'It must be good for Catholics to work alongside other Christians—it must be a more realistic environment than a straight RC Church school.' An Anglican teacher, speaking from experience of working in the Catholic school involved in the merger, thought that the Roman Catholics might have lost part of their distinctive tradition of devotion in the amalgamation—for example the distinctive habits of nuns, crucifixes and statues of saints adorning the building, the sign of the cross at assembly—but that in compensation the Roman Catholics now seemed to have emerged from a previously rather ' narrow' environment.

Even if some staff interviewed in 1981 thought the ecumenical influence on the pupils generally might not be that noticeable in terms of their behaviour, one science teacher commented that the ecumenical atmosphere helped pupils to appreciate both sides of a question more easily. Assemblies and services were singled out by staff as a reflection of the Church school ethos. Another teacher remarked:

> Being able to attend religious services with teachers and pupils, and having assemblies where religion is an integral part, have some influence on your thinking and attitudes or behaviour in the school. Having chaplains present and pupils whom you see and relate to in the parish also affects you.

When asked whether staff were made aware that some pupils were committed Christians, a biology teacher added: 'An altar boy in most classes would be able to explain how a poppy seed is dispersed by a "censer" mechanism.'

Several staff, especially in the humanities subjects, commented that religious and moral issues often arose in their lessons, for example the Reformation's place in history, social issues reflected in English literature. In modern languages, particularly at the sixth-form level, a teacher commented: 'Christians have responded well to Mauriac, but have been hindered by preconceptions in studying Sartre.' In physical education, issues such as honesty, loyalty to team members, no foul play or cheating, were singled out for special emphasis. In science the teaching on contraception, abortion, population control, respect for plant and animal life and for one's own body were all considered topics raising religious and moral questions. A Roman Catholic science teacher remarked: 'You are aware you have to give both sides of the picture, an Anglican and a Roman Catholic perspective, and encourage students to think through the issues for themselves.' It is clear that many teachers at St Bede's made a conscious effort in their lessons to discuss moral and religious issues in a Christian context. Several form tutors in 1981 said that they encouraged such discussion in form periods (e.g. on issues such as bullying or stealing) and that senior pupils often wished to compare viewpoints on contemporary events in the news.

In relation to counselling, staff were asked to what extent they were aware of their pupils' religious views or backgrounds. Replies varied. On the one hand there was the answer 'I make a point of finding out at the beginning of the year', or 'I feel advice would be pointless unless you know the student's background and beliefs'; on the other hand, 'I make a principle of not asking', and 'I have not found this makes much difference'. While some suggested that they were not as aware as they should be, one teacher added 'I would particularly want to be aware of their religious background if asked about contraceptive advice'. Another said 'Denominational issues only arise if I need to ask which chaplain the child would like to talk to'.

In conclusion, it is clear that both the overt and the hidden curriculum were influenced by the Church school context, though it would be difficult to quantify this influence. While a joint Church school might reflect a wider range of viewpoints than a single-denominational establishment, the issues for discussion were similar. It might be that the pupils at St Bede's were unable to see their environment as anything other than normal compulsory education; they were not comparing it with other ways of doing things. But, as one teacher suggested, 'It would be most interesting to see whether those children are taking an active part in ecumenical activity within the community, ten, twenty, or thirty years from now'.

2. ST BEDE'S SCHOOL: TEN YEARS ON, 1991–92

New developments in ecumenism

We have got to get the theology right first: what is God's will for the Christian Churches and then where does St Bede's fit in? (Julian Marcus, 1992)

These words of the Anglican headteacher appointed in 1985 to succeed Dr Dineen are reminiscent of the original manifesto of 1972 which, at a time when ecumenical hopes were running high after the Anglican/Roman Catholic Commission's eucharistic agreement, envisaged a united Christian school blazing a trail for ecumenical collaboration at the parish and lay level. Marcus continued:

> It is important to make ecumenical schools a microcosm of what the Churches are doing ecumenically. This means that St Bede's needs to take seriously the role of the Free Churches in the ecumenical movement and rethink its constitution to reflect Churches Together in England.

By 1991 St Bede's exuded confidence in its own success. The school had expanded its staff and pupil roll under its new headteacher and had become increasingly oversubscribed. New buildings had been approved but only after a debate in Parliament, a petition to No. 10 Downing Street (9 July 1986) and a meeting with two Secretaries of State: Sir Keith Joseph expressed surprise when he met the governors' delegation as it was the first time he found both an Anglican and a Catholic bishop supporting the same school! The buildings had opened in September 1988 and were dedicated in March 1990 by the Anglican and Roman Catholic diocesan bishops, and the school was anticipating the arrival of 11-year-olds in September 1993, when the age of secondary transfer was to be lowered from 12-plus to 11-plus across Surrey. Like most schools, St Bede's was coping with financial constraints (under Local Management of Schools), having the third-lowest per capita funding in the LEA and was reviewing its position in relation to grant-maintained status (GMS). In May 1992 the governors decided not to seek GMS for the immediate future, taking into account the imminence of 11-plus transfer and the need to lease extra accommodation from the LEA.

The issue of the Free Churches' involvement in St Bede's became part of the governors' agenda during 1991–92. The implications for pupil admissions, financial contributions, religious education, chaplaincy and community relations were significant. Although in practice under former heads, Free Church children had always been welcomed in reasonable numbers, there had been 'a modest but steady rise' in Free Church applicants, averaging 12–13 per cent and, in 1991, even amounting to 17 per cent of the intake. The governors, in monitoring the admissions balance over the years, had not seen this as an issue for comment, other than to question whether the Free Churches should contribute to the school's maintenance costs (a question also asked of some local Anglican Churches: Anglican deanery policy was that each parish should demonstrate its responsibility to the Christian community by basing its contribution on parishioner numbers rather than on the number of children attending St Bede's; not all parishes regularly fulfilled their obligation). No trust deed for St Bede's had specified formal arrangements on admissions or staffing, which were by less formal agreement and tradition, allowing for greater flexibility in changing circumstances.

In practice, the rise in Free Church pupil admissions coinciding with greater oversubscription to the school generally, had meant that 'fringe Anglicans and other religions' had increasingly been excluded. The proportion of Roman Catholics meanwhile had remained steady between 25 per cent and 32 per cent, averaging about 28 per cent. The head acknowledged the danger that St Bede's could be accused of being a Christian middle-class ghetto in which 'Christians kept the best school to themselves', a view he considered detrimental to good community relations. This perception was reinforced when the local Muslim imam was unable to gain admission for his child in 1991. Table 3.1 gives some indication of the changing admissions pattern over ten years.

Table 3.1 *Pupil admissions by denomination*

Denomination	1982 Whole school %	1982 Year 8 %	1992 Whole school %	1992 Year 8 %
Anglican	63.2	70.5	51.7	44.5
Roman Catholic	28.4	20.5	28.6	38.1
Methodist	3.1	3.6	4.2	4.7
Baptist	1.9	0	4.4	4.7
United Reformed	2.0	1.3	3.2	4.2
Other Free	0.1	0.5	5.9	3.4
Salvation Army	0.3	1.3	0.1	0.4
Other/none	1.0	2.3	1.9	0
Total no. of pupils	1,075	224	1,186	236

In September 1990 the national ecclesiastical bodies came together to form Churches Together in England, the successor to the British Council of Churches; but this time the Roman Catholics were included as full members (in accordance with a recommendation from the National Pastoral Congress in Liverpool, 1980). Although St Bede's had to all intents and purposes seen itself as a recognized 'Local Ecumenical Project' (LEP), even to the point of including that logo unofficially in its publications, no formal covenant had ever been drawn up. The rather narrow criterion for LEP recognition under the Churches' Council for Local Ecumenical Projects in England meant that the governors' request in the early 1980s had been turned down, since it was not associated with a formally constituted Free

Church Federal Council. When the criteria were widened in the mid-1980s to include schools, St Bede's, Redhill was added to the database at the request of the then chair of governors, although no sponsoring body was specified.

On the Roman Catholic side, meanwhile, the appointment in 1983 of a 'conservative' Catholic as local parish priest, whose prime interest was to safeguard (more perhaps than to share) the Catholic tradition and to assert the rights of his parishioners to send their children to their Catholic school, had created some problems for new ecumenical developments. 'Manpower difficulties' in the diocese were said to explain the appointment, and a few years passed before the bishop could find an appropriate replacement, to accord more closely with local lay Catholic feeling. There were objections to St Bede's celebrating 'parallel' eucharists which moved the bishop—also under some pressure from very conservative Catholics—to request that they cease in 1985 after Julian Marcus' appointment as headteacher.[9] Even if not disallowed by the 1983 code of canon law, they had been leading to mis-understanding in the parishes as they 'were not part of the local ecumenical experience,' commented the bishop (*Church Times*, 22 January 1993). One Roman Catholic member of staff in the RE department reflected that the parish priest 'thought he was being ecumenical, but felt he had to fly the flag for the Roman Catholics: the new one is much more ecumenically minded and supportive'.

Undeterred by such difficulties and inspired by the imminent establish-ment of Churches Together in England, following on the 1987 *Swanwick Declaration* that 'as a matter of policy at all levels and in all places, our Churches must move from cooperation to clear commitment to each other in search of the unity for which Christ prayed', the headteacher published a paper in May 1990, entitled *The Next Step* (Marcus, 1990). Marcus saw his role not just as an 'educational manager' but as a 'promoter of the school's ecumenical vision'. He argued that

> if St Bede's is to be faithful to the will of our Lord, to be true to the ecumenical inspiration of Vatican II, to participate in the mission of the Church through the Inter-Church process, to demonstrate as an LEP genuine 'commitment' as 'official policy at every level', then the Free Churches must be offered representa-tion on the foundation.

He proposed that, while the school's instruments of government were being amended, it would be appropriate to invite Free Church representatives as observers to governors' meetings, and to request a 15 per cent financial contribution to the school's maintenance costs in line with the average

[9]Phil Dineen, the previous head (interviewed in January 1993), suggested that the bishop could not have stopped them earlier as she would have considered this a resignation issue.

percentage of Free Church pupil admissions. The headteacher's paper was discussed by the governors' Christian Education sub-committee, and the chair decided to consult the Anglican and Roman Catholic bishops.

The discussion paper caused consternation in both diocesan circles. The Southwark (Anglican) diocesan director expressed his deep concern that the proposals would 'rock the boat' (memorandum of 4 July 1991), and in particular that the Roman Catholics might reconsider 'their future involvement with the school if the present Trust was changed'. He argued that the head did not carry the full support of his governors, especially the Roman Catholics, whose diocese of Arundel and Brighton had 'continually and openly indicated their opposition'.

His anxieties were confirmed by a letter from the Roman Catholic area dean to his diocesan director of schools (8 November 1991) following the autumn governors' meeting, expressing fear that the diocesan involvement and therefore its authority were being eroded. The area dean voiced concern that the chairman of governors, although admitting the need for great sensitivity, believed that the governors had the 'legal right to alter the foundation', and only a 'moral obligation to take the views of the Trustees into account'. His letter sought Catholic diocesan advice on four main issues:

1. that the school was founded primarily to take the Anglican and Catholic children in the area, 'not because of a passionate desire to set up an Ecumenical School. There is a difference between a Joint School and an Ecumenical School. . . . Both dioceses still see the school as a Joint Foundation—nothing more';

2. that the Foundation cannot be altered without the agreement of the trustees of both dioceses;

3. that the presence of larger numbers of Free Church children does not imply corresponding representation. 'Representation surely hinges on the Foundation, not the other way round';

4. that 'Free Church members are welcome provided there is room', but 'we are now reaching a position where baptized Catholics (and Anglicans) are excluded', in spite of the bishop's statement that all baptized Catholics are entitled to Catholic education;

The area dean's views clearly formulated Roman Catholic anxieties that agreement to official Free Church representation might water down the school's commitment to the Roman Catholics and Roman Catholic commitment to the school. It was a single priest's view, but represented an influential voice.

Other views were aired in a joint memorandum to their respective bishops by the Anglican and Roman Catholic diocesan directors of education in 1991. They shared the concern that any admissions policy by which Free Church children were admitted to St Bede's at the price of excluding Anglicans or Roman Catholics, must have emerged 'without the agreement of the parishes and diocesan authorities who financially and otherwise established and have sponsored the school'. The Free Churches had traditionally felt their contribution to be in the non-denominational state-provided county sector: 'if that traditional approach is no longer accepted Free Church policy, that must be clearly thought out and its implication spelt out for us all'. While the informal involvement of Free Church ministers in St Bede's had been no problem, 'we are quite clear that the arrangements of St Bede's school should not be used for non-educational ecumenical engineering'.

The memorandum also clarified the diocesan directors' view of the vision and purpose of St Bede's:

> We still feel that there is something peculiarly valuable about the common trends in the ecclesiastical dimension which can bring Anglicans and Catholics very closely together. At St Bede's school, the sensitive approach to sacramental worship and Religious Education has protected and developed this crucial aspect. It has not been done in any exclusive or narrow way. We feel confident that the contribution and importance of other denominations and non-Christian faiths have neither been neglected nor belittled. But such a tolerant and balanced approach need not, in our view, require a dismantling of the delicately established joint Anglican/Catholic basis to the school.

The directors regretted that 'any advice which we offer can now, if desired, be interpreted as being negative to ecumenical developments or, specifically, hostile to the Free Churches'. Nevertheless, they strongly advised their bishops:

(a)   to affirm their support of the present joint Anglican/Catholic foundation to the school;

(b)   to support the diocesan directors' concern that Anglican and Catholic children might not be offered places in the school as a consequence of places being given to non-Anglicans and non-Catholics.

A special meeting of the governing body was called on 1 February 1992 'to discuss in full the ecumenical role of the school', based on a draft document drawn up by the headteacher entitled 'An Ecumenical Covenant for St Bede's School': this noted the necessity of requesting the Secretary of State

---

[10]Ironically 'ecumenical' was the original title proposed in the early 1970s, later amended to 'united'. This is attested in the archives of the diocesan lawyers. Legal advice in 1992 suggested that the Secretary of State would be unlikely to agree to the amendments of the Foundation if the foundation governors and trustees were opposed.

to alter the school's Instruments of Government in order to include Free Church foundation governors, and to change its name from a United School to St Bede's Ecumenical School.[10] Before the meeting, the Anglican diocesan director had written to all Southwark foundation governors, reiterating the main points made in the joint memorandum to the diocesan bishops. A parallel issue was emerging about whether power lay primarily with the dioceses or the governors.

The governors' meeting was later described by the chairman as 'helpful and productive'. Keen to assert their rights under the 1988 Education Reform Act, they unanimously resolved:

> it is the firm desire of the Governors of St. Bede's School for its foundation to be enlarged to include formal Free Church representation so that the school can reflect our membership of Churches Together in England.

It was agreed that wider discussion be undertaken as to the provision of a Free Church chaplain for the school; that Free Church denominational RE be included in the curriculum from September 1992; and that the governors begin consultations with the bishops and diocesan authorities with a view to including Free Church representation in the Foundation. These resolutions and consultations were reported to parents at the annual governors' meeting on 2 April, when no parent asked any questions on this issue. Subsequently a joint meeting was held with both diocesan ecumenical officers on 7 July, and further meetings were planned with the two bishops.

The question raised was bound to be a thorny one. On the one hand, the school saw the proposals for Free Church representation as a great ecumenical opportunity for St Bede's to be become 'a dynamic force for ecumenism' in establishing a new kind of Local Ecumenical Project. By June 1992 'the Free Churches in Association with St Bede's' had been set up (in parallel to the Anglican deaneries structure) to appoint school governors and a chaplain, and to accept the moral commitment to pay expenses. The chairman of the local Free Church Ministers' Fraternal wrote to his colleagues, in November 1992, that St Bede's 'offers a point where we can overcome our denominational and theological differences in a common concern for children's education and well-being'. Meanwhile, however, the response from both bishops had been discouraging. They referred the issue back to their diocesan directors, insisting that it was 'largely an educational matter'. Julian Marcus expressed impatience with the dioceses' preoccupation with ecclesiastical power and bureaucracy; to him the question was primarily theological, about 'the will of God' rather than about 'territory and power'. Nevertheless the diocesan directors urged caution, realizing that amending the trust deeds would be contentious (and therefore expensive), and that it would be easy to unsettle Roman Catholic confidence in the school, particularly in the matter of admissions, a view independently confirmed by two Roman Catholic governors.

The chairman of governors in June 1992 acknowledged these concerns as sensitive and complex, and conceded the importance of 'pacing any new developments carefully'. The significance of the matter was illustrated by remarks of the pupils themselves. One sixth-form girl, reflecting on her first impressions of St Bede's at the age of 12, regretted that, as a Methodist, she was always put with the Anglicans: 'the first message the school conveyed to me was that Methodists were not important'. A young boy, asked in the bus queue by a senior teacher on the pastoral team why he did not get a bus pass to Epsom, explained that, as a Methodist, he was not entitled to the free pass given to Anglicans and Roman Catholics; the boy behind him in the queue commented, by the way of helpful explanation, 'You see, Miss, he's the wrong religion'.

Staff also expressed a variety of views. Members of the RE department in 1992 considered that Free Church children had a higher profile than ten years previously: they were keen to have their own identity and proud of their tradition. The Roman Catholic chaplain, then a nun appointed in 1988, explained that she had learnt much about differences within the Free Churches since she came to St Bede's: 'The Methodists seem to be similar to us and the Baptists so different.' She was impressed by the Free Church children, for example in running their own prayer group: 'their faith is so strong'. She understood the reservations of the Catholic diocese because St Bede's had so often been the focus of attention. But having seen integrated schools in Northern Ireland, like Lagan College, succeed in creating ecumenical schools which included the Free Churches without the need of diocesan structures, she felt herself drawn to the head's vision for St Bede's.

An evangelical Anglican senior colleague, however, felt hesitant about formal Free Church representation. She questioned whether it was really the role of the school to bring the Churches together. She felt that St Bede's' first priority was to run a successful school with an academic and Christian ethos, thereby demonstrating to the Churches that different communions can work together: 'We don't need to become one Church because we are all one now, as part of the one body of Christ; the school should demonstrate that unity.' Her reservations, which she admitted were practical rather than philosophical, included the risk of upsetting the dioceses who had invested so much in the joint school ('there are a lot of sensitivities'), the fact that not all Free Churches were affiliated to Churches Together in England (e.g. the independent evangelicals), and the absence of a Free Church body to shoulder its obligations to the school, though it was some reassurance to her that the new association might turn out to be sufficient.

Two established members of staff, both high Anglicans, independently drew attention to a far from unimportant theological issue. As Anglicans they often found themselves identified as Protestants rather than as Catholics, and therefore were seen on the same 'side' as the Free Churches. However, in their theological position, they personally felt much closer to the Roman Catholics. This self-understanding was difficult to make comprehensible to the evangelicals as well as to traditional Catholics conditioned to regard all Reformation Churches as a rebellion against divine authority. The issue of Free Church representation was perhaps as much about personal perceptions, including self-perceptions, as it was about structures and constitutions.

The Curriculum and Religious Education

THE CURRICULUM

Curriculum development in 1991–92 was understandably dominated by the National Curriculum and post-16 expansion. Like most Church schools, St Bede's had to manage both Key Stage 3 and 4 implementation and its implications for staffing, resources and in-service training, as well as ensure that religious education retained its prime position as a core subject through to GCSE for all students. In the sixth form, expanding numbers of students staying on beyond compulsory school-leaving age had necessitated the development of courses appropriate for a wider range of ability. In 1992, 23 A levels together with 4 AS levels, GCSE (mature), secretarial studies and the City and Guilds Diploma in Vocational Education were offered. Students from other 11–16 Surrey schools, faced with the option of college courses, were also free to transfer into St Bede's' sixth form. One new sixth-former entrant from a practising Anglican background said he had been attracted by the school's reputation for 'good teachers who made you work'.

In addition, the school was involved in the Technical and Vocational Education Extension scheme (operating in Years 10 and 11 in September 1991) and in piloting Records of Achievement in Years 8 and 9. St Bede's contributed more students than any other school in Surrey to the Duke of Edinburgh Award Scheme, and had extended its international exchanges (already established with Europe and New York) into Tanzania. The head even considered such Third World links as 'the essence of what a Christian school is about; much more significant than the ecumenical question'.

A senior colleague considered that the school's academic reputation had grown over the decade: it was now more sought after by parents wanting high academic standards, with some still inclined to see it as 'the next best thing to private education'.

We now offer three languages [Spanish was added in 1989] and science has blossomed. Students are awarded Oxbridge places each year. There's now a better boy/girl balance than ten years ago when it was still seen as the ex-girls' school.

It is not surprising that St Bede's was ambitious to enhance its academic reputation both locally (having once been known as a 'secondary modern') and nationally, now that league tables were all part of marketing.[11] A parent governor commented that the school had no choice in the current climate since parents were so critical about results; but she wondered whether it had swung too far the other way: 'I think St Bede's is excellent for able children, but I'm not so sure now about the less able. How can a Christian school keep the right balance?'

RELIGIOUS EDUCATION
Religious education, as ten years previously, was seen as central to the curriculum. In the school's booklet *Information for New Parents*, the section 'Religious education in the classroom' extended across more than three pages—the only curriculum area to be considered in such depth. Major staffing difficulties in the mid-1980s (including a two-year interregnum[12]) had been overcome, and the RE staff appeared confident and professional in their discussion of departmental issues. The 1992 HMI inspection team invited into the department commended it for 'sound scholarship and Christian commitment'. Designated RE classrooms in the new building had raised morale and put RE in a stronger position across the school. HMI described the department's resources and displays as 'excellent'. One teacher, who had been attracted by 'the most exciting RE job in Britain', claimed that it had largely lived up to his initial impressions.

RE staff had felt it was important to be academically demanding, as standards throughout the school improved. They had switched to the more challenging London and East Anglia Group GCSE syllabus with encouraging results and increased A-level take-up. One lower-sixth student commented: 'French A level gave me the ability to speak a language, but RE made me think.' An interesting new Cambridge modular course for A level had allowed the flexibility of building up credits towards A or AS certificates over its two-year programme.

---

[11] St Bede's was cited in the 1991 *Parents' Guide to Good State Schools* as one of the 300 best schools in Britain (Clark and Round, 1991, p. 235) and placed top in the Surrey section of the 1992 national GCSE league tables.

[12] The school had experienced some difficulty in making a satisfactory appointment as head of department in 1985. As a result, a long-serving member of the department became acting head of department for two years.

The next priority for the head of department (appointed in 1987) had been to bring the syllabuses up to date, which, despite the considerable efforts of colleagues in the meantime, had not in his view kept pace with contemporary developments. In 1991–92, for the general RE in Year 8, pupils studied an introductory course on Old and New Testament themes, followed by a topic on pilgrimage to include aspects of Christian history.[13] In Year 9 a course on three major world religions (Judaism, Hinduism and Islam) was justified to parents with the observation: 'Unless students make a serious study of faiths other than their own, they cannot be said to be religiously educated'; they need to understand faiths encountered in society to avoid racial or cultural prejudice. Setted pupil groups were rearranged to facilitate mixed-ability teaching throughout Years 8–11 to obviate 'bottom set' labelling; this presented staff with additional demands to ensure appropriate differentiation and match to pupil capability.

The overall structure of religious education established in 1979 seemed to have held up well. The integration of denominational teaching with the GCSE syllabus on 'Christianity and Family Life' had continued, with pupils 'willing to address denominational differences openly'. Segregated denominational RE (DRE) in Years 8 and 9 continued (and continues) to be the subject of debate. The common syllabus framework (for example all pupils studying the sacrament of baptism simultaneously) and its main topics had largely been retained. At the staff restructuring in 1990 the teacher promoted to second-in-department had been given responsibility for the DRE joint scheme of work, and faced similar difficulties to those of 1979 in identifying appropriate teaching materials. Some material from *Weaving the Web* (Lohan and McClure, 1988) had been helpful, but staff felt their own syllabus was more strongly developed. She produced a resources and suggestions pack after consultation with governors and colleagues, but was deeply discouraged when the official governors' meeting was inclined to dismiss it as merely 'photocopied material'. The timetabling of one double DRE period every fortnight created a lack of continuity, but offered a lesson of reasonable length for teachers to get to know their students. To encourage the children to distinguish 'general' from 'DRE', a new marking scheme of effort grades was introduced. The department also hoped to address the problem of pupil motivation on a non-examination course by reporting pupil progress in DRE through the new Records of Achievement.

As occurred ten years previously, the staff felt bound to ask what was the continued justification of separate denominational teaching. A senior teacher acknowledged that the original 'tramlines to establish boundaries' were no longer needed since the school was now more confident and open in

[13]This continued the successful tradition of pilgrimage in the steps of St Bede in the north-east of England during summer half-term, started in 1983.

religious matters, but she admitted that sensitivities still existed—
'nevertheless that is no reason not to keep asking the question'. Some RE
staff found classroom management of DRE with Year 9 students very difficult, but also said that it had to be retained for 'political reasons'. In 1992
the governors resisted a senior management proposal to remove it by September 1993 to allow more time for the National Curriculum.

A Roman Catholic in the department commented:

> Until the Roman Catholic Church gets its educational structure right, we'd have
> a fight to remove it; but progress has been made. The parish now takes responsi-
> bility for the teaching of the sacraments; the gaps to be bridged are between
> communion/confirmation and adult catechetics. I feel strongly that catechetics
> should be done in the parish and the home—it's the parents' job to teach the
> catechism.

Such views appear to be supported by the educationists associated with the
National Project for Religious Education in the Roman Catholic Church.
The Catholic chaplain agreed that

> we are doing a stop-gap in DRE until the parishes are ready. Although holy
> communion and confirmation preparation has already been taken out of the
> schools across the diocese, the school is still expected to do its part. The danger
> is that if catechetics are wholly removed from schools, will the Church see a need
> for Catholic schools at all? I personally think Church schools can be justified by
> communicating an effective Catholic ethos, since a 'religious' way of life is
> caught, not taught. The role of staff is critical here, in their relationships with
> pupils and their personal example. Parents will be looking for results in their
> children's morality and lifestyle.

The Catholic chaplain and staff felt under pressure from both sides. The
contemporary political climate promoting school distinctiveness and
parental choice in education, as in the 1992 White Paper *Choice and Diversity* (DfE, 1992), together with more conservative Catholic circles lobbying
for a return to a traditional catechesis, encouraged parents to expect more
from their school in terms of religious formation. At an open forum during
Cardinal Hume's visit to St Bede's in March 1992, one Catholic parent
commented that she did not feel her children were receiving enough
catechetics at school, the only time when there was a 'captive audience'.
When a Roman Catholic RE teacher suggested that this was primarily the
parish's responsibility, the parent replied that the parish was not teaching it
either. The Cardinal expressed the hope that the school would take some
responsibility with the parish for Christian nurture. Several Catholic staff
recognized the value of the Cardinal's visit in marking the hierarchy's positive commitment to ecumenism, but felt frustrated that 'there had been no

real discussion of Roman Catholicism in the ecumenical context'.

However, it would be misleading to suggest that the only perceived purpose of DRE was to keep Catholic parents happy. Catholic RE staff acknowledged that the community needed to be reassured by seeing Catholic teachers teaching Catholic children, but they did not see DRE as 'narrow catechetical nurturing, even if that's the way we are expected to see it'. The RE staff felt the real value of DRE lay in the teacher–pupil relationships and explicit Christian atmosphere of the classroom, where children felt better able to talk about their own personal exploration of faith than in general RE, and the chaplains could be present to answer their individual questions. Yet the possibility of tension is well illustrated by the following anecdote: one Catholic teacher said she greatly valued the opportunity for staff and pupils to be able to acknowledge their own shared community, for example by saying a prayer together in class; however, she had found herself biting her lip when the Catholic chaplain tried to insist that the children learnt by heart part of the Catechism, a task which she, like others in single Catholic schools, considered to be the role of the home and parish.

It would also be misleading to imply that DRE was primarily for the benefit of the Roman Catholics. Anglican staff felt equally strongly that DRE had an important role in ensuring that both Anglicans and Catholics had an understanding of their own traditions within an ecumenical Church school. 'They need to realize that an ecumenical school is two traditions coming together' and 'to know the difference', one teacher commented. Both Anglican and Roman Catholic staff said they explained each other's distinctive denominational characteristics to their DRE classes. At the same time, the Anglicans recognized that most pupils interested in learning more about their own Churches in their denominational groups were likely to be attending their parish Sunday school and therefore to need less specific nurturing than the Roman Catholics whose Church teaching still tended to be based in school. Again they wanted to create an atmosphere in the classroom in which children felt confident to talk about their own religious perceptions and understanding.

Meanwhile, unplanned but significant, a new development in DRE had taken place since the autumn of 1991. It became apparent in timetabling for the 1991–92 academic year that the headteacher would be unable to fulfil his teaching commitment to the Anglican DRE programme in Year 9. To cover the classes, a qualified teacher from the local United Reformed Church was brought in and the teaching groups restructured to place all Free Church pupils in one group. By accident, Free Church DRE had been established. This arrangement continued 'fortuitously' into 1992–93, informally creating a specific Free Church teaching presence in the school. As a senior teacher pointed out, the Free Church parents often needed as much reassurance as the Roman Catholics about entrusting their children to a joint

Anglican/Roman Catholic school where they might not always expect to meet a favourable estimate of the Reformation.

While this development gave the Free Church pupils more confidence in their own identity, and strengthened the argument for some official Free Church representation on the governing body, the move also reinforced the separate denominational structure in the RE department. Since all Free Church children admitted to St Bede's (like most Anglicans) were likely to have been closely involved in their own Sunday schools, the DRE classes were appropriate less for passing on knowledge than for providing an opportunity for pupils to explore their own faith in a sympathetic environment.

There is little doubt that, over the last ten years, the 'political' justifications outweighed the 'educational' considerations for continuing separate denominational teaching at lower secondary level. Maintaining the confidence of parents and Churches was of paramount importance, in spite of the educational difficulties of limited resource materials or managing large classes of 14-year-olds for non-examination courses once a fortnight. On the other hand, the integration of denominational teaching into the GCSE syllabus in Years 10 and 11 had been successfully established, giving a sense of assurance that specific denominational issues could be addressed in an ecumenical context.

RE staff looked optimistically towards the future: perhaps after the new Year 7 children had settled into St Bede's, it might become possible to negotiate fully integrated RE for Year 9, whilst retaining DRE for Years 7 and 8. Although this move had so far been resisted by governors, staff shared the founders' hope expressed seventeen years earlier, that what can be done together in worship and RE 'will be allowed to increase and expand naturally as the staff feel it right'.

The broad principles of religious education at St Bede's, as formally stated by the RE department, appropriately conclude this section:

> Religious Education must not seek merely to present factual information about religion. It must also encourage students to experience religion at first hand. Only then can children be led to make a realistic choice about their own religious views. This is a difficult aim to achieve by itself; rather it is part of an on-going process to which the worship of the school, faith of the home, and the teaching and practice of the Church all contribute.

School chaplaincy and ethos

THE CHAPLAINCY ROLE, WORSHIP AND COMMUNITY LIAISON

In February 1990 the governors advertised for a new Anglican chaplain with the following responsibilities, which may be read as the priorities identified over ten years' experience:

(a)   to be a pastor and enabler to the whole school community involving home visiting, parish liaison. . . ;

(b)   to lead the Anglican and support the Free Church staff and students within the school, helping them to have a deeper sense of their vocation and responsibility; presiding at the eucharist; leading other worship, developing lay leadership in the spiritual life of the school, encouraging and participating in diocesan activities;

(c)   to lead and guide ecumenical services within the school;

(d)   to lead discussion groups of students in the second year and sixth form weekly and help staff with denominational religious education lessons;

(e)   to assist health education staff with Anglican perspectives on moral and ethical problems.

These tasks were expected to occupy three days per week in term time; the chaplain would also assist in a local Anglican parish and could be offered some part-time teaching (thereby receiving accommodation and additional remuneration). The new chaplain took up his post in September 1990, spending three days in the parish and three days in St Bede's, with a third of the latter also as a part-time teacher in the RE department, marking an interesting new departure. Trained as a counsellor and with previous school chaplaincy experience, he believed he had established himself effectively in both pastoral and academic roles. He commented that working in the class-room enabled him to develop good relationships with pupils and to gain the respect of staffroom colleagues.

He had been particularly attracted to the job because it offered teaching and he found no difficulty in the dual role of teacher and counsellor: 'I expect high standards academically but children talk to me confidentially as a priest: it's not a problem.' With regard to the relationship between the two chaplains, himself and the Roman Catholic sister, he thought that they complemented each other well: the sister seemed more effective with chil-dren than staff whereas he, as a trained teacher, felt at home in the staff-room. 'She is more child-orientated, whereas I counsel teaching and non-teaching staff all round the school.' The Roman Catholic chaplain also felt that they worked well together: she especially enjoyed the relaxed atmos-phere when pupils spent lunchtimes in the chaplaincy room, while her Anglican counterpart met colleagues in the staff canteen. The head con-sidered the balance of a man and woman in the chaplaincy 'a great blessing to the school'; although initially he had been concerned when the Roman

113

Catholic bishop did not offer a priest, in practice the sister had enhanced the confidence of local Catholic parish clergy in the school by inviting them in to celebrate the eucharist.

Other staff saw the chaplains' pastoral role as a valued complement to their own. The only occasion when staff criticisms of chaplains were voiced both in 1982 and 1992 was, understandably, when services ran over schedule causing disruption to lessons. Sometimes year heads might refer a child for chaplaincy support; on other occasions the chaplain would alert pastoral colleagues to a family crisis or bereavement. The governors' published policy on health and sex education, as required under the 1986 Education Act, informed parents that 'students' conversations with chaplains are always regarded as confidential, although parental involvement will follow where necessary in almost all cases'.

On the issue of *worship*, the best organization was dependent on establishing effective relationships with the pupils. In 1988 when the Roman Catholic sister arrived, Roman Catholic clergy expressed concern over the pupils' voluntary mass arrangements, which had reverted to the time prior to the start of the school day in the chaplain's room, at 8.20 a.m. before most of the school buses had arrived. Few children were attending, and the services were rushed to beat the registration bell. The previous chaplain had been unable to drum up support even on days of obligation. The head therefore agreed with the sister's suggestion to move the Roman Catholic weekly eucharists back into assembly time on Tuesdays, an arrangement soon followed by the Anglicans on Wednesdays. When for pragmatic reasons it was later felt that both services should take place on Tuesdays, the two chaplains amicably agreed to hold their respective eucharists in alternate weeks. They could not have anticipated the result: so many pupils chose to attend both Anglican and Roman Catholic services each week that they had to transfer to a larger space in the gym, and its unsuitability has led to the consideration of building a chapel. Since both chaplains related well to each other and to the pupils, they created what one form tutor described as a

> lovely atmosphere where everyone feels welcome. . . . I am particularly surprised at some of the 'lads' who go. They would not have gone to the chaplain's room—it was too intimate—but now they will ask you openly, in front of their peers, if it's Eucharist today.

As in all eucharistic services, the pupils were encouraged to receive communion if the priest of their own denomination was celebrating (and they were regular communicants) or to receive an individual blessing.

The voluntary non-eucharistic services for the entire school, usually held twice a term, were also well attended in 1991–92, attracting large numbers of lower-school children and up to 50 per cent and 40 per cent of Years 10 and 11 students respectively. One senior teacher reflected: 'Worship has really taken off in the last four years. We cram so many children in, I am sometimes even worried about Health and Safety, but I prefer that to what went before.' Several staff commented on the atmosphere of unity and Christian fellowship in these joint services, which until 1989 had been denominationally separate, one year head recalling 'the feeling of them and us' when he had first come in 1987—'the school was not trying hard enough then'. Another wondered if it might be better if the services were mandatory: 'Older students are often reluctant to go because it is crowded; or is that adolescent inertia?'

One particular incident showed how much progress had been made ecumenically. Soon after her appointment and unaware of Protestant sensitivities in this area, the Catholic chaplain enthusiastically encouraged the children to join in saying the 'Hail Mary' at a joint service; it would not have occurred to her that there could be anxiety about an acclamation made up of two sentences of Holy Scripture. One Anglican RE teacher remarked:

> The Anglicans would probably have said it if they had known the words! It marked a turning-point for the school because Anglicans earlier on would certainly have taken offence. At least the GCSE course now covers these differences.

It was common practice to make at least one of the termly joint services a eucharistic celebration, following either the Anglican or the Roman Catholic rite. On Ash Wednesday 1992 all pupils were able to receive the imposition of ashes on the forehead, whereas in 1982 the Catholic children came out of their separate service trying to brush off the ash so that they did not appear different from their peers. The chaplains actively encouraged pupil attendance and staff willingly participated; one Roman Catholic teacher explained how, supported by their sympathetic local priest, she had overcome her personal lack of confidence to assist in giving a blessing to the children who did not receive communion.

By 1992 each end of term was marked by a special service for staff, at which colleagues who were leaving selected their own hymns or readings, regardless of whether they themselves were practising Christians. One teacher saw this as indicative of a 'sense of common purpose among staff and a commitment that all individuals were valued in the school's Christian community'.

The 'parallel' eucharists that had provided such important ecumenical opportunities in 1981–82 were no longer celebrated after 1985 when the bishop decided to withdraw his support for these services. Several staff and parents, including Roman Catholics, expressed regret, commenting that they had been a valuable witness to Christian fellowship. One Catholic parent reflected that shared communion 'would be good, but it seems to be an issue which is bigger than us. The children can't understand why not.' A

St Bede's student of 1982 (who went on to Cambridge to read theology) recalled the experience even in 1992 as one of the most powerful and exciting in her time at school. At the memorial service held for Canon John Montague, the first chairman of governors, in November 1992, Julian Marcus reflected that it was 'John's greatest grief' that the Roman Catholic bishop stopped these services. One RE teacher also recalled 'they were one of the best things St Bede's ever did'. The pain among Anglicans and Roman Catholics was still deeply felt seven years after these services had ceased and the previous headteacher, Phil Dineen, thought the decision had seriously set back ecumenism in the local area. As more local ecumenical developments take root in England and other official ecumenical bodies evolve, this issue of 'parallel' eucharists which maintain the current rules on intercommunion needs to be addressed.

In the decade since 1981–82, the chaplain's task of *community liaison* had hardly become less onerous. The 1992 prospectus recorded:

> Our students come from about 80 local parishes and churches. Liaison with these is a formidable but rewarding undertaking . . . The School chaplains often make home and Church visits where they can offer support and liaise also with parish priests and ministers.

The chaplains continued to work within the parish communities, the Anglican priest having specific parochial responsibility as assistant minister. Both preferred the local parish work to involvement in official diocesan or deanery activities. The organization of the annual parish day for Year 8 (previously second-year) pupils reinforced the chaplains' commitment to the community, linking school with home and parish and facilitating further ecumenical co-operation between local churches.

The possibility of broadening the chaplaincy team in 1993 by the appointment of a Free Church chaplain added another dimension, and affected the balance established (sometimes precariously) over the past few years. There had always been a latent question of churchmanship, particularly among Anglicans; the chaplain was High Anglican, his predecessor was Low Church evangelical. But the situation was more complicated if one Free Church chaplain was expected to represent the interests of both Methodists on the one hand and 'house' Churches on the other. The head of RE felt that, although there was a risk of Free Church 'in-fighting', he was hopeful that because the Anglican/Roman Catholic balance had worked so well, even at a time when the local Anglican parish was deeply evangelical and the local Roman Catholic parish traditionally Irish and conservative, the Free Church chaplain should be able to fit easily into the team.

Over ten years, the chaplaincy role at St Bede's had evolved considerably. The pattern of worship had been developed, community links enhanced and relationships with staff and pupils strengthened. But in the final analysis, it was the quality of the chaplain's ecumenical vision as well as personal commitment which seemed most significant. In 1992 the Roman Catholic chaplain reflected:

I'll never be the same again. Living through the fruitful tensions and consequences of being truly ecumenical means that you've got to take your theological vision beyond just being nice to non-Catholics. The prophetic role is not a comfortable one. I make mistakes. But when I talk to Catholic chaplains in other schools, I am certain that St Bede's is really trying to live out what it means to be a Christian school.

SCHOOL ETHOS: SHARED CHRISTIAN VALUES

It is interesting to review the way in which St Bede's saw its Christian ethos ten years on in 1991–92. The school governors remained explicit in their endorsement of the school's aspiration to a Christian ethos. For example, the 1992 prospectus specified the first aim of the school as follows:

To provide for students and staff a Christian setting in which to experience the Gospel, to grow, explore, and nourish their faith (lived out at home, at church and in the world), to treasure and indeed test the traditions of their own denominations, while learning to work for the unity of the Christian Church; and in which to be helped to gain respect for other people who may have different likes, attitudes, and characteristics, or who may be of other races, cultures, and religions.

The annual Governors' Report to Parents of April 1992 also emphasized this: 'We hope that concern for our Christian witness underpins all that we do.' The report went on to instance school worship, community service, charity fund-raising and Third World links as areas for practical expression of that witness.

The school's two leaflets for prospective parents and staff devoted a full section to 'The religious life of the school'.

As St Bede's is a Christian school, religion obviously has more importance than it would have in a county school. However, our aim is not to indoctrinate but to join pupils in a religious quest that asks fundamental questions about the meaning of human life and about our individual and social values. . . . For staff and pupils who are committed Christians, there are frequent opportunities to explore faith and celebrate in worship our corporate life. Although not all our teachers belong to a Church, we hope that all will value a Christian way of life and share our concern to provide an exciting and relevant curriculum, within a caring pastoral framework which nurtures the individual and his/her growing intellect, beliefs, ideals, and emotions.

117

This extract was common to both leaflets, for parents and for staff. However, that for parents also included the sentence:

As a Christian school we are able to take committed stances upholding Christian values, for example in personal sexual behaviour.

That for staff included the comment:

In practice, colleagues who are committed people but not churchgoers seem to fit happily into St Bede's and its ambience and certainly do not feel pressurised!

The importance of pragmatic marketing had not been missed by the management.

Self-evidently the teaching staff had a significant influence in their commitment to and understanding of the nature and ethos of an ecumenical Church school. We have seen in the previous section the way in which the chaplains were responsible for setting the tone in Christian relationships both within and outside the school community. Several commented that the school had a higher proportion of committed, caring staff than a county school and, as at Lagan College, that there appeared 'less gossip and intrigue', 'less militancy' in the staffroom. One member of the staff replied, 'I cannot really put it into words; it's just a feeling I get that the atmosphere is more caring'. The presence of the chaplains also prompted a comment from a probationary teacher: 'Some pupils make use of the opportunity to discuss problems with the chaplains, which relieves the pressure on staff.' The staffroom was seen as 'by and large united'; despite the extra pressures of educational initiatives in recent years, colleagues still seemed willing to be involved in all aspects of the school. Admittedly one regretted that some of the new graduates coming into the profession appeared to be 'more out for themselves than for the kids'. One deputy head felt the general spirit of the school had improved over the years, helped by the new buildings and the more motivated pupil intake:

The atmosphere is one of cooperation and care. You rarely hear a teacher shouting. The children are not tightly disciplined because they do not need to be. Exclusions are very exceptional.

Another senior colleague added that the pressure to improve academic achievement had in no way lessened the school's Christian ethos.

A number of staff had chosen to apply to St Bede's because of its ecumenical dimension. One senior Roman Catholic teacher, with experience in Catholic and county schools, felt the joint school was theologically and educationally more balanced than Catholic schools without an ecumenical presence. He valued the opportunities offered to staff and students to exchange religious ideas, improve their understanding and overcome prejudices—those atavistic memories which do much to keep groups apart.

Even if the younger children do not notice it is ecumenical, they know it is Christian in ethos. Because they have no point of comparison, they do not know the significance of ecumenism, but the older ones can understand it. It could have a real influence on them later in life, even if they do not attend Church.

Another colleague argued that he was 'more of a Catholic' because he knew more about Anglicans: he had witnessed a militant Protestant demonstration outside an ecumenical service in Liverpool Cathedral in 1967, and wanted to work to get rid of that kind of hatred.

Celebrating and cherishing the differences is important rather than challenging them in a confrontational way; but you cannot be a Catholic in today's world without the ecumenical dimension.

Staff also commented on their pastoral responsibility. In the programme of personal and social education,[14] taught by all form tutors to their own tutor groups, moral issues were bound to arise. A senior curriculum specialist emphasized that, while details may be different, the key thing was common agreement on the Christian principles underpinning moral values. After all, it would be misleading 'to suggest that all Anglicans believe this or all Catholics believe that'. In 1992 one head of year felt able to say that, in his experience, the children related well to each other, whether Protestant or Catholic: 'I have heard children on occasion use racist remarks or be inhumane in other ways, but never criticize another's religion.'

If back in 1982, there had been some concern that the outward signs of a Catholic school (such as crucifixes and statues, nuns in habits) might be lost in the joint school, by 1992 every classroom displayed (after consultation) a simple wooden cross, handmade by the technology staff at the request of the head when the new building opened in 1990. One teacher pointed out:

We are more relaxed now; the new form rooms have display space where children can put up crosses, icons, crucifixes, or pictures as they like. One pupil on a school trip to Israel asked if she could buy an icon specially for her classroom wall.

A local Anglican priest and school governor commented: 'It wouldn't work to import an artificial Anglican or Roman Catholic atmosphere into the school.'

It might be feared that St Bede's was in danger of becoming a Christian 'hothouse'. In 1992, however, a senior teacher (an Anglican evangelical) thought this was appropriately counteracted by the highly professional

[14]The governors' 1989 statement of policy on personal, social, health and sex education states, on contraception, 'the Roman Catholic position is made quite clear that while in the last resort this is a matter for the conscience of individual Catholics, only the "safe period" is approved by the Church', and on abortion, that all Churches 'start from a belief that human life is God-given and therefore sacred'.

119

chaplaincy, and by the fact that even in the evangelical Christian Union the children meet others with different views, and the Union was seen as open to anyone who valued Christian fellowship:

> I do not know whether the children there are Anglican or Catholic. Usually the pupils lead the sessions, but even the Catholic chaplain has been known to ask kids to give their personal testimony.

One head of year commented wryly: 'There's no proselytizing here; we are not breeding zealots.' Another made the point that

> the issue is not whether you are an Anglican or a Catholic; it is more whether you are a believer. Although there is some normal peer group pressure not to take part, those who want to be involved in Christian activities are not treated differently; it is accepted as normal. One boy recently described his visits to an elderly lady for his Duke of Edinburgh Award Scheme as 'part of Christian life'; and the sixth-formers being interviewed for the post of Senior Student talked about their Christian activities openly and without embarrassment.

Confident but not arrogant in their Christian beliefs and way of life, these young people seem to exemplify the achievement of St Bede's in balancing personal commitment to their respective Churches with ecumenical understanding.

3. LOOKING TO THE FUTURE

> The school is successful in many ways, it is popular and has a clear notion of its identity and place in the local and wider community. High standards are set and mostly achieved; examination results are good. However, there are aspects of the school which need to be addressed in order to ensure that all pupils are challenged both academically and personally, that staff can adapt to curricular change and development and the school can build on its present success. (HMI Report, March 1992)

St Bede's has come a long way since it opened its doors in 1976. Despite a difficult amalgamation, inheriting outdated split-site accommodation, an uneconomical sixth form and an ex-secondary-modern curriculum, the school has now established itself as a thriving and successful educational Christian community. When schools are suffering 'innovation fatigue' with the implementation of the National Curriculum and financial Local Management, the parental demands of middle-class suburbia (exacerbated by published league tables and issues such as selection by pupil ability or aptitude) encourage oversubscribed schools to 'rest on their laurels'. The increasing emphasis on awareness of Third World issues across the curriculum (such as St Bede's links with Tanzania) might be sufficient challenge for generally affluent Surrey children. One member of staff commented: 'Perhaps St Bede's might prefer not to take too many risks.'

To be recognized as a 'quality' school with a reputation for academic excellence and a caring ethos is one achievement, but to what extent is St Bede's able to give a lead in ecumenical education? One Roman Catholic on the pastoral staff in 1992 thought that the school was still at a developing and evaluating stage and questioned whether it ought not to be doing more to advertise its pioneering ecumenism: was it reluctant to attract too much attention for external 'political' reasons? The move to incorporate formally the Free Churches into the foundation is indeed courageous if it can retain the confidence of the Anglican and Roman Catholic communities in the process.

How far can an ecumenical school celebrate the diversity of Christian traditions and at the same time advocate full co-operation in unity? If this is difficult for mature adults, how much more so for young people at school? To what extent should pupils' attention be drawn to denominational distinctions? Explicit clarification of different interpretations of Christian doctrine are incorporated into St Bede's RE and moral education programmes, although (as one deputy head noted) 'youngsters will ask ecumenical questions in any subject'. The predominant ethos is undoubtedly Christian rather than exclusively denominational. The *Church Times* entitled its full-page article on the school (22 January 1993) 'No labels by request: St Bede's is a place simply for Christians'. Even the chaplains had some difficulty in defining religious understanding in narrow denominational terms: for example the Roman Catholic was surprised to find her High Anglican colleague shared beliefs she had previously considered exclusively Roman (e.g. Real Presence); yet she found his evangelical predecessor more akin to her in his approach to evangelism and moral questions, even if some of his doctrinal beliefs seemed very different. While respecting and valuing different traditions, St Bede's offers a challenge to those who would seek a false sense of security within safely categorized denominational identities.

The need, however, to show that St Bede's ecumenical co-operation builds on the foundations of distinctive denominational traditions is particularly important for the Roman Catholic community. If Catholic parents are still expected to ensure their child's education in a Catholic environment, St Bede's has to fulfil all the criteria of a good 'Catholic' school. As one Roman Catholic colleague explained, 'It's like a stick of Brighton rock: you have to see "Catholic" through every area of the school'. Endorsement has been evident in the long-standing support for the school by the Bishop of Arundel and Brighton, and recognized by Cardinal Hume's visit in March 1992; but a senior Roman Catholic teacher highlighted the problem:

Some of the RC clergy are reluctant collaborators, concerned primarily that the 'Ark of the Covenant' should be kept intact. . . . They don't want convergence;

reluctant co-operation is as far as they'll go, because the Vatican still insists that only Catholics have the whole truth.

He had also heard concerns expressed by parents in his local parish that Anglicans who only go to church to have their children admitted to St Bede's might prevent Catholics being accepted; or that their children will be reluctant to talk about their own faith and practice in an environment where not all pupils are 'believers'. Allaying such unfounded fears is a vital task of the Catholic chaplain, governors and staff, helped by the regular visits of local Catholic clergy to celebrate mass. However, other Roman Catholic parents were equally adamant that they had deliberately rejected a narrow Catholic education for their children: 'I couldn't believe my luck to have St Bede's', said one.

The question of a Catholic 'imprimatur' is not only important for the outside community; it is also an issue for staff, particularly since Church school appraisal schemes tend to focus on their distinctive religious ethos. St Bede's governors' sub-committee had to balance the more open Anglican approach to appraisal (based on good LEA practice) with the more denomi-national Roman Catholic guidelines, in devising appraisal criteria appropriate for an ecumenical school. Yet Phil Dineen reflected on her time as headteacher: 'The key issue was to ensure that the school was acceptable to both Churches without prostituting ourselves in the process.'

St Bede's has moved forward both educationally and ecumenically since 1976 under the leadership of three visionary headteachers. In 1992, several staff and governors commented that the head, Julian Marcus, was 'an energetic change-agent who leads from the front', 'a zealous missionary who would like to see the school promoting ecumenism by bringing the Churches together'. He himself acknowledged that it was tempting to drift into ecumenical 'navel-contemplation' rather than to recognize ecumenism as outgoing 'mission and service'. Yet all concerned were aware that St Bede's must not go ahead too fast: it should educate rather than confront, lest it become isolated from its founder Churches.

The challenge posed by St Bede's is significant:

> Our covenant is not about the assimilation of differences, but about the sharing of gifts. We accept that there may be tensions and difficulties in implementing this intention. We acknowledge that it will require prayer, sacrifice, understanding, good will, tolerance and determination from all involved. (Draft Covenant, June 1992)

This chapter has attempted to demonstrate that such qualities, characteristic of the school since its inception, have been developed and strengthened over the years, providing the Churches with a powerful example of ecumenical co-operation in action.

4

Education in the Northern Ireland context: background issues

PREFACE

The complexity of Northern Ireland in terms of its history or politics, let alone education, should have been enough to dissuade any interested writer from including a case study of an 'ecumenical school' in Belfast. However, the explicit co-operation between Lagan's early pioneers and colleagues at St Bede's, Redhill, was important in exploring a shared understanding of ecumenical education in different contexts, and it is interesting to review their respective development. The issues in Northern Ireland, while different from those in England, are nevertheless informed by the education debates at Westminster and among Christian educationists across Britain. There are links across the water at individual, institutional and national levels.

Unlike Redhill, Northern Ireland has attracted extensive media attention and volumes of research reports on the historical legacy and the effects of segregated education. This and the following chapter draw on these studies, which provide relevant statistical information together with historical and sociological perspectives. Here I move forward to focus on the potential of integrated schools to bridge the social and religious divide and on the attitudes of both Protestant and Roman Catholic Church spokesmen whose influence is still considerable across their communities. When ecumenical relations between the Churches are more defensive than in England, undermined by centuries of bitterness and particularly over two decades of violence fuelled by religious hatred, it is not surprising that the Churches' prime concern is to protect their own proper interests.

This study traces the determined progress of parents and children in seeking a viable alternative to the segregated school system, and the hesitant moves by politicians in supporting an evolving policy for integrated education—hesitant because it is accompanied by the almost certain risk of antagonizing those with vested interests in preserving the status quo. Lagan College's progress in manoeuvring around seemingly insurmountable barriers is a story worth telling.

1. HISTORICAL BACKGROUND

The mould of education in Northern Ireland has been hardened over a long period in a climate of political fumbling, suspicion, violence, fear and disillusionment at the abandonment of promises whose fulfilment became too complicated. Such a mould is difficult to break. The problem has been tersely stated by John Darby, a sociologist at the University of Ulster:

> The history of Irish education is unremarkable except for occasional pioneering experiments and the regularity with which crises accompanied any attempt to alter existing educational practice. What is remarkable is how frequently the crises have been the result of the same dispute—the extent to which the Churches should control the schools. The most constant thread running through the saga is the deep-rooted suspicion of Catholics towards the state control of their schools. (1976, p. 123)

One cannot plausibly suggest that these suspicions have been without foundation. King Henry VIII, in his self-appointed position (then, under intimidation, conceded by Convocation and by Parliament) as 'supreme head under God of the Church of England and Ireland'—a title as offensive to his more Protestant subjects as it was to Roman Catholics—instructed his Anglican bishops in Ireland to establish schools 'for to learn English'. The native Irish had no enthusiasm either for the breach with Rome or for the intrusion of an alien language, and their fusion of national identity with Catholicism was massively reinforced by the Church of England's further shift in a Protestant direction under Edward VI and Elizabeth I, this stage being but a pale prelude to the dismantling of Anglicanism under Oliver Cromwell and his ruthless policy of oppression in Ireland. Even in the seventeenth century, Irish Catholics were offered the stark choice of education in schools run by Protestant charitable trusts or no education at all. The learned Anglican Jeremy Taylor (1613–67), Bishop of Down and Connor, remarked that the Irish Roman Catholics used to justify their refusal to listen to Anglican theological argument about the papacy or the decrees of Trent with the impregnable consideration that they were unfamiliar with the English language (Taylor, 1664, vol. 6, p. 176). There were already religious grounds for distrusting schools sponsored by the English government.

In the nineteenth century the situation improved. The British administration attempted to establish a system of integrated education for 5–11-year-olds in Ireland. This was to be secular, religious education being outside the normal school day. Lord Stanley, Chief Secretary for Ireland and responsible for bringing in the Irish Education Act of 1831, enacted the compromise by which children of all denominations were admitted to schools receiving a government grant; children were taught moral and literary education together and separated for religious instruction taught by their own local clergy. He declared that 'admitting children of all persuasions should not interfere with the particular tenets of any'. Although the Churches, including the Roman Catholic Church, acquiesced in the proposals and accepted them *faute de mieux*, neither Protestants nor Catholics could feel any enthusiasm for the Act. The Protestants, especially the Presbyterians, wanted to use the Bible during 'secular' instruction and Roman Catholic parents were apprehensive that their children might be exposed to Protestant proselytization if they were educated side by side with zealous evangelicals. Under great pressure, the government of the time was forced to allow the national schools to abandon the intended neutrality and in practice to become denominational schools.

The situation is well summarized by Norman McNeilly:

> By a strange paradox, the Roman Catholic Church which at first had largely supported the 'mixed' or 'integrated' principle, had by the end of the nineteenth century become strongly opposed to it. On the other hand, the Presbyterian Church, the Church of Ireland, and the Methodist Church, which initially had opposed the 'national' system, decided to support it—but only when the 'mixed' principle had been effectively defeated in practice. (1973, p. 2)

The tensions and violence up to partition in 1921 bequeathed a long legacy of mistrust and unease in the six counties to which 'Ulster' was now reduced. The British government had long intended Home Rule, but the vehemence of Edward Carson and the Ulster Protestants demonstrated that the price of carrying the policy through would be high.

The Protestants of Northern Ireland drew the lines to ensure that their interest was given legitimacy as the democratic will of the majority of the people. As Maurice Hayes, a former ombudsman and local government boundaries commissioner for Northern Ireland, commented:

> One result of partition was that Protestants tended to see expressions of Irish culture as belonging wholly to the Catholic community, and indeed as having

125

been hi-jacked for political ends; and because Britishness was so often expressed in terms of Englishness, Catholics tended to see this as something imposed on society, as an initiation test which they could not pass, or would not enter. (Hayes, 1990, p. 8)

In 1923 the government attempted to provide for Northern Ireland an integrated system of education at primary level (5–11 years). Ignoring Sir Robert Lynn's recommendation for denominational religious instruction in schools, Lord Londonderry as the first Minister of Education proposed that religious education was to be forbidden in school hours, and teachers were to be appointed without reference to their religious denomination. It was hoped that the Churches would be willing to transfer their schools to the new local authorities established by the Act. Such hopes were naive in their optimism. As John Darby commented, 'With rare ecumenical spirit, all the churches opposed the Act' (1976, p. 126).

The Roman Catholic Church was determined to retain complete control of its schools and to repel all attempts at interference. This determination can only have been increased by smouldering resentment at partition. The hierarchy immediately declared the Act unacceptable, insisting on a separate denominational system and control of staff appointments. By 1930 teachers' salaries and half the school capital and maintenance costs were paid by the state.

The Protestants felt that the Act was a betrayal of what they had fought for in the Home Rule crisis: a guarantee that their children would be educated as Protestants. They demanded assurances that Roman Catholic teachers in state schools would not constitute a 'subversive' influence on their children. Because of the past acceptance of Bible-based religious education, they were already in a position of some strength. By the time their schools were transferred to the new local education authorities in 1930, they had created a system of management that also allowed them to retain effective control over their schools, a position strengthened by the 1930 Education Act, which gave the transferors' representatives at least half the seats on school management committees. They also forced the government into supplementary legislation in 1925 and 1930, which permitted teachers in the transferred schools to give Bible instruction daily.

In this way entrenched positions were taken up by both sides, and down to the present time there has been little substantial change in this situation. Admittedly, there was realization that the consequences were not ideal, since the Belfast Education Committee meeting on 20 January 1928 recorded dissatisfaction among Protestant clergy at the policy of 'setting up a dual system of education, one system for Roman Catholics, and another for those of any or no religion to which Protestants are compelled to conform'.

The 1947 Education Act (Northern Ireland), based on the 1944 Butler Act, introduced compulsory free secondary education for all. As in Britain, it ushered in a new exciting era of expansion and development. Captain Terence O'Neill, ex-Prime Minister of Northern Ireland, commented in his autobiography that the Protestant political parties were slow to realize that this 'would produce a new Catholic intelligentsia which would be quite unwilling to put up with the deprived status their fathers and grandfathers had taken for granted' (1972, p. 137). The education authorities implemented a bold programme of school building, creating 'intermediate' schools for the 80 per cent of children over the age of 11 who were not selected for grammar schools. It is noteworthy that the Director of Education for Belfast submitted a report to his committee as early as 9 January 1953 proposing comprehensive secondary schools which would provide 'suitable courses of secondary education for all ranges of ability' (a plan rejected by the Minister, possibly under pressure from conservative institutions and grammar school interests); later in October 1953 he even proposed abolition of the 11-plus qualifying examination, because of its inadequacy as an instrument for selecting children for the tripartite system of 'Intermediate, Technical and Grammar Schools' (a proposal rejected by his committee). In his history of the Belfast Education Authority, Norman McNeilly commented that the qualifying examination was 'in practical operation little different from the grading of cattle or pigs, but with fewer dependable criteria' (1973, p. 113). Nevertheless, the 11-plus test remains today a key factor in the education system of Northern Ireland and, it is sometimes argued,[1] has provided a vital impetus to the pioneering parents in the movement for integrated schools to launch an alternative system for the post-primary education of their children.

Relations between the Protestant Churches and the local education committees generally improved after 1947. Although the resented requirement on *all* teachers in committee schools to give Bible instruction had been withdrawn (against the Protestant Churches' wishes), the inspection of RE was allocated to 'ministers of religion and other suitable persons' (1947 Education Act, 3, 21(5)). The dual system had *de facto* established itself as a reality since Roman Catholic schools refused to transfer to state control. The more constructive contribution of Protestant churchmen on the Belfast Education Committee in the post-war period prompted Norman McNeilly to speculate that there might be 'new channels of communication between the two parts of the dual system enabling them to come closer' (1973, p. 228). Such views have come to seem over-optimistic as the twenty-first century approaches, and the Protestant Churches have again articulated their concern that their position in 'controlled schools' is being eroded by

[1]For example by Alex McEwan in Caul (1990), p. 139.

government policies for improving Catholic 'maintained' education provision and enhancing the integrated sector.

From the late 1960s, public opinion favouring some integrated schooling became more vocal,[2] as segregation in education was mountingly seen to be one of the root causes of the perpetuation of community conflict. In 1966 Prime Minister Terence O'Neill even commented publicly at Corrymeela, an interdenominational Christian centre, that 'a major cause of division rises from "de facto" segregation of education along religious lines'—a courageous statement from a government leader which is likely to have cost him some votes, since it certainly implied that educational separation brought social difficulties and that he wished to see the segregation ended.[3]

In 1971 the Presbyterian General Assembly passed a formal resolution declaring that 'integrated education would best service the social, economic, and educational needs of the community'. But the tender plant of hope and confidence was crushed by the progressive elimination of consensus and middle ground in Ulster politics. People of reason and moderation proved unable to deliver the goods and, particularly after the bloodshed in Derry in 1969, the violence of the IRA and the Protestant paramilitaries exacerbated the tension. London became convinced that it had to shoulder the burden of ruling Northern Ireland directly and, after 1974, services like education fell under the control of larger area boards directly answerable to the Secretary of State, thus reducing the power of local councils, many discredited by stories of scandalous bigotry and discrimination.

Despite the deeply discouraging political climate, the goal of establishing some integrated education had not been lost to sight. In 1973 a group of mainly Roman Catholic parents, whose children were attending state schools, met to form the 'All Children Together' movement. On the ground that these children were not being enrolled at Roman Catholic schools and therefore could not be given 'admission cards', they were in effect being refused confirmation by their bishop, Dr Philbin of Down and Connor. When his announcement was read out publicly in several parishes at the Sunday mass, public concern and sympathy markedly increased. The parents decided to take on responsibility themselves for running Sunday classes of catechetical instruction and even managed to persuade a sympathetic bishop to hold a special confirmation in a neighbouring diocese in 1978. The All Children Together movement had passed a resolution in 1974 to become inter-denominational in response to many requests from Prot-

[2]National opinion polls for the *Belfast Telegraph* (1967, 1968) and *Fortnight* magazine (1972) showed a majority in favour.

[3]O'Neill (1972), p. 79. His remarks were criticized by the Cardinal but supported, surprisingly, by a Nationalist MP.

estant parents who wished to show solidarity with their aims. The move-ment stated its aim as follows:

> to seek the establishment of shared Christian schools where parents so wished (opinion polls show the majority in favour), bringing together the two main Christian traditions and the two cultures in their fullness, in close cooperation with the Churches, knowing that where children grow up together in mutual respect they will no longer fear and hate each other. The members are convinced that Christ does not divide: he is the one solid ground of unity. They desire to awaken in their children a faith and love of God and man that is unitive, ecu-menical, exciting, unfettered. (Lagan College Report, 1981–3)

At the same time, the Minister of Education in the power-sharing Executive at Stormont (set up after the Sunningdale agreement of 1973), the Rt. Hon. Basil McIvor (later first chairman of the governors of Lagan College), pub-licly stated his belief that 'the mixing of school children would contribute to the reduction of community tension in Northern Ireland'. McIvor looked back on the situation of 1974 in the following terms:

> I recognised the hesitation of the Churches arising from the understandable anxiety about the religious upbringing of their children in schools not under their management, but asked them earnestly to consider the very special needs of Northern Ireland and to join the power-sharing Executive in a constructive approach to meeting those needs. I had in mind the possibility of a new manage-ment arrangement which could be accepted by either 'controlled' (State) schools or 'maintained' (Catholic) schools, leading to a system of shared schools which would operate alongside the existing system. (McIvor, 1984)

He went on to quote from his speech in Parliament as recorded in *Hansard* (30 April 1974):

> We would consider the possibility of changing the law to facilitate another class of school . . . in which the two groups of Churches would be equally involved in management. Obviously the details . . . will have to be worked out in consulta-tion with the interested parties before political proposals for legislation can be formulated.

In his autobiography *Memoirs of a Statesman* (1978, p. 242), the late Brian Faulkner recalled McIvor's proposals being brought to the power-sharing Executive. Initially the members from the Catholic Social Democratic and Labour Party (SDLP) had reservations about some details of the scheme but they supported the principle and, in the second meeting of the Executive to debate the matter, gave McIvor's scheme full support.

> Once the decision had been taken, no one wavered from collective responsibility even when the Cardinal and the Catholic bishops launched a strong attack on

the whole idea after publication. But the hopes of dealing with this important problem, like many other hopes for Ulster, died with the Executive.

Nevertheless the 1974 decision showed that a Northern Ireland government, in which both Catholics and Protestants participated, could act to allow for shared schools. The plan cohered with power-sharing.

Under the pressure of the Protestant workers' strike in May 1974, designed as a challenge to constitutional authority, and with the effective failure of London to help the Executive, the Stormont government resigned.[4] Direct rule from Westminster was imposed. The minister responsible for education in Northern Ireland declared that because of a lack of 'substantial agreement in favour of the idea', the government was not continuing with the plan for integrated education. Bishop Philbin wrote in his 1975 Lenten pastoral: 'short of banning religion altogether, there is no greater injury that could be done to Catholicism than by interference with the character and identity of our schools'.

Yet by 1977 a 'cautious policy of charitable neutrality' established the principle that the reorganization of secondary schooling 'should not create nor perpetuate barriers against integrated schooling' (cf. the Dunleath Act of 25 May 1978).[5] A working party of representatives from Protestant and Catholic Churches had even advocated integrated sixth-form colleges and nursery schools, ecumenical RE, exchange of teachers and 'agreement that the churches should promote pilot schemes and research projects to find effective ways of bringing together Protestant and Catholic young people at school level'.[6] It is noteworthy that at several stages the proposal for some integration attracted interest as long as there was no interference with the segregated schooling of 5–16-year-olds.

The fact that by 1980 none of these ideas had been taken up suggested that 'everybody's business had become nobody's business'. Even the 1980 Chilver Report interim recommendation to amalgamate the Protestant and Catholic teacher training colleges fell on deaf ears (only the two single-sex Catholic colleges merged in 1985). As Gallagher and Worrall observed in 1982, in spite of discussing the issue of integration, the Churches seemed 'unconvinced at a deeper level than that of a passing thought'. These authors were drawn to the conclusion that 'irrespective of the ideology,

[4]Basil McIvor later revealed that, as the violence increased, Protestants involved in the strikes admitted to him privately that they would probably have given in if he had 'held on for another two weeks'. It was probably one of the British government's worst decisions.

[5]The government's 1977 proposal for comprehensive reorganization was blocked by grammar school interests.

[6]The Report of the Joint Churches Working Party (set up by the Catholic hierarchy and the Irish Council of Churches), *Violence in Ireland* (1976, p. 86).

both in the short and foreseeable longer terms, integrated schooling in Northern Ireland is "not on"' (p. 171).

2. A QUESTION OF IDENTITY

It is not perhaps surprising that the Roman Catholic minority should manifest a siege mentality in struggles to retain their educational strongholds in a hostile environment. Yet the Protestant majority are equally defensive. The historical legacy sketched above may be part of the reason; but the cause may also lie in the strange, 'bifocal' vision created by the position of Northern Ireland in relation to the Republic. While Protestants are in the majority in the north, they feel under threat from Roman Catholics who politically and spiritually consider themselves united to Dublin and thus in a majority position in relation to Ireland as a whole. Each body therefore considers itself in the position of an embattled minority, and driven, if not entitled, to take up a defensive stance when invited to co-operate.

Much has been written in the attempt to break through this psychological impasse. For example:

It cannot be too often repeated that conflict in Ireland is not a religious conflict between Protestants and Catholics as such, but between two sets of people who happen to be one Protestant, the other Catholic. That religious differences have been involved on each side and at every stage to evoke a crusading spirit, to explain the depravity of the enemy, and to stiffen and perpetuate hostility, is true. But, fundamentally, it was for political and military reasons that Catholics were persecuted and Protestants planted; it was in obedience to economic theories that Catholics were made destitute and starving; it was as the landless that Catholics took to the gun against the property owners, of whom many, as a result of English policies, were Protestants. (Bishop John Austin Baker, 1984)

Or Eaman O'Ruaire in the *Irish Times* on 30 October 1981:

The Unionists are trapped in a siege mentality. The folk memories of the massacres of the 17th century linger in their collective sub-consciousness. They feel threatened by coercion from without and by subversion from within. Some of them have a gut intuition that they are fighting a losing battle against the tide of history, but that only serves to fuel their desperation. Many of them suspect that Britain is going to abandon them.... Until those fears are removed, the Ulster Unionists will remain psychologically and politically inhibited and therefore incapable of making any movement or granting any concession that would facilitate a solution of the Northern Ireland conflict.

A writer in the *Economist* of 2 June 1984 observed:

> The Protestant community has come to prefer direct rule to power-sharing with the Catholics. The Catholic community prefers direct rule to the return of the Protestant ascendancy. There is a premium on the status quo and on behaving irresponsibly towards any British initiative.

In his comprehensive survey of research into the Northern Ireland community, John Whyte commented:

> Nowhere else does one find the lethal mixture of a large minority with a well-founded and deeply-felt sense of grievance, and a narrow majority with justifiable anxieties about what the future may hold. (1990, p. 219)

Catholic grievances have been well documented (cf. the 1969 Cameron Commission which pointed to housing discrimination, gerrymandering, the B Specials, the Special Powers Act and failure to obtain redress from complaints). The segregation of residential areas, particularly in Belfast, has polarized communities to provide 'a base for self-defence', whereas 'there has been a high correlation between integrated housing and the absence of overt community violence'.[7]

In employment, discrimination is recognized by the Fair Employment Agency as a serious problem, primarily because of the powerful 'informal networks of recruitment'. The 56 per cent gap, identified by Compton's researches in 1981, between Protestant and Catholic unemployment levels is difficult to explain 'apart from discrimination or unequal opportunities'.[8] The deputy director of the Council for Catholic Maintained Schools (CCMS) commented that, although he had an excellent working relationship with the Belfast aircraft company Shorts, which was keen to raise the number of applications from Catholics (then only 8 per cent), Catholic school-leavers either did not want to apply because the training centre was located in the Protestant area of East Belfast or, if they did, the company found that too many lacked the basic skills—an issue the CCMS has been trying to address with Catholic schools.[9] Interestingly, the principal of Lagan College reported at a conference in June 1992 that the local information published for employers regarding the religious affiliation of schools from which they recruit pupils had to acknowledge that, unlike other

[7]Darby (1986), p. 29. See also Poole (1982).

[8]David Smith, in a 1987 report for the Standing Advisory Committee on Human Rights, vol. 1, p. 39). A view confirmed by McWhirter (1989a).

[9]See also ch. 7 of Cormack and Osborne (1983).

schools, Lagan College is distinctive in that 'no assumptions about religious affiliation may be drawn from pupils attending this school'.[10]

Yet the question of identity is of paramount importance. As the British government recognized:

> The majority of the population of Northern Ireland think of themselves as British. They regard themselves as part of the social and cultural fabric of the United Kingdom and their loyalty lies to the Crown. . . . There is also a substantial minority within Northern Ireland who think of themselves as Irish, whether in terms of their identity, their social and cultural traditions, or their political aspirations. . . . This difference in identity and aspiration lies at the heart of the problem of Northern Ireland; it cannot be ignored or wished away. (*A Framework for Devolution*, 1982, paras 15–17)

'It's all about identity', commented an interviewee to Dervla Murphy. 'Who's what? If everybody in Northern Ireland could answer that question without hesitation, we'd be more than halfway to a solution.'[11] There is an unspoken rule that one never asks another person in Belfast what religion they are, yet it is the one question everyone wants answered, because that religion is the shorthand note of the other person's education, background, and often his political views.[12] A Catholic taxi-driver commented that, with the name Gabriel, he was often hassled at police road-blocks in Belfast: 'No Protestant has a name like that!' The principal of Lagan College explained that, since his own surname Flanagan was usually a Catholic name, his Protestant allegiance sometimes confused prospective parents. (He commented that previous generations of his family must have 'taken the soup', i.e. converted to Protestantism at the time of the Famine.) The Catholic head of religious education in 1992 emphasized that the children at Lagan are as keen as everyone else to find out one's religion, yet will disguise the question, as in the more legitimate form, 'What football team do you support, sir?' 'Once they have satisfied their curiosity and have identified what you are, they just get on with the lesson.' The significance of religious identity is endorsed by John Hickey in *Religion and the Northern Ireland Problem*:

---

[10]'In Northern Ireland a person's religion, academic success and social standing can be weighed up by knowing where he went to school. If these are not the best years of an Ulsterman's life, they are some of the most important': Stephen Castle in *Seven Days* magazine, 20 November 1988.

[11]Murphy (1978), p. 126.

[12]See also Cairns (1987).

While differences in the social structure between Protestants and Roman Catholics are being slowly eliminated, the importance of the other difference—religion—is being increasingly emphasized. Conflict now centres upon the distinction of religious belief and the 'world-view' based upon it. (1984, p. 105)

John Whyte takes this further by suggesting that the two communities' objections to each other are based on different perspectives (1990, p. 106). For Protestants the fear is religious in that an autocratic Catholic Church claims the authority of Rome, not merely in preserving the *depositum fidei* but also in dominating the state south of the border, as illustrated by its opposition to the least relaxation of the laws on abortion or birth control in the Republic. For Catholics, the objection is more political and economic, with resentment at the Protestants' political outlook and tight grip on power, as illustrated by their opposition to the Anglo-Irish agreement since 1985. Whyte stresses that 'the task of statesmanship is to devise arrangements whereby the opposing sets of anxieties and grievances can both be assuaged' (ibid., p. 173).

Segregated schools are often cited as having 'an important role in socialising children into sectarianism. The symbols, practices, friendships which are part of a normal school may, in a divided society, reinforce the divisions' (Darby and Dunn, 1987, p. 95). While there are some curricular differences between Catholic and Protestant schools (e.g. in Irish language teaching, and whether they play rugby or Gaelic football), it is often through the hidden curriculum that the most influential messages are reinforced. Dominic Murray's 1985 study showed how two schools (one Protestant, one Catholic) initiated children into separate customs, and attitudes, even entitling one chapter 'The three Rs: religion, ritual, and rivalry'. In the Protestant school, British identity was emphasized by close partnership with the government's education officers and the daily raising of the Union Jack. A Catholic teacher commented: 'They fly the flag down there to show that they are the lords and masters and we [Catholics] should be continually aware of it' (Murray, 1985, p. 113). The Catholic school, on the other hand, was suspicious of government 'intruders' giving advice and displayed its own religious symbols. A Protestant teacher commented: 'It's hard to escape the view that a special show is being put on for our benefit. . . . They must know that these are the very things that we object to, yet still they are flaunted everywhere' (ibid., p. 114).

These attitudes and anxieties need to be addressed if community defensiveness and group rivalry are to be overcome. Recent initiatives on inter-school links and 'Education for Mutual Understanding' may go some way towards breaking down barriers. A Protestant primary teacher involved in these schemes expressed cautious optimism:

When I took my class to the Catholic school to work together on an environmental topic, they played happily together in the playground, although one Protestant Dad (an RUC policeman) had refused to let his child go because he did not want him to hear the bad language of the Catholic children. I also had to forbid the kids to come into school on the day of the visit sporting the regalia of Protestant football teams; but I couldn't stop them wearing red tops, white shoes, and blue trousers!

Murray's research, however, in recognizing the importance of identity symbols in segregated schools, led him to doubt the effectiveness of integrated education in overcoming the deeply ingrained differences in politics and culture. Would integrated schools 'prohibit any overt signs of religious or cultural aspirations? Which (if any) identity would be fostered? Would all clergy be deprived access? Which flags should be flown? Which prayers said? Which games played? Which songs sung?' (1985, pp. 134–5). How these issues were addressed in the first integrated school in Belfast can be seen in the story of Lagan College.

5

Lagan College, Belfast: 'experiment' in Northern Ireland

Lagan College is not going to bring peace. That will only come when children grow up and have no reason to kill each other because of religion. But the process has started. Lagan College has broken the mould. (Chairman of Governors, quoted in *Newsweek*, 21 May 1984)

CHRONOLOGY OF MAIN EVENTS

1973–74	'All Children Together' (ACT) movement founded
1974	Power-sharing Executive collapsed
1978	The Dunleath Act provided an 'integrated education' option
1981	ACT decision to open Lagan College for pupils 11–16; Sheila Greenfield appointed as principal
1982	Lagan College moved to Church Road, Castlereagh
1984	Lagan College became a 'voluntary aided maintained' school (85 per cent government capital funding)
1987	Terry Flanagan appointed as principal Northern Ireland Council for Integrated Education founded
1989	Education Reform (NI) Order proposed 'grant-maintained, integrated schools'
1980	Lagan College became 'grant maintained' (100 per cent government capital funding)
1991	Lagan College opened on new single site at Lisnabreeny House, Castlereagh

1. THE LAGAN COLLEGE STORY

The integrated schools, like Lagan College, would not pretend they have 'the answer to the Northern Ireland problem', but they point to the fact that 'goodwill and moderation' have not solved it either. Terry Flanagan, Lagan's principal, at a conference in Cambridge in June 1992, quoted Dr David Hempton of Queen's University, Belfast:

> Somehow enmity must be embraced, irreconcilable objectives seen as such. In short, Christian love and truth must not be allowed to degenerate into wishful thinking and idealism.

Flanagan continued:

> The challenge is to create schools where truth as seen by people holding different beliefs can be freely told to others and accepted and valued by them. It is the challenge of creating school communities where unity consists of 'reconciled diversity' and not uniformity. Such unity will not require that I accept that which I cannot in the interests of facile eirenicism.

These views are reflected in Lagan College's prospectus, which states that

> it was the intention of the founders of Lagan College that as well as being an integrated school for pupils of all abilities, Lagan College should also be a Christian school. They believed that Christianity was not 'per se' a cause of our divisions and that properly practised it could prove a source of healing in Northern Ireland.

Such affirmation of religious diversity is also highlighted by a former pupil, later at the Queen's University:

> My friends there came from different social and religious backgrounds, and I learned that while we were not exactly the same, the differences between us are not enough to justify the suspicion, misunderstanding and fear that has divided our community.

How successful has Lagan been in bridging the sectarian divide?

2. THE EARLY YEARS

The managers of a new school face the vital task of addressing key issues in securing a firm foundation for their educational community. These issues for Lagan inevitably included the political dimension and relations with the Churches, alongside those related to academic structure, curriculum design, religious education and community liaison. This section focuses on these specific issues in turn.

Political Issues

In Ireland a new nation is being born out of a strife that will, as enlightenment grows, enliven a whole people to a whole new way of life. This new nation is not born in the minds of violence. It is born in the minds of a few prophetic people who have the imagination and creativity to reach beyond the narrow confines of laneways of thought and move into new highways of enlightened cooperation.

So wrote Cormac O'Connor of Co-operation North, an organization begun in the Republic in 1978 to promote links between the Republic and Northern Ireland.

Although they might shy away from any description so grandiloquent, the founders of the All Children Together movement could be described as 'prophetic' in the sense that they both look to the future and wish to ensure that in certain respects it is not like the present and the past. In 1979 their mission was 'a voice crying aloud in the wilderness', a plea that for the sake of their children the traditional views of a segregated structure and denominations could be rethought. Their pressure on the government, along with that of some Protestant spokesmen concerned with education, brought about an important change in the law. The Education (Northern Ireland) Act 1978 gave legal authority for the creation of a third integrated sector in the Northern Ireland system, alongside the maintained (mainly Catholic) and controlled (mainly Protestant) sectors. The intention was to allow ministerial approval for a school to become integrated if Church representatives on the school management committee took the initiative, and if 75 per cent of the parents hoped to keep their children on at the school. Tony Spencer, then a trustee of All Children Together, observed that the Protestant Churches and area boards had previously been able to declare boldly to him that they were in favour of integrated education, confident that legislation to make it possible was still remote and unlikely in the future. In 1978 their bluff was being called; they had not realized that, if they were not careful, they would get what they were asking for.

The high hopes generated by such a change in the law were not long in fading. No kind of encouragement came from the Churches, and it soon became evident that a newly established integrated school would have to start life as an independent and therefore fee-paying school. Such a school would have to demonstrate its viability over three annual intakes before 'aided' status (attracting 85 per cent government funding) could be considered. Only Throne Controlled Primary School in north Belfast attempted to follow the 'integrated' possibility offered by the 1978 Dunleath Act; because of falling rolls it was threatened with closure, so the attempt was made from weakness rather than from strength. No Catholics joined the staff or the governors, no Catholic children enrolled and it finally closed in August 1985.

Notwithstanding the cold feet of Church leaders, some opinion polls indicated a substantial proportion (over 60 per cent) of the Ulster population in favour of integrated schooling in principle, even if, in practice, only about 30 per cent would actually wish to send their own child to such a school.[1] Fuelled by frustration and impatience, and fearing with reason that their initiative would go the way of so many others, the All Children Together (ACT) movement established in 1979 a charitable trust

for the advancement of integrated education, where desired, in Northern Ireland and for the benefit of the children of Northern Ireland in the provision for them of a system of integrated education, where desired, as an addition and alternative to the existing system of Catholic maintained schools and de facto Protestant controlled schools.

At the annual general meeting of the movement on 23 March 1981, a group of parents, faced with the prospect of their children leaving segregated primary schools to transfer to segregated secondary schools, persuaded the trustees to try to open a shared school the following September. Although there was some concern in ACT about moving from the model of a successful pressure group to take on an additional role as a development group, two parents (who were also trustees) argued that their children could not wait any longer. One put it bluntly at the subsequent trustees' meeting: 'Would Lagan open in September with ACT or not?' The recommendation of the annual general meeting was eventually accepted, and the decision made to establish a governing body, to seek a principal, and to raise the money for the cause.

It was decided that the fees would initially have to be set at £625 a year and, to enable children from deprived and often more sectarian areas to enrol, it would be necessary to offer bursaries. This meant that substantial funds would have to be sought, and an international campaign began, led by an indefatigable Anglican nun, Sister Anna. The balance of Protestants and Catholics among pupils, teachers and management was considered a high priority, the parameter being set at 60:40 respectively.

The sense of urgency was strong and the reason for it noteworthy. One

[1] See the Survey report in *Fortnight* 178 (1980). Protestants tended to be more supportive than Catholics.

Catholic parent described the problem thus. He had always been clear about the need for a 'change in culture' and had deliberately sent his eldest two children to Protestant grammar schools 'in order to mix with Protestants'. However, he found that no concessions were made for his Catholic daughter who reported that, in the first term of French, the class recited 'Nous sommes Protestants'. His third child, who had failed the 11-plus and gained a fee-paying place at a different Protestant grammar school, remembered the music teacher losing patience with the voluntary chapel choir in which she had enrolled, saying, 'You sound like a choir on the Falls Road'. When this parent, taking part in a radio broadcast, explained that he had Catholic children who went to Protestant schools, his son burst into tears because his 'cover had been blown'. 'We learnt through their experiences what had to be avoided.' Disillusioned with his own ecumenical experiment, which merely showed how inadequately the Protestant education system treated the Catholic children it took in as part of its 'open door' policy, he committed himself to find an alternative education for his youngest daughter, who had, as expected, failed the 11-plus in March 1981. Undoubtedly two motives were present: to obviate the choice of secondary intermediate school for his middle-class child, but also to protect her from the 'sectarian' culture of the exclusively Catholic school.

As the summer of 1981 progressed, the Protestant and Catholic communities were further polarized by the Maze hunger strikes. Nevertheless, the parents and trustees pushed forward with public meetings, fund-raising, searches for a site, and the appointment of a principal whose salary they could not at that stage guarantee to pay. Tony Spencer, a Roman Catholic and a lecturer at Queen's University, recalled: 'It was unbelievable the support we got. People would stop you in the street, in the post office, and say "What a marvellous thing you're doing" ' (*TES*, 14 September 1984). As the principal appointed (Sheila Greenfield) observed, the parents knew that if they were slow to act, it would be too late for their own families; and that was why they went ahead so rapidly.

The impetus had now become too strong to resist. In order to offer integrated education to all children, the college had to step outside the normal Ulster 11-plus selection procedure. It had to open its doors to children of all abilities, boys and girls. Because of the total commitment of the parents from the start, the school enjoyed sustained support in all its activities. Especially in its first year, parents took responsibility as dinner supervisors, cleaners and bus drivers. The first intake of 28 pupils moved into a Scout centre with two teachers (whose salaries were paid by charitable fund-raising) and at the end of each day had to pack everything away into cupboards. The deputy principal recalled his relief when the Scouts removed their Union Jack from the room without being asked, before the pupils moved in. The camaraderie of those early days remains alive in the school. One pupil ten years later remembered that only a flimsy curtain separated the two classes: 'The whole school knew if you had not done your homework!'

The attitude to integrated education shown by ministers in the Northern Ireland Office can only be described as hesitant. The Department of Education in Northern Ireland insisted that Lagan must pay its own way without state aid for a full three years to prove its viability, which may sound reasonable until one recalls that such a policy would not naturally or automatically be applied to a new Roman Catholic aided school. The resentment felt by the Lagan pioneers was understandable.

> It is particularly annoying to be told that parents are able to choose the sort of school they want for their children, when there are only two choices, both committing children into segregated systems. (Newsletter of the All Children Together movement, June 1983)

The government did not want to put taxpayers' money into projects which few citizens of the land wished to have. The Northern Ireland Parliamentary Under-Secretary, Nicholas Scott, a man with considerable parliamentary experience in the Conservative party, commented:

> we are in favour of integration, but not by imposing it on people. Since it is the wish of the majority that children be educated in accordance with their own ethos, integrated education is not on for the foreseeable future. (Newsweek, 21 May 1984)

This utterance conveyed the impression that if integrated education was not for everybody, the government was unwilling to help anybody to have it, even if they wanted it. Politically the reserve of the Northern Ireland Office was intelligible as a cautious reaction in face of the manifest fears of both Protestant leaders and the Roman Catholic hierarchy, whose co-operation cannot be unimportant to the government of Ulster.

Nevertheless, in the three years as an independent school, the cost was estimated at more than £500,000, and there is no doubt that had state aid been withheld in April 1984 when monthly expenditure reached £20,000, the school could have had no option but to close. Intense political pressure from such powerful figures as James Callaghan, Lady Plowden and others was brought to bear upon the Secretary of State, James Prior. Tony Spencer, then Lagan treasurer and a founder parent, recalled a private interview with Nicholas Scott, in which the Minister gave his personal assurance that the school would achieve 'maintained', voluntary-aided status by the following April. Lagan College survived.

But the financial position was not yet secure. The trustees were torn between keeping the school on its site in Church Road at Castlereagh (to which it had moved from the Scout centre in January 1982) and allocating

141

funds to mobile classrooms as the school expanded further, or conserving its limited resources to make possible the 15 per cent down payment on the purchase price of a new building. The local council, which could hardly be invulnerable to subtle political pressures, placed obstacles in the path, all for reasons which to the council looked legitimate and to the college governors looked 'technical'. They objected to the school's expansion on its existing site, so that, by September 1985, the new intake of four classes of 11-year-olds had to be housed in an annexe five miles away, provided by the Education and Library Board, and travel to use the specialist facilities in the afternoons. In the event, as temporary planning approval expired in 1988, the governors had no choice but to move to a new site.

The negotiations of the governors with the local council illustrated the point that, though the school had support from some weighty Ulster Protestants, it did not command the support of all. One might also expect that the lack of enthusiasm for the school manifested by the Roman Catholic authorities may have contributed to the degree of support which it found among some Protestants. The governors hoped that, as falling pupil rolls led to amalgamations and closures, a redundant school building in south Belfast might be made available; but in the end no school was closed. They investigated more than 130 sites with the help of a property committee (representing parents, governors, estate agents etc.) before successfully negotiating with the National Trust to purchase a 99-year lease on the 18.5 acres of Lisnabreeny House, nearby in Castlereagh. By September 1987, 200 pupils were accommodated in semi-permanent mobiles on the new site, with over 500 still at Church Road. The school was finally reunited on one site at Lisnabreeny in September 1991.

It was not until 1989 that the government finally gave formal recognition and approval to 'integrated education' in the Education Reform (NI) Order, following consultations throughout 1988. Based on the policy of extending the principle of parental choice (in Britain already enshrined in the 1988 Education Reform Act), it announced that its new proposals for grant-maintained schools attracting 100 per cent government funding could include a specific category of 'grant-maintained integrated schools' which would demonstrate 'a strong commitment to and progress towards full integration between Protestant and Roman Catholic pupils' (Department of Education for NI, 1988a, p. 19). There was vehement opposition from the Roman Catholic Church, which had recently established its own Council for Catholic Maintained Schools (CCMS), and was lobbying against the 'injustice' of still having to find the 15 per cent of capital funding for their schools. The Catholic lobby was understandably incensed that the government should be favouring the new integrated status with 100 per cent funding, particularly as the Northern Ireland curriculum proposals required a considerable expansion of specialist facilities in science and technology.

'The threat to the Catholic school system ... may be even greater, especially in the light of recent government legislation, which effectively discriminates in favour of alternative forms of educational provision.'[2]

The Protestants too were unhappy. They were concerned that a third (grant-maintained) sector in education could undermine their powerbase position in relation to 'controlled' schools and divert funding. This anxiety was articulated, for example, at the General Synod of the Church of Ireland in Dublin in May 1992, when clergy claimed that their role and influence had diminished since 1989, and that the pupils in state schools—almost all Protestants—were 'getting a raw deal'. Nevertheless, on behalf of the Church of Ireland, Archbishop Robin Eames of Armagh acknowledged that 'the view my Church has taken is that, where parental choice signifies that they want the experiment of integrated education to take place, then it ought to be'.

During the consultation period, the *Times* leader of 8 October 1988 commented that the government's claim for an encouraging level of support for integrated education was 'less than the whole truth. . . . The government must know that there is nothing like a consensus in support of integrated education and that powerful vested interests of all kinds from both sides of the religious divide are ranged against it.' In 1989 the government had probably decided to gamble that the time was right to come out in official support of the few integrated schools, still struggling financially on charitable donations. The fact that no denominational interest would wish to be seen opposing the principle of parental choice was advantageous politically, and the offer of 100 per cent funding for grant-maintained integrated schools could bring kudos to ministers under pressure to be seen taking positive action to ameliorate one of the apparent causes of Northern Ireland's troubles.

When eventually the Order was enacted in February 1990 to enable funding to come through by September, the recently formed Northern Ireland Council for Integrated Education (NICIE) breathed a sigh of relief. The chief executive, Fiona Stephen, recalled the tension of trying to run five integrated schools, one secondary and four primaries,[3] with no budget to pay staff salaries or purchase the required new sites: 'it was a seat of the pants job'. In May 1991 the Minister, Lord Belstead, also agreed to offer grant aid to assist NICIE in supporting further developments in integrated education across the province. By the beginning of 1992 over 3,000 children

---

[2]Council for Catholic Maintained Schools (1990), p. 5. Catholic schools were themselves finally offered 100 per cent government funding in 1992.

[3]Excluding Lagan, which by 1986 had already been granted voluntary-aided status: nevertheless their 15 per cent governors' contribution was difficult to raise.

were being educated in planned integrated schools, more than 1 per cent of the school population.

The Churches' response

Analysis of the Churches' response to integrated ecumenical education is inevitably a piece in the complex jigsaw of the intertwining interests of religion and politics in Northern Ireland. We may attempt to examine the Protestant position first.

THE PROTESTANTS

Protestant supremacy has not only meant permanent control of the government by the enforcement of the majority view in the name of democracy (leaving the minority with the sense of being excluded from equal participation). It has also meant a belief in a superior social position and a difference of economic status and opportunity. The traditional Unionist and Orange convictions, expressed with force and clarity by the Revd Ian Paisley, clearly show the fervour and commitment of Irish Protestantism in the North. Dervla Murphy commented:

> The average Northern Ireland Protestant is convinced that his forefathers were God-fearing, diligent, sober, honest, thrifty settlers whose virtues entitled them to take over the neglected lands of the superstitious, lazy, drunken, sly, shiftless natives. (1978, p. 100)

She went on to quote an example of the bigotry which this conviction can produce:

> A fourteen year old Protestant boy, horrified to discover that his French oral examiner was to be a nun, telephoned his mother. 'No child of mine will ever be examined by a Taig', she replied. 'And don't worry about your exam. I'll be on to the Education Authority now this minute.' That fourteen year old attained instant fame as the hard-done-by opponent of pernicious ecumenism. (Ibid., p. 101)

Murphy suggested that Protestant bigotry was, or at least appeared, far more entrenched, abrasive and aggressive than the Roman Catholic equivalent. Evangelical assurance encourages Protestants to suppose that they speak and act with the right of God on their side; by contrast 'Roman Catholics derive from their membership of the Roman Catholic Church an inner assurance which makes their bigotry that much less aggressive'. One person's devotion is another's fanaticism, and it is difficult to accept that Murphy's antithesis can be entirely fair. The two communities seem to be equally misinformed about each other's beliefs and traditions of practice, and equally ready to misrepresent one another: 'the two dominant cultures, are so mutually antipathetic that any demonstration of one is perceived to be an assault on the other' (Murray, 1983, pp. 238–55). In relation to the integration of education, the opposition of Protestants appeared veiled, whereas suspicion, not to say direct opposition, had been unconcealed on the part of the local Roman Catholic bishop.

This disapproval by the Catholic hierarchy let the Protestant Churches off the hook in several ways. First, Protestant ministers in the non-episcopal Churches are chosen by their congregations, and it would be difficult for them to follow a line independent of their flock.

> The great majority of church members in Northern Ireland ... instinctively expect their ministers to support the traditional sectarian parties which on each side are supposed to give political expression to true Christianity as they see it. (Gallagher and Worrall, 1982, p. 200)[4]

Since the Protestants fought long and hard to protect their own interests in education, they were as reluctant as the Catholics to take any risks with the status quo. Secondly, the Church of Ireland ministers had to watch their backs for fear of undermining their position *vis-à-vis* the Republic. As a minority community south of the border, they have argued forcefully for the protection of their own schools and denominational teaching. They therefore had to be cautious in their stance on integrated education north of the border or in appearing to undermine the Catholic minority's defence of their schools in Northern Ireland.

Nevertheless, the Churches publicly responded to the government consultations leading up to the Dunleath Act 1978. The Presbyterians had already passed two resolutions in favour of integrated education. The Methodists recognized it as 'one step toward improved relationships'. The Church of Ireland welcomed the initiative:

> It will be difficult for anyone who is sincerely concerned about growing understanding between our two communities not to wish the Minister well in an experiment, which demands of all participants the willingness to take a calculated risk for the possible greater good of the whole community.

The main Protestant Churches had also developed effective ecumenical links with their colleagues through the British Council of Churches—of which the Roman Catholic Church was not a member—and therefore, it was argued,[5] had a broader ecumenical perspective than either the Catho-

---

[4]Also Darby (1986, p. 130): 'I would alienate half my parish if I invited a Roman Catholic priest to my church', said one minister.

[5]Gallagher and Worrall (1982), p. 211.

lics or the Free Presbyterians.[6] It is not without weight that the Anglican Archbishop of Dublin, H. R. McAdoo, played a major part in the agreements of the Anglican/Roman Catholic International Commission articulated in the 'Final Report' of 1982. Therefore, when Lagan College was opened, offers of assistance with the pastoral and denominational support for the children were forthcoming. Although they would be hesitant about their status as official representatives of their respective Churches, the Protestant chaplains from the Presbyterians, Methodists, Anglicans, Baptists and non-subscribing Presbyterians[7] gave willingly of their time to ensure the Lagan children received pastoral encouragement.

THE ROMAN CATHOLICS

Roman Catholic teachers working on the staff of Lagan College fervently wished that their own Church could more openly offer support to so courageous a venture, but it is not the way of the Irish hierarchy to yield ground. The inveterate hostility to mixed marriages remains (the RC Church in England and Wales eased its rules on 6 April 1990) and insistence on the *Ne Temere* decree enforcing the Roman Catholic upbringing of the children has only in recent years required no written undertaking. Protestant reservations were not lessened by the vehement opposition of the Roman Catholic hierarchy to the decision of the Dublin government led by Garret Fitzgerald that it was politically necessary to make artificial means of birth control more freely available, partly on the ground that the exposure of unwanted children is far worse (*The Times*, 18 and 22 February 1985). The Roman Catholic Church in Ireland has not always been so hostile to the presuppositions of contemporary society. In the first half of the nineteenth century Gallicanism had more following than ultramontanism among members of the hierarchy, and there was less use of language that appears authoritarian. In 1826 the Roman Catholic Bishop of Kildare and Leighlin, James Doyle OESA (bishop from 1819 until his death in 1834), declared:

[6]This group, led by Ian Paisley, has been vociferous in opposition to ecumenism. At the Martyrs' Memorial Church on 26 January 1975, Mr Paisley said: 'The Lord will not deliver Ulster while her people do not realise that there are strange gods among us in the form of ecumenical clergy.... who would lead the Protestants of Ulster astray' (*Irish Times*, 27 January 1975).

[7]Non-subscribing Presbyterians are mainly found in Ireland. In the eighteenth century they split off from the Presbyterians who required ministers to sign the Westminster Confession, claiming that the authority of the Bible was all that should be recognized, not any interpretation of it; they then moved towards Unitarianism and Arianism, deciding that the doctrine of the Trinity is absent from Scripture. Their links with British Churches are with the Unitarians.

I do not know of any measure which would prepare the way for a better feeling in Ireland, than uniting children at an early age and bringing them up in the same school, leading them to commune with one another and to form those little intimacies and friendships which often subsist through life. (Select Committee, 1830, VII, pp. 426–7)

This surprising declaration belonged to a time when Catholic emancipation was being urgently pressed at Westminster and when the Roman Catholics in England were striving to reassure public opinion that Catholicism was not seditious or treasonable to the Crown.[8] But in the twentieth century it is hard to imagine that so optimistic and 'progressive' an opinion could come from a member of the Irish hierarchy. The bishops had real grounds for apprehension that too great an enthusiasm for integrated education could result only in injury to Roman Catholic schools, to which Roman Catholic parents ought to be sending their children rather than to places like Lagan College. Roman Catholic parents who chose to send their children to Lagan were put under moral pressure. Their action looked like disloyalty to their Church, tantamount to surrendering the heart of the faith in favour of religious indifferentism. Back in 1976 the Catholic hierarchy had given unexpected prominence to education in the *Directory on Ecumenism in Ireland* (Catholic Hierarchy, 1970), acknowledging the challenge presented to their schools by the ecumenical movement and the tragic conflict in Northern Ireland. However, they argued that

the replacement of Catholic by interdenominational schools in Ireland would not contribute to overcoming the divisions in our midst. . . . We must point out that in such schools the full Catholic witness is inevitably diluted.

Bishop Cahal Daly himself endorsed the official line in an article on 'Ecumenism in Ireland' in the *Irish Theological Quarterly* (1978).[9] However, dissenting Catholic voices were beginning to be raised to these utterances of the hierarchy. Father John Brady, the Jesuit director of the College of Industrial Relations, wrote in 1978: 'There are no insuperable difficulties about educating Catholic and Protestant children in the same school.' If the Catholic Church was 'prepared to pursue its legitimate interests in educa-

[8]For example Archbishop Wiseman (to the Select Committee on Education in Ireland, 1836): 'It might easily be managed to give Protestants and Catholics a common education, reserving religious education of their respective classes to their own pastors.'

[9]Cardinal Cahal Daly, now Archbishop of Armagh, was previously Bishop of Down and Connor from 1982. Before this he was Bishop of Ardagh and Clonmacnois for fifteen years, having previously served for 21 years lecturing on scholastic philosophy at Queen's University, Belfast.

tion through participative structures, at least in some instances and on an experimental basis', it would be saying 'in deeds rather than words that they do not wish to perpetuate the divisive social structures of Northern Ireland'. This concession that integrated schools could be recognized as 'experimental' was finally offered in 1982 by Cardinal O'Fiaich, then Cahal Daly's predecessor as Archbishop of Armagh,[10] in the *Irish Times* (30 January 1982).

The official policy of theoretical detachment and practical discouragement created acute difficulties for Roman Catholic parents sending their children to Lagan College. During the first year or two of the school's life, these parents put their shoulder behind the success of the project, and for the time being tolerated their Church's position. As the Catholic parents became more vocal, their sense of frustration at lack of support from their parish clergy could increasingly be felt. At one meeting in November 1982 they formally expressed the hope that their Church would make appropriate arrangements for their children's catechesis.

It cannot be easy for Roman Catholic bishops anywhere to give their priests and people a strong lead that they do not wish to follow, and in Ireland the difficulties must be considerable for any sensitive pastor among the hierarchy. Bishop Daly did not feel able to speak in favour of integrated education, and indeed his response highlighted some practical disadvantages: it meant 'bussing' children out of their communities, an artificial exercise; single-denominational schools were more representative of their neighbourhood community, and provided pupils with a stronger sense of identity and security, facilitating the natural partnership of parish, home and school, which a distant integrated school could hardly hope to do. That objection, however, was more obviously valid for particular areas like the Protestant Shankill or the Catholic Falls (where no one could seriously suggest the establishment of an ecumenical school) and loses much of its validity out in the more mixed residential areas of south Belfast where Lagan College is situated.

The Roman Catholic approach to ecumenical education was more than cautious. They seemed to feel that they had everything to lose, little to gain. Monsignor Colm McCaughan, later director of the Council for Catholic Maintained Schools but then secretary of a diocesan education committee, decisively commented to a reporter from the magazine *Newsweek* (21 May 1984): 'Integrated education is a facile solution to an extremely complex problem. I cannot give encouragement or approve of it.' Bishop Daly himself formulated the same negative attitude in a radio phone-in programme after the New Ireland Forum in February 1984: 'I do not see integrated

[10]On 16 January 1978 O'Fiaich had also commended the appointment of a Protestant to the management committee of a Catholic grammar school.

education as the way forward.' An institution such as Lagan College was tolerated with difficulty as a possible alternative for a few interested parents, but they were in effect tolerated only because they were so few. Thus Bishop Daly's response to Senator (later President) Mary Robinson during the Forum was reported in the following terms in the newsletter of the All Children Together movement:

> The Bishop said the Church did nothing to oppose the efforts of people to promote inter-denominational schooling. But such a development affected very few people and left unaffected those who needed this kind of mixing most.

The newsletter commented with unconcealed regret:

> We remain saddened that some priests and nuns who are willing to be involved in religious education and pastoral care for children not in attendance at Roman Catholic schools, do not feel free to do so.

The Catholic deputy principal of Lagan College felt disappointed that in 1984 Bishop Cahal Daly still held the negative view that integration was not the way forward. 'If only he could be persuaded to go so far as to grant "experimental" status—like O'Fiaich—and the experiment is judged to have been successful, the implications would be important.'

It became evident that the official Roman Catholic policy locked the Church into a circle from which there was no escape. On the one hand, the bishop's reason for seeing no solution in ecumenical education was that it could affect only a few. On the other hand, the quantity of ecumenical education which did exist was tolerated only to the degree that the minimum number of Catholic parents shared in it. In an age when support for serious and profound ecumenical engagement is the policy of an ecumenical council and of successive popes, it is impossible for a Roman Catholic bishop to disapprove of ecumenism without flying in the face of his own authorities. But the division in Ulster between Catholic and Protestant is a wound going so deep that there is not much room for the principle that Christians should do together what they are not absolutely required to do separately.

By the summer of 1984 nothing had been done to answer the parents' cry for help. They requested regular meetings and a celebration of mass perhaps in a church in the city centre; their requests were met with a quiet refusal. Roman Catholic priests wishing to respond positively feared being sent into a kind of 'internal exile' in much the way that has been experienced by Presbyterian ministers determined to build a bridge to Roman Catholic communities.[11] (The Ulster phrase for this is 'sent to Rathlin Island', a rocky outcrop off the north-east coast of Northern Ireland.) At Christmas

[11]See Revd David Armstrong (1985).

1983, when the school included Roman Catholic representatives among the invitations to its carol service, it was necessary to negotiate a private under-standing that any priest who attended would not be subjected to penalty or discipline: yet in 1985, 1,000 attended Lagan's carol service in a Catholic church on the Falls Road. One consequence of the Church's attitude was a genuine concern among Lagan's Roman Catholic parents that their children might lose their distinctive Catholicism. The official policy of the hierarchy seemed to be that Roman Catholics should not go to Lagan College for fear of losing or diluting their loyalty to the Church, whereas their policy of coldly ignoring the institution seemed specifically designed to bring about the consequence they feared. In Roman Catholic schools, a class mass would normally be held at least once a term. On days of obligation pupils at Lagan who attended mass in the morning necessarily arrived later at school because no celebration at the school was authorized. The Roman Catholic parents felt that this deliberate policy was at variance with the pastoral care which they expected from their Church.

The Roman Catholic head of religious education even produced a dos-sier of quotations from authoritative Catholic documents to inform discus-sion of the topic 'May Catholic parents choose Lagan College?' and these were cited to vindicate the parents' view. Three quotations suffice to illus-trate the strength of the contention:

> Acknowledging its grave obligation to see to the moral and religious education of all its children, the Church should give special attention and help to the great number of them who are being taught in non-Catholic schools. (Vatican II, Declaration on Christian Education, *Gravissimum Educationis*, 28 October 1965: Flannery, 1981, p. 732)

> The fact that in their own individual ways all members of the school community share this Christian vision, makes the school 'Catholic'. (Sacred Congregation, 1977, p. 14)

> In situations where, for one reason or another, Catholics and members of other churches are educated together, every attempt should be made to diminish the inherent disadvantages for religious formation. It is to be hoped that whatever Church is in charge of such schools would agree to arrangements by which children of other denominations could receive a religious education in accord-ance with the requirements of their own churches. (Catholic Hierarchy, 1976)

The situation presupposed in the last quotation is evidently that of Roman Catholic children educated in schools with a Protestant affiliation. But the principle should apply *a fortiori* in the case of a school of integrated charac-ter. It might have been easier for the Roman Catholic parents if the cool policy of detachment had been replaced by complete negativity: a reluctant toleration made for peculiar difficulties. As the number of Roman Catholic children educated in integrated schools increased, however, the Church authorities could less easily dismiss them as a small minority problem created by parents of little judgement who had opted out of the Roman Catholic educational system in defiance of their priests and pastors. As integrated education continues to expand, the hierarchy could feel more threatened, resulting in outright opposition to ecumenical developments in education. Alternatively the Church authorities may be moved to take seriously and positively the parents' desire to see an authentically Catholic education within an integrated framework. In the meantime, the balanced, interacting triangle of relationships of home, school and parish has one piece missing.

Initial academic issues

Just as education intrudes into Irish religion and politics, so politics and religion intrude into Irish education. What might seem to external observers to be a straightforward set of issues on curriculum or teaching method comes to take on another dimension. This is especially the case in the context of integrated education.

At Lagan College the parents of the first three annual intakes paid fees. In all private fee-paying schools, parents feel entitled to a considerable say in the teachers' decisions affecting their child. The first Lagan parents, who by acting as dinner supervisors, drivers or cleaners were responsible for keeping the school open at all, naturally felt a proprietary concern. Built into Lagan's constitution was a Parents' Council, which would channel communication from parents both to the school and to the governing body. As one parent recalled, this had the positive effect of educating the parents along with their children into what integrated education meant in practice; it also provided a forum for discussion and at times heated debate. The parent governors were often able to defuse situations which would otherwise have gone straight to the governors. In the early stages, this 'conflict-resolution' framework is said to have proved invaluable.

In Northern Ireland selection at 11-plus is the norm. To pass this qualifying examination is to enter the door of opportunity. The competition for places in the grammar schools is fierce. There must be few parents willing to endanger their child's established path to success through the grammar schools by taking the risk of an integrated experiment. In consequence, a fair proportion of early Lagan parents were those whose children failed to pass the 11-plus examination but who, mixed in with higher motives, saw Lagan as a superior option to, and even an escape from, the secondary modern or 'intermediate' system. Accordingly, parental ambitions and expectations ran high. Lagan's staff could not avoid facing demands that in their view may have seemed unrealistic. The chairman of the governors commented that the heart of the problem was 'to show that integration can go with a demonstrated commitment to excellence'.

The situation was exacerbated by constraints of size. The school was not large. Although nineteen subjects were offered to the first public examination cohort of 59 pupils in 1986, such a tiny proportion of these pupils was capable of achieving O level that mixed-ability teaching was necessary; staff's lack of expertise in this methodology meant success in O level became more difficult for those children who might achieve it. The converse of the problem appeared in the study of English literature, where only O level could be offered because the set texts for CSE courses were different and the two courses could not be taught to one group.

The balancing of pupil ability with parental expectation put the staff under severe pressure. Teaching a class of mixed ability was for many of the staff a new experience: in the majority of cases they had taught only within the selective Ulster system, and had little or no opportunity for retraining in the delicate task of stretching the more able and supporting the slow learners sitting in the same class. The first principal, fortunately, had a real understanding of an all-ability comprehensive school and encouraged the staff in mixed-ability methodology.

The principal wisely did nothing to encourage parents in unrealistic aspirations, but had to recognize the problem that the public success of Lagan was likely to be judged by its examination results. With GCSE syllabuses still in the future, she had to provide the opportunity for O-level as well as CSE teaching. Her sensitive formula in reply to enquiries was that 'results will be good for the ability of the pupils'. There is no school which does not face a dilemma here. The advertised curriculum offers courses to suit all abilities, yet it is the traditional academic bias which attracts parents to send their children to the school in the first place: few headteachers have not been asked on an open evening whether Latin is on the comprehensive school curriculum. An excessively academic approach has rapid repercussions in the breakdown of classroom discipline; where children cannot cope with a subject they are most likely to express their anxiety in disruptive behaviour. Parental ambitions create a situation where the best interests of the children are at odds, from the school's point of view, with the requirements of a public relations exercise. In Northern Ireland, more than in most places, the choice of priorities here is exquisitely painful.

The curriculum

What could seem more straightforward than the three Rs? Or in Church schools is it four Rs? Yet oversimplification of this kind is inappropriate for any school, and for an ecumenical institution damaging. As the experience at Redhill in suburban Surrey shows, in the context of a two-denominational school, religious education is far from being the only subject to need thought and scrutiny.

Single-church schools are often homogeneous in their pupil intake, so can feel free to reflect a specific culture and ethos in their curriculum. Nowhere is this more evident than in Roman Catholic or Protestant schools in Northern Ireland. Although there are practically no native speakers of the Irish language in Northern Ireland, Roman Catholic schools regard Gaelic as their birthright and guarantee it a place alongside continental languages in a way that Protestant schools would not.[12] Music may also reflect different cultural backgrounds: Catholics include a strong Gaelic tradition uncongenial to most Protestants. Another case in point is literature. The integrated school has to attempt sensitively to maintain the balance between two distinct cultural and social traditions.

If religion may appear rather marginal to the difference of tradition in music or Gaelic, that cannot be true of history. Through their reading of the past, rival communities defined themselves. The history syllabus, especially the Reformation, contains 'dynamite' for an ecumenical school, and in Ulster the contemporary tensions perpetuate misinterpretations and myths about the causes of the confessional divide.[13] But anxiety about the teaching and history of the Reformation pales into insignificance beside attempts to teach the Battle of the Boyne or the Easter 1916 uprising to a mixed class of Belfast Protestants and Catholics. In state schools, Irish history is frequently seen as an adjunct to English history since, after all, the great political decisions of people in power have normally been made in England, seldom in Dublin. In the past, though now much less so, Roman Catholic schools have preferred to treat Irish history as the story of noble heroes maintaining national culture and feeling under an alien and oppressive foreign rule. The Irish story is told in terms of Catholicism defining the identity of the people, suffering through the centuries from Tudor monarchs, Cromwell and the penal laws. The phenomenon is not, of course, unknown in England where the latent assumption that somehow Protestantism and English nationalism are linked is less dead than some imagine.

[12]My Catholic taxi-driver in the Falls Road waxed lyrical about the success of the one 'Gaelic-medium' primary school in Belfast (I only found out later that the deputy principal at Lagan had sent his children there). Comhaltas Uladh, a non-political and non-sectarian organization founded in 1926 to encourage the teaching of Irish language and culture, took 'an active interest in the teaching of Irish in Lagan College at its inception'.

[13]The same Catholic taxi-driver was adamant that discrimination against Catholics arose from 'Protestants not being told the truth about 1916'.

Lagan had the good fortune that one of the founder teachers had previously been a history teacher in a Catholic grammar school, and the experience had led him to the conviction that social tension is perpetuated by rival 'nationalisms' in the way people understand the past of their society. This understanding determines their sense of identity. His job must have been among the more exciting and taxing in Northern Ireland. He felt that if he could involve children from both confessions in looking at the evidence together, he would elicit a frank exchange of opinion and 'gut reactions' which, in terms of educational experience, could prove creative. He described how his ideas were put to the test one Friday afternoon when all pupils in the first three years at Lagan were involved in a lively debate on 'This house believes the plantation of Ulster was a good thing'. In the context of an integrated community where the children know each other well, and with an experienced teacher handling the exchanges, such encounters help each side towards mutual co-operation and comprehension. Significantly the Northern Ireland Curriculum Council subsequently drew on this teacher's expertise in devising the cross-curricular theme of 'Cultural Heritage', with specific links into the RE and history programmes and 'Education for Mutual Understanding' (see *Religion in Ireland: Yesterday, Today and Tomorrow* curriculum materials trialled in 1990: Lambkin, 1990).

Comparable controversy can enter even the playing fields. In general terms Protestant grammar schools follow the English public school tradition of rugby and cricket, whereas Catholic schools teach Gaelic football. To add to the confusion, Protestant matches are held on Saturdays, while Gaelic football kicks off on Sundays—in the eyes of Puritan Presbyterians an additional sign of profanation.[14] Soccer is mainly the prerogative of secondary modern intermediate schools. The integrated school is left either to dilute its limited resources by offering a selection of sports right across these choices, or to opt for the more common sport, soccer. Present policy at Lagan favours the sensible compromise of soccer and Gaelic football.

Back in the staffroom, the geography teacher, reflecting on the sensitivities necessary for teaching a mixed group of Catholics and Protestants, commented, 'I feel I have gently to correct the pupil who instinctively refers to Ulster as "our province". We also had an interesting discussion on employment patterns in this area, when a pupil asked why so few Roman Catholics were employed by a particular firm.' It is evident that the teacher's own sensitivity is crucial. Lagan College is fortunate in attracting a high proportion of committed teachers who are willing to explore the conflicting

[14]This issue 'jeopardized if not ruptured' a relationship carefully built up over seven years between Unionist and SDLP councillors in Londonderry in 1980 (cited by Gallagher and Worrall, 1982, p. 222).

aspects of their Ulster heritage. The fact that nearly a third came to Lagan at the price of a drop in salary or status decisively shows their commitment to the ideal for which the school stands. One Catholic teacher wrote: 'Knowing that there would be no official approval from the Catholic Church, in going to Lagan College I felt I was going into a kind of exile.'

Severe pressure was experienced by the staff, especially during the autumn term 1984. The long delays in permission to erect mobile classrooms meant an emergency staff meeting in the last week of August to decide whether or not to cancel the new intake of 11-year-olds due to arrive a week later. The only alternative was a 'crazy proposal' put to the staff: increase the class sizes by contracting the number of classes; rewrite the timetable; move the staff to a small boiler room to free another classroom; place two classes back to back in the assembly hall; and commit staff to a lunch-duty every other day. Since the other option, of cancelling the intake, would have played directly into the hands of Lagan's opponents, the staff agreed to the proposal. Many teachers would have thrown in the sponge under that excessive strain. But Lagan's highly principled staff were led by a headteacher whose determination for Lagan to succeed was not easily undermined.

Religious education and chaplaincy

RELIGIOUS EDUCATION
Religious education in an ecumenical school requires a particular degree of consideration when it is located in Northern Ireland. Lagan College published a statement of its aims in this field as being 'to meet the requirements not only of parents belonging to the main Christian Churches but also those of other faiths or none'. In its attempt to respond to individual needs, the school offered parents a choice for their child of attending assembly and inter-denominational acts of worship or of withdrawing. Similarly they could withdraw their child from all RE classes, or ask for them to attend only shared classes in RE without receiving 'denominational care' from a chaplain.

The school's prospectus outlined three main elements in the RE programme:

(a) the history and ideas of the major religious and philosophical traditions, intended for all pupils in the school;

(b) the common Christian tradition;

(c) church-specific, doctrinal, moral and ethical traditions and sacramental practice, intended for children of major denominations where desired.

155

The prospectus informed parents that they were free to withdraw their children from any of the three elements, but 'would be strongly encouraged to allow their children to attend at least the (a) element'. In practice none completely contracted out. In 1985 the percentage of pupils in the school worked out at 42 per cent Catholic, 41 per cent Protestant, and 17 per cent uncommitted denominationally. This last group, who tended to opt out of the 'denominational care', could be lapsed Catholics or children of mixed marriages. Some parents, like those in mixed marriages, felt that when it came to a two-choice denominational decision, they preferred to sit on the fence. At Lagan, unlike St Bede's, that was (and is) a possible option. However, one Roman Catholic parent, mother of six, wife of a priest of the Church of Ireland, commented that the parents' decision to commit the children to the 'denominational care' of one particular chaplain was essential, for it reflected the position in the 'real' world and was important for the child in creating a sense of Christian identity. (In her own family, three children were brought up as Roman Catholics, three as Church of Ireland.)

Religious education in the first year (11-year-olds) provided an overview of the structure of Christianity. Each chaplain from the various denominations (Church of Ireland, Presbyterian, Methodist, Baptist and the Roman Catholic sister) was interviewed by each class, 'so we learn about *all* religions' (as the pupils put it). Visits to particular churches were organized—to the RC church in the autumn term, to a Protestant church in the spring. Two Protestant girls commented on the Roman Catholic visit, 'The main differences were the coloured windows, confessional boxes, and the statues of Mary. They have mass instead of an ordinary service.' A boy in the same class optimistically thought that 'learning about all religions' would help to solve some of Northern Ireland's problems and to reduce violence. In the second and third years, pupils followed the development of early Christian communities and major world religions for two periods a week.

DENOMINATIONAL CARE
A specific period was regularly set aside for 'denominational care' in small groups with a visiting chaplain. This provided a vital contact between the Churches and the school, ensuring that the line of communication with individual families was kept open.

A lively second-year Catholic girl said that she enjoyed her sessions with Sister Clarke, but wished they were more frequent: she felt the difference between Protestants and Catholics was that 'Roman Catholics go on more about Mary'.

Lagan's statement on religious education underlines the purpose of 'denominational care'. The chaplains' job

is pastoral rather than teaching, to build up a relationship with pupils of their own flock, to encourage and support them in growing in their own tradition as they progress through the College. The Chaplains can help pupils to grow to be more committed and articulate members and representatives of their own denomination. For Catholic pupils this means the sort of experiences, liturgical worship, retreats etc., they would have in a maintained school, and for Protestant pupils pastoral care that would be complementary to Sunday School.

In fact, the decision was made at Lagan's inception to appoint a chaplain for every religious denomination represented by a pupil in the school. 'In the first year this meant finding a Baptist chaplain for our only Baptist pupil!' recalled the deputy principal.

The evident intention was to give reassurance to Lagan's parents that, far from finding a diluted religious education, their children would discover an enrichment through integration which would encourage personal commitment to a specific Church, not indifferentism. The suspicion is common among watchers of ecumenical communities that the end-product is a drift away from the particular devotion found in denominational religion into a vague, uncommitted, grey version of Christianity. In effect the opposite is more often the case. Somehow the juxtaposition of two communions compels individuals to analyse their position and, from an anchorage in their own tradition, to develop a more open appreciation and understanding of others' views.

One founder parent commented: 'We spent as long trying to recruit chaplains as we did teaching staff.' The aim was to provide 'reassurance to parents that their children would not be proselytized; pastoral support for staff and pupils; advice on RE and the role of religion in the school; and to represent the goodwill of the Churches in an integrated school'. Particularly on the Catholic side, the chaplaincy issue was contentious. A Catholic parent recalled his frustration when the then bishop Cahal Daly said that he could not possibly spare a priest for Lagan when he did not have sufficient for Catholic schools: 'But we weren't asking for a priest. We only wanted his support for a chaplain.' With no support from the hierarchy, those who volunteered to assist had to do so privately, mainly from religious orders, and even then were the object of criticism. One nun appointed to an RE post was forced by the bishop to resign. The Redemptorist priest who organized a mass for the Catholic parents was ordered to cease. Eventually in 1984 a retired nun, Sister Clarke, joined the chaplaincy team at Lagan and remained for eight years, during which time neither the bishop nor her community hindered her work, yet equally gave her no moral support. In her report on the Catholic chaplaincy (February 1990), she described how she came to the school with an interest derived from her Corrymeela connections, enthusiasm for its ideals, 'yet with no precedent for my role as chaplain. . . . My first few months were a challenging learning experience for me; coming from the Catholic system into an emerging integrated system, the focus on integration absorbed most of my time and attention.'

In the early days of Lagan, special attention had to be given to the support of Roman Catholic parents. Protestant parents had no difficulty with the role of the Church in the child's religious formation through Sunday school. The Catholics on the other hand were used to the school taking a central role and needed reassurance through a series of evening meetings that their child's Catholic identity would be safeguarded and strengthened. A founder Roman Catholic parent recalled 'umpteen discussions with Catholic parents to allay their fears, at which the Catholic deputy principal was a tower of strength'.

Staff too needed encouragement in clarifying Lagan's Christian ethos. At a residential weekend for all staff in Donegal in September 1985, they focused on how to create a school community 'animated by a spirit of liberty and charity based on the Gospel' (cited from *Gravissimum Educationis*, 8: in Flannery, 1981, p. 732). They identified formal ways such as occasions for worship or prayer and religious symbols round the school, but also informal ways in the quality of relationships between staff, pupils, parents and governors. These opportunities for staff to discuss openly and honestly were invaluable in establishing the school on a secure Christian foundation.

Lagan College had two heads of RE, one Roman Catholic, the other Protestant. In distinction from the few Protestant schools that had incorporated 10–20 per cent of Roman Catholics within their community, Lagan had to do more than 'accommodate' denominational differences. The challenge to an ecumenical school was to provide opportunities for sharing together religious experience and commitment in an atmosphere of trust, honesty and humility. An integrated community could provide that opportunity for religious questions to come out into the open, for convictions and prejudices to be aired, so that commitment was not seen as an expression of hurtful rivalry but as a power for healing in a deeply polarized community.

Community relations

A school's success is to some degree related to its reputation in the community beyond its walls. An 'ivory tower' policy is rarely the concomitant of success. For Lagan College it was not merely success but survival which was at stake.

From the first, Lagan was dependent on its supporters, without whom it would never have got off the drawing-board. Parents, politicians, clergy and laity, persuaded that the mould of segregation must be broken, found their individual voices coming together in the formation of the All Children Together movement in 1974. Their pressure, as we have seen, was instrumental in getting the law changed to allow for shared schools. Their support for opening the school in 1981 evoked a response in the surrounding community: the Scouts offered their new centre as a site for the school's first term, and parents both ran the tuck shop and cleaned the floors. When new accommodation intended to be ready for September 1983 was incomplete, the director and staff of the Ulster Folk Museum offered their education centre as a base for the new intake of 77 pupils. The school's neighbours at Castlereagh, a factory and public playing fields, allowed generous use of their car parking areas, especially when builders were occupying much of the school site. Equipment for laboratories and workshops was forthcoming from local business and industry. Extensive media coverage stimulated an international interest in the school's development.

Lagan's early students were encouraged to go out into the community, to visit different churches and exhibitions, and to participate in inter-school sports competitions. By 1985 Lagan had twice won the senior section of a schools' history competition aimed at promoting community understanding and tolerance, organized by the Churches' Central Committee for Community Work in association with the *Belfast Telegraph*. Speakers from the All Children Together movement encouraged co-operation across the religious divide at many meetings around the province. The Department of Education for Northern Ireland issued a circular on *The Improvement of Community Relations: the Contribution of Schools* (1982/21), commending an area in which Lagan had clearly taken a lead.

PARENTAL LIAISON
On the school's behalf the most effective influence in the community was the parents. Many of them persevered in the early years at considerable cost to themselves. One working-class Roman Catholic mother had been anxious and hesitant over choosing a secondary school; when Lagan was given publicity, an open-minded Roman Catholic primary headteacher gave her the brochure saying that it might provide the answer. She took a job in a factory kitchen to earn a contribution to her son's education at the integrated school. 'We decided that no matter what else happened, Christopher was going to that school. . . . My son should meet people from all walks of life' (cited from *Newsweek*, 21 May 1984). One Protestant grandmother was apprehensive about the Roman Catholic influence on her grandson if he enrolled at Lagan. In his first year the mother persuaded the grandmother to help with school cleaning, and through contact with the spirit of the school, she became fully converted to the idea. The mother, while in sympathy with the aims of Lagan, came from a Presbyterian background; she was not herself a practising Christian. She found Lagan's open-door policy to uncommitted parents a relief in the sectarian divide of Ulster's education system.

The sociologist and founder parent, Tony Spencer, commented in inter-

159

view that parental involvement was important for three reasons: first, parents should not 'expose their children to the experience of integration without having that experience themselves'; secondly, 'the more interest and involvement the parents have in their children's education, the more effective the school will be as a formal socializing agency'; and thirdly, their involvement helps to spread 'the effects of integrated education throughout the human life-cycle', i.e. to more than one generation at a time.[15]

One brave couple with four children had a particular reason to support Lagan College. As a policeman, the Catholic father lived in constant danger. He sent his son to Lagan partly because he wanted coeducational mixed-ability teaching, but primarily as the only way to escape what he saw as the overwhelmingly republican influence of teachers, priests and peer groups in Catholic schools. He expressed the opinion that 'Cardinal O'Fiaich favours the IRA, does nothing to support those priests who press for a more balanced line, and certainly has no control over the gunmen'.

Nevertheless, the parent in question was by no means uncritical of Lagan College. The crowded accommodation and the question-mark over the future site of the school created a sense of insecurity even among parents who had lived 'hand-to-mouth' from 1981. In relation to religious education, he felt that the sessions with Sister Clarke allowed for insufficient catechetical instruction; and he was worried about his son studying Christianity with a Protestant teacher, who knew less about Roman Catholicism than some of his pupils. These reservations were comparable to those articulated by Catholic parents at Redhill, gradually coming to terms with the recent emphasis on greater parental responsibility for children's catechesis.

On one occasion an anxious Protestant mother telephoned another when her son failed to arrive home from school one afternoon. They decided to drive over to the republican New Lodge district of Belfast to see if the boy was at the flat of his Roman Catholic friend. In the darkness they were stopped by a group of young men, hands in pockets, who allowed the boy's mother to check the flat while they stayed with the other by the car, lights out. The boy was later found back at home, but the experience was unforgettable for the mothers.

Support for parents, especially those under such pressures, had to be part of the school's role. Like other ecumenical ventures, Lagan College organized meetings or retreats for parents, such as the weekend held in September 1983 at Corrymeela near Ballycastle. Free discussion ranged from education to religion, from unemployment to worship, with the aim of 'fostering a community spirit of integration beyond the school'. What was likely to be a long-drawn-out process had at least started successfully.

[15]See also 'Arguments for an integrated school system', ch. 7 in Osborne et al. (1987b), p. 109.

RELATIONSHIPS WITH OTHER EDUCATIONAL INSTITUTIONS

A matter of major importance for Lagan was to have good relations with its feeder primary schools. These were a vital link into the community, and there was a wide variety in their responses to contact with Lagan. A founder member of staff, responsible for primary school liaison, saw her task as twofold: first to find out about prospective pupils as individuals, to assess how they would fit into the academic and religious balance of the classroom; and secondly to put Lagan 'on the map' so far as the primary sector was concerned. Increasing numbers of Protestant primary schools asked for the college prospectus; but when there were more than 40 'feeder' schools to visit, a warm welcome could not be taken for granted. Among Roman Catholic primary schools there was overt hesitation. One headteacher commented that her parents were free to do what they liked, but she felt that in sending children to Lagan they were making a mistake; another top form teacher confided that she was convinced Lagan was a step in the right direction but would get into trouble for saying so. Two Protestant primary schools answered Lagan's request for a visit with the reply that it was not convenient; one principal felt that there was no need for a visit because written records could be sent on, although they never were.

On one visit to a Roman Catholic school run by Christian Brothers, the Lagan teacher was astonished to be greeted and blessed. The principal clearly took the view that the child in question would survive far better in a small school like Lagan than in a tough secondary modern school (with RC affiliation). Another principal asked anxiously about religious education: would Lagan provide catechetical teaching? Was there provision for clergy to come into the school?

Among primary schools there was concern that oversubscription meant that not all pupils could be assured places; this is a problem common to all institutions with a popular draw. The question whether there might be intimidation in the school was not. One young boy from the UDA stronghold of a Dundonald estate on the outskirts of Belfast felt confident, however, that he had nothing to fear in being educated alongside Roman Catholics: 'I've got big brothers.'

One seemingly trivial matter became a significant mark of the confidence that Lagan College came to feel. Apprehensive about the reaction of the community, pupils during the first year in 1981 wore unmarked black blazers without distinctive insignia. By the autumn of 1984 their blazers sported a badge with the Latin motto *Ut sint unum* (from John 17:21—'a motto in English would have been as divisive as one in Irish', said the deputy principal), and a school scarf was introduced—black with bright red and yellow stripes. The children could now take pride in their uniform.

2. LAGAN COLLEGE: IN ITS TENTH YEAR 1991–92

We seek to free our children and future generations from the sad suspicion, from the cynicism of despair and of futile gloom, all too prevalent in Northern Ireland today and which has been imposed on us more forcibly in the last two decades.

So spoke the first chairman of governors, the Rt Hon. Basil McIvor, to a packed assembly hall at the opening of the new school building at Lisnabreeny on 25 October 1991. He paid credit to staff, children, parents, local community representatives, Church leaders, government ministers and officers, benefactors both national and international, without whom Lagan College could not have come into being and integrated education might have remained no more than a vision. In particular, he acknowledged the support of Dr Brian Mawhinney, Minister of State at the Northern Ireland Office, in his successful efforts to procure the £3.3 million from the government towards the new building.

The principal, Terry Flanagan, wrote this in his newsletter to celebrate the occasion:

The first part of the story has ended. The sceptics had been wrong. In the ten years between, there was much to be excited about, and to be discouraged about, and to hope for and to despair of ever achieving. One thing was certain during the years of split sites, inadequate accommodation, and lack of those things which other schools took for granted, and that was the certainty that the education of Catholic and Protestant children together by teachers from both sides of the community was the right thing to do, and that the Lagan College experiment would succeed.

There could be little doubt that the college had 'succeeded' if judged by the criteria of pupil numbers and staff recruitment. To move from 28 pupils and 5 staff in 1981 to 740 pupils and 47 staff in 1991 was no insignificant achievement for a secondary school which, for its first few years, was wholly dependent on charity, competing for children in a province where parents demand high standards of educational excellence. The second principal, Terry Flanagan, took over the leadership of the college from Mrs Sheila Greenfield in September 1987 when already over 500 pupils were enrolled. In 1991 over a hundred applications had to be turned down for lack of space in the first year alone. The scheduled expansion to over a thousand boys and girls, including a full sixth form, was gradually to take place as new buildings 'came on stream', replacing the temporary hutted accommodation with humanities and business studies suites, science and technology laboratories, and a sports hall. The charitable trust meanwhile continued to raise funds to support two full-time chaplaincy appointments and to finance the establishment of a worship centre in the school as part of the building programme.

Over ten years after the creation of the school, the parameters of the discussion had hardly changed. Yet the seeing eye was not quite looking at the problems in the same way and both circumstances and status had altered. In the following section we reconsider the political issues, the Churches' response; academic, curricular and the religious dimensions; and the relations with the surrounding community.

Political issues

On 14 April 1987 the chairman of Lagan's governors said in a press statement: 'Lagan College is a native growth, and it is to be hoped that it will not lack the tending and watering which will bring it to full flower in as short a time as possible.'

In March 1988 the Department for Education in Northern Ireland published a consultation document entitled *Education in Northern Ireland: Proposals for Reform*. For the first time it acknowledged the government's support for schools which demonstrated a 'strong commitment to and progress towards full integration between Protestant and Roman Catholic pupils' (para. 57). It offered integrated schools (i.e. schools with at least 20–25 per cent pupils in the minority communion) the specific option of grant-maintained status, enabling them to claim 100 per cent capital funding from government. Additionally

> in grant-maintained integrated schools, given the Government's commitment to support and encourage integrated education, enrolments would not necessarily be constrained by the school's existing physical capacity, and normally it would be the intention to give the highest priority within the capital programme to projects involving the provision of necessary additional pupil places. (para. 62)

This statement not only marked a clear policy change in the government's commitment to integrated education (moving from a 'hands-off' policy to one of specific support), but also singled out integrated schools for preferential treatment as regards expansion to meet demand.

These proposals seemed to be the answer to Lagan College's prayers over the previous decade. At last their efforts were being officially recognized and commended, and the opportunity to be relieved of the massive fund-raising responsibilities of the previous years seemed welcome.

The immediate reality, however, turned out to be rather different. The proposals for 100 per cent future funding came too late for Lagan and the strenuous toil of its supporters and, ironically, sabotaged much of the essential fund-raising efforts for other integrated schools in the meantime. In practice they 'rolled a boulder in the path of Lagan College and probably other integrated schools. By holding out the promise of paying for Lagan's new school *eventually*, the motivation behind fundraising has been damaged ... the building fund has slowed to a trickle.' So wrote the secretary to the appeal in the Lagan College newsletter for June 1988.

The other 'sting in the tail' was the issue of control of an integrated school when it adopted grant-maintained status in order to attract 100 per cent government funding. The repercussions of the change in status for diocesan education policy or parental control were considerable, and the Roman Catholic Church in Northern Ireland, like its counterpart in England and Wales, has already expressed concern about a policy which allows its schools to 'opt out', warning of the danger that 'opting out' might allow undesirable political factions to take control of their schools.

Integrated grant-maintained schools face a comparable dilemma. In consequence of 'opting out', the foundation and trustee governors of the school (who would be understood to have special responsibilities for keeping it true to its initial ideals) no longer hold the overall majority on the governing body where additional places are offered to elected parents. This gives parents, on a ballot as low as 20 per cent, the power to change an integrated school into, for example, a county school or a Roman Catholic school at some time in the future. The anxiety that the advocates of integrated education may have gained only a hollow victory is understandable.

Because of these considerations the future of integrated schooling in Northern Ireland is still far from clear. In a society already marked by suspicion, anxiety is hard to exorcize. However for Lagan's governors, the offer of 100 per cent funding could not be turned down since it secured the financial position. The strong moral pressure on government ministers to provide capital funding for their 'flagship' integrated school was also strengthened when it became one of the first grant-maintained schools in the province. The governors' concern about the balance on the governing body and the ability of particular interest groups to exercise control has not in fact proved contentious. In 1991, the chairman of governors commented that although the nine foundation governors were not the majority, the six elected parent governors had retained an appropriate denominational balance, and the six governors appointed by the government have hitherto been chosen after the consultation with the Foundation, with three elected teacher governors making up the full complement of 24. Lagan College's bursar also suggested that, although, as Lagan was an opted-out school, he could not expect support from the Local Education and Library Board, in practice he was able to seek helpful advice from its officers on a range of financial and administrative matters. As government policy becomes clearer in relation to the management of grant-maintained schools, no doubt this situation will need to be kept under review. It is not easy to draw out Leviathan with a hook.

The Churches' response to government policy on integrated status also had to be taken into account. The Roman Catholic authorities were incensed that this new sector received 100 per cent funding while they still struggled to raise their statutory 15 per cent funding to support their aided schools. The Council for Catholic Maintained Schools, in its response to the report of the Standing Advisory Committee on Human Rights (SACHR) in September 1991, wrote:

> The Council accepts that the statutory requirements of the Common Curriculum have resulted in a large number of new capital projects being urgently required in Catholic maintained schools. It endorses the [SACHR] view that 'the financial burden will fall on a community which suffers high levels of social deprivation.' In the interests of equality of opportunity, the Council calls on Government to consider this particular initiative as a special case and provide for it to be funded fully by Government and at no cost to the Catholic community. (Council for Catholic Maintained Schools, 1991, p. 1)

At the same time the Catholic authorities were keen to retain hard-won control of their schools and hesitant to follow the route of the Scottish hierarchy whose decision to allow their schools to be 100 per cent state funded since 1969 is thought to have resulted in a gradual erosion of the power of Catholic education authorities (*Catholic Herald*, 29 May 1992). Despite these fears and hesitations, in November 1992, after negotiations, an 'historic agreement' was reached that the government would provide 100 per cent capital funding for Catholic schools in return for overall control of governing bodies, heralding 'a new era of trust', according to Bishop Edward Daly (*TES*, 13 November 1992). The bishop's confidence seemed founded on the fact that the parent governors would all be committed Catholics who would not wish to alter the school's ethos.

The Protestants too resented what they saw as preferential funding meted out to integrated schools, while other sectors had for years been knocking on the Exchequer door. The representative of the three main Protestant Churches (Methodist, Presbyterian and Church of Ireland), speaking at a seminar on integrated schools in 1991, also strongly objected to the exclusion of the Churches from a management role in integrated schools—a view he reiterated to his Church of Ireland Synod in June 1992:

> I regard it as a blatant breach of historic and legally binding agreements. And I regard the Conservative administration policy in education, in this respect, as included in the 1989 Order, as being divisive, extremely insensitive and hurtful. I perceive such attitudes as being a slur on the track record of many church representatives.

He went on to insist that 'schools do not need to opt out of the controlled sector to become integrated', praising local initiatives which welcome Roman Catholic pupils, teachers and governors into controlled schools. Like the Catholic hierarchy, he welcomed the government's encouragement for the National Curriculum cross-curricular themes of 'Cultural Heritage' and 'Education for Mutual Understanding' in all schools. He emphasized the need for equality of treatment for the controlled sector: if the government was willing to fund a Council for Catholic Maintained Schools and the Northern Ireland Council for Integrated Education, 'the time is overdue for a body to provide a similar focus for controlled schools'. It seems therefore that the government's explicit endorsement of integrated education has ruffled the feathers of both Protestant and Catholic Churches, whose reaction is to regard it as a 'cuckoo in the nest'.

A further important issue is raised by the government's formal recognition of grant-maintained integrated status: is an integrated school by definition one that describes itself as Christian or religious? Or might the government encourage in the future secular integrated schools? There is already public debate about the religious nature of an integrated school. At the Education and Library Board's conference in October 1989, reported in *Education* (27 October 1989), a Protestant spokesman declared: 'The creeping secularization implied in the proposed grant-maintained integrated status is no cure for sectarianism.'

Lagan College goes out of its way to acknowledge religious diversity and is very explicitly Christian—though at the same time it 'welcomes on an equal footing, pupils of religions other than Christianity, and those who come from homes which do not subscribe to a religious view of life' (cited from the 1990 prospectus);[16] it therefore offers an attractive refuge for parents in mixed marriages or where religious allegiance has been rejected, whether out of intellectual conviction or even from disgust at religious sectarianism and its consequences. Some other integrated schools, however, which would also consider themselves Christian, tend to play down the importance of religion, no doubt because of its divisive potentialities. This was recognized by the Church of Ireland General Synod's education spokesman, who commented to his local synod in June 1992:

> Some schools do attempt to engage with the realities of both main religious traditions in Ireland, whilst the attitude of others would indicate a more secular approach—a virtual 'plague on both your houses' attitude towards the two Christian traditions.

However, the principal of one school, identified as being in the second category, commented:

[16]Note that this admissions criterion is not shared by St Bede's, Redhill.

Northern Ireland is not ready for a secular school; it won't be for twenty years. Religion is built into the culture ... Yet I don't believe for one second that the problem is religious. No one has ever been shot because of their views on Transubstantiation.... The problem between Catholics and Protestants is not that they do not understand each other's theology. It is because they are afraid of each other. It is all about perception. If people feel threatened, they will attack or run away.

He acknowledged that there may be different models of an integrated school: if people saw Lagan as more overtly Christian than his school, so be it. He preferred to emphasize the importance of the hidden curriculum in developing pupils' self-esteem, thereby increasing their understanding and respect for each other.

Seamus Dunn of the Centre for the Study of Conflict at the University of Ulster (Coleraine) discussed these issues:

All the existing planned integrated schools describe themselves as Christian schools in spite of the fact that, in most of them, there are parents who do not describe themselves as Christians. It is clear that the emphasis on the Christian nature of the schools arises out of the deep (Christian) religious convictions of those involved. But there is also the view that, since most people in the Northern Ireland culture define themselves in Christian terms, there would be general reluctance to support a secular school and even outright opposition to it. (Dunn, 1989)

Dunn even suggested that here the old joke about people defining themselves as Catholic atheists or Protestant atheists holds true. He continued:

The aspiration that all religions be cherished should be seen alongside the view that the schools are nonetheless Christian schools. In Northern Ireland, where the numbers of non-Christian religions are small, this is uncontentious because there is no threat.

However, he speculated that a school dominated by a secular ethos, in so far as the majority of its pupils and staff would be atheist or agnostic, might have little to contribute to improving community relations for the reason that it would not effectively be an integrated school: the discussion of these matters is just beginning.

This issue has also been addressed by the Northern Ireland Council for Integrated Education. In answer to the 'misconception' that 'integration is creeping secularization', the chief executive commented: 'All integrated schools are based on Christian foundations.' At the Cambridge joint schools conference in June 1992 she confirmed that NICIE's approach to religion, as declared in its published *Statement of Principles*, is Christian rather than secular and that, since the government required integrated schools to have an appropriate balance of Protestants and Catholics, they must by definition be 'ecumenical'. The principal of Lagan College questioned, however, whether it is possible for them to be truly 'ecumenical' as long as the Churches refused to become involved. It would be ironic if the Churches, in their single-minded determination to defend their own denominationally oriented schools in preference to the integrated Christian institutions, found that by their absence the integrated sector became dominated by secular interests and government control.

The Churches' response

In the period since Lagan College began, the position of the Churches has not radically shifted. Both Catholic and Protestant Church spokesmen continue to insist that the maintained and controlled sectors respectively are and will remain their prior concern. Yet there have been important if subtle changes of emphasis in the Churches' response to the development of integrated education.

There seem to be three issues on which the Catholic and Protestant leaders agree: they claim that their own single-denominational schools encourage integration; they insist on the importance of control and influence in their schools; yet they respect the right of parents to choose the school which best suits their child. We may briefly consider each of these claims.

First, the Protestants have always been in the position to claim that integrated schools are unnecessary since their controlled schools are open to all, welcoming Catholics as much as anyone else; but they acknowledge that *de facto* their ethos is predominantly pan-Protestant (the opinion of the education spokesman of the Irish Council of Churches). The Catholics, on the other hand, have argued that far from being divisive, their schools care about 'reconciliation and love in our community'; they have an obligation to encourage an 'ecumenical spirit with sister schools of different traditions', to implement and extend inter-school co-operation, and to develop projects for peace and mutual understanding (see Loughran, 1987). What these two viewpoints do not take into account, many would say, is the inherent sectarianism of a segregated system in Northern Ireland, evidenced in the research of Darby, Dunn, Murray and others; such a system cannot acknowledge the enrichment of diversity nor accept another tradition on equal terms. The function of religious separation is to make the most characteristic features of Catholicism and Protestantism in Northern Ireland a series of negations of the alternative.

Secondly, both confessions argue that they must have control of their schools. The Protestants have kept 'transferors' rights' on the governing bodies of controlled schools, and are arguing with the government to allow the establishment of a Council for Controlled Schools, parallel to the Council for Catholic Maintained Schools set up in 1989. (As noted earlier, the point surfaced in the General Synod debates of the Church of Ireland in May 1992.) They tend to be more suspicious of the 'creeping Irishness' implied by the Education for Mutual Understanding (EMU) initiative, for example, since it might undermine their emphasis on preserving a British identity. This observation appeared to be confirmed when the 'Religion in Ireland' project was being given a trial at Lagan College: the Protestant children were made more anxious than the Catholics when the work disclosed that the differences between the denominations were less than they had been brought up to believe. It has even been argued, for example by Duncan Morrow (1991), that Protestants are less threatened by integrated education than by EMU because integrated education 'is portrayed as the end of control over education by the Catholic Church and the very public objections of the Catholic hierarchy to integrated education have encouraged this view' (*Tablet*, 16 February 1991).

Canon Houston McKelvey of the Church of Ireland has regretted that a consequence of the opposition of the Catholic Church to integration has been that the government has gone for grant-maintained status, so that now no Church has a controlling influence in the integrated schools. Such an erosion of power must be unwelcome.

The third issue on which the Churches agree is that of parental choice. As has been noted, the government's Parent's Charter and other initiatives to enhance parental choice in education have been acknowledged by both Protestants and Catholics but only warily, again because of the implicit threat to Church control in education. Once, however, they have agreed the principle, it can be applied as much to the rationale for developing integrated schools as for preserving segregated ones. Catholics argue that the parents' decision to have their child educated in a Catholic school is a religious decision based on 'a theocentric view of reality' (Loughran, 1987), though probably few parents would think of expressing it in such terms, and in any event it is hardly distinctive of Catholicism. Cardinal Daly, when interviewed for *Fortnight* magazine, remarked:

> The very high proportion of Roman Catholics who deliberately and freely choose Catholic Schools for their children is a very effective way of showing that this is what they believe is in their circumstances the best form of education, which they themselves desire in exercise of their parental choice. Others make a different choice—that's fine. I'm not crusading against integrated education. I am a fervent believer in the value of Catholic education. (13 September 1991)

These comments certainly reflect a change, even if only a hesitant and reluctant one, from Cardinal Daly's marked disapproval of 1984. However, the right of Catholic parents to choose integrated education remains difficult, since they are officially choosing also to take on 'personal responsibility for their child's religious formation', because (to quote Mgr McCaughan, director of the Council of Catholic Maintained Schools) 'they are opting out of a full Catholic education'.[17] The judgement that only a Catholic school can provide Catholic education is shared by Bishop Patrick Walsh of Down and Connor, but he observed that parish support for integrated schools was increasingly becoming a priority. Unlike the experience of the Lagan pupils in early days, he hoped that his parish priests would take seriously their bishop's insistence (e.g. at the priests' conference in spring 1992) that children in integrated schools needed more support in Catholic formation, not less.

Lagan's principal reported that Bishop Walsh had given permission for a Jesuit priest to assist in a day conference for fourth-year pupils at the college in June 1992. Nevertheless the bishop refused to give his approval to the appointment of a Passionist father as Lagan's Catholic chaplain in September 1992, in spite of the fact that the man concerned had already taken up the post with the knowledge of his superiors: the Passionist Order was eventually willing to allow the chaplain to remain at Lagan for the academic year 1992–93. The bishop considered that it was contrary to Church policy to appoint a priest to the post, although he was prepared to consider a non-ordained religious. Have the days passed when Lagan parents in his diocese could describe themselves as 'left in a spiritual no man's land'? It is too early to speculate whether or not the principles of reconciliation and ecumenical spirit advocated within Catholic schools might be equally applicable outside them.

The Churches still face a number of difficulties in their response to integrated schools like Lagan. Protestant ambivalence may be explained by three factors. First, Protestants do not speak with one voice. On policy there are wide disagreements. For example, the non-sectarian Alliance party openly supports integration, while the Official Unionists would prefer schools to reinforce 'the British dimension'. A Church of Ireland spokesman privately observed that when the Church of Ireland was trying to encourage ecumenical co-operation with Roman Catholics, it was 'unhelpful if the Unionists publicly voiced strong anti-Catholic opinions'. Secondly, Protestant ministers are generally less at home in schools than their Catholic counterparts. Their theology of conversion seems more appropriate in the context of Sunday schools (though probably only about 17 per cent of

[17]See Mary Kenny, *Tablet*, 10 February 1990: 'the Roman Catholic Church has embarked upon a propaganda exercise to promote Catholic schools specifically and, in some cases, to be uncooperative in administering catechism, First Communion or Confirmation classes to Catholic children in integrated schools'.

children attend these) than in the pan-Protestant culture of controlled schools, let alone integrated schools. Thirdly, it is observed that the Protestant school is closely linked with its own local community in a way the integrated school cannot be because of its wider catchment area. (The same would apply, of course, to Catholic schools in Catholic areas, but the point seems not to be noted so much by Catholics.)

Canon McKelvey suggested that integration which arises naturally by consent (for example when a local Church of Ireland school chooses to have a Catholic on the governing body to represent the interests of the increasing numbers of Catholics moving into the area) is superior to that 'imposed by any government'. The 'sensitive local negotiations' which led to the establishment of the first integrated controlled school (Brownlow in Craigavon) offered a case in point; however, the local board representative governors (Protestants) were forced to resign in July 1992 for not supporting integrated status. Bishop Gordon McMullan, Anglican Bishop of Down and Dromore, noting Lagan's progress, nevertheless felt that the school's public relations had concentrated more on the media than on the local community and its people: 'it must also guard against being isolated, a problem exacerbated by its geographical position in the more rural area beyond south Belfast' (personal interview, October 1991). By contrast, Colin Irwin's research noted advantage in its site beyond Belfast's main residential area, where the college was less likely to draw pupils from a community 'with a social class or sectarian bias' (1991, p. 15).

The Catholic Church's response to integrated education has tended to be more officially clear-cut. Although there are still priests who put undue pressure on parents,[18] many now feel that the priority is to make Catholic schools sufficiently attractive in terms of both academic excellence and Catholic nurture to make such pressure unnecessary. This links with the conviction that Catholic schools are the only choice for Catholic parents because religious education must permeate every aspect of school life. Bishop Walsh commented that it is not enough to have separate RE on the timetable, even if it is taught by Catholic teachers, since this separatist model does not recognize the implicit formation of children through the school's pervasive Catholic ethos. This view is also found in Loughran's

---

[18]The depth of feeling can be sensed in the rhetoric of Fr Denis Faul at Maynooth (28 February 1989): 'Catholics who do not send their children to Catholic schools inflict a grievous wound on the children by depriving them of a uniquely precious gift—an education with a 2,000-year-old perspective on religion. These parents endanger their faith and they are helping to betray the faith of the coming generations by failing to support Catholic schools now. Who gave them leave to opt out of the Catholic community for selfish or snobbish reasons? Their duty is to support Catholic education and strengthen it for the coming generations. This is the only way they can fulfil the promise given in Baptism.'

article of 1987 on 'The rationale of Catholic education': 'There is no catechism which can make a school into a Catholic school. It is rather the existence of a Catholic school which makes catechesis possible.'

One problem with this is that it may presuppose a rather more monolithically Catholic society than actually prevails in modern Ireland. A Catholic teacher who had worked in Belfast Catholic schools for many years even considered the bishop's view to be 'fiction': if it was once true of the hidden curriculum, 'it did not exist any more, because the religious orders were less and less involved in education', he argued. However, even if this is too pessimistic, a second question is how can we know that this Catholic ethos may not also be present in integrated schools? Bishop Walsh conceded that it was difficult to define; but he would expect to recognize it by the presence of statues or crucifixes.[19] However, he had never visited an integrated school to judge for himself; he felt he already knew that it could not exist there. A third—and from an ecumenical point of view the most significant—question is whether an integrated school may not create a genuinely Christian ethos in which the different denominations would participate equally.

Another difficulty arises from the traditional role of the Catholic priest in schools. Unlike Protestant ministers in relation to controlled schools, priests are regular visitors to Catholic schools. Their theology of nurture is naturally at home in the school setting where every teacher is viewed as a catechist. The deputy director of the Council of Catholic Maintained Schools admitted, however, that Catholic priests are unaware what catechetical programme is being taught at integrated schools like Lagan College, nor are they encouraged to find out. He went further in insisting that it would be 'an act of disbelief' for them to go into an integrated school since 'we cannot become involved in something over which we have no control or authority'. If a visit did take place, the Catholic priest would not be there as of right as he would be in a Catholic school. Nor could he indicate to Roman Catholics that integrated schools might be as good as Catholic ones. A related issue was highlighted by Mgr Bartley on Ulster Television (22 January 1989): Catholic schools put central emphasis on the mass, prayers to Mary, and preparation for the sacraments. 'This cannot be done adequately in a mixed school without offending the religious sensibilities of other Christians.'

Thirdly, even if they wanted to, Catholic schools could never become partners in joint ecumenical schools since there are no Protestant Church schools with which to amalgamate, unlike the situation in England where the Catholic and Anglican Churches both retain their own schools. Bishop

---

[19]Note that Christian symbols were deemed important at St Bede's, Redhill in the 1991 refurbishment and in Dominic Murray's 1983 research in Ulster schools.

Walsh explained that this was a further reason why Catholics felt uneasy about integrated education, because the Church was not involved from the start. However, he acknowledged that Catholic opposition had forced Lagan to start as a 'new' school without the Churches' support, even if it had wanted it. As we have already noted, there is some paradox here, namely that a ground for Catholic opposition to Lagan is that in the college's conception and birth the official Catholic Church was absent, when it is also conceded that that absence was a reflection of Catholic opposition *ab initio*.

In legal terms it is hard to refute the claim that the only constituted Church schools in Northern Ireland are Catholic. But in moral terms the claim is less plausible. Lagan College's founding purpose contains the aspiration to be truly 'ecumenical' and the school aims to draw on the support of all the Churches from which its pupils come, the Catholic Church no less than the others.

Academic issues

Ensuring that Lagan College's policy of an 'all-ability pupil intake' allows each child to fulfil his or her potential is perhaps of even greater importance ten years on than it was at the start. The difficulty in the early days was to establish the school's reputation for academic success with children who for the most part had failed the 11-plus. In her newsletter of March 1987, Sheila Greenfield was able to report that Lagan's first public examination cohort in 1986 had acquitted itself well: 'No pupil left school without some examination success. 93% achieved five or more CSE passes, 67% achieved an additional GCE Certificate, and 29% achieved GCE passes or CSE 1 equivalents in four or more subjects. (It is worth noting that only 5% were given an A grading in the selection test aged 11.)'

As parental confidence increased, so more bright children whose parents were committed to both integrated and comprehensive education were enrolled. As one third-year girl's parents commented, Lagan brought together these two ideals for their daughter's education. However, when she passed the 11-plus, their friends and grandparents expressed incredulity at the choice of Lagan College. The parents had to cope with local prejudice, for example that 'at Lagan College their daughter would come into contact with working-class children'; or the primary school headteacher who advertised details of every high school's open day except Lagan's. Parents with such personal commitment to integrated education were also likely to be keen to ensure that their daughter was offered every educational opportunity. Like her mother, who has a first-class degree in languages, the girl was hoping to study two modern languages in her third year. However, when she was offered only Irish (alongside French) instead of Spanish because of a timetabling problem, the parents insisted: 'We turned down a grammar school place to send her to Lagan; she must be offered two languages as she would be at a grammar school.' Within two days Spanish was reinstated for the third-year pupils.

The principal was adamant that 11-plus selection created a separate but no less divisive fault line than that created by culture, religion and politics. In Northern Ireland, as is recognized by the Fair Employment Agency, too high a proportion of children leave school with no qualifications. Lagan aims to bring children together from all backgrounds and all classes, but has to achieve good examination results if it is to attract the full cross-section of parents. The principal acknowledged: 'It may be the best known school in Northern Ireland, but it is not yet the best.' Looking forward to the next ten years, he identified the importance of clarifying the implications of an all-ability school. Public perception was that it meant mixed-ability teaching; but increasingly Lagan staff felt that 'setting by ability' would be more appropriate, for example in languages and mathematics. Although the earlier divisiveness of GCE and CSE had been removed by the arrival of the common 16-plus examination, he saw real dangers for all-ability schools if, as in Great Britain, the government were to allow grant-maintained schools to adopt grammar school status. He expressed apprehension that the new generation of Lagan parents and governors might be pressurized into reassessing the admissions criteria and selecting on grounds of pupil ability (whether by the 11-plus or the Key Stage 2 assessment tests).

Equally the government's policy on open enrolment may allow grammar schools, faced with falling rolls or under-utilized capacity, to offer places to more children who previously would have failed the 11-plus. It was estimated in 1988 that the percentage of pupils in grammar schools in Northern Ireland was likely to rise from 27 per cent to 35 per cent, a prognosis that could weaken Lagan's ability to attract more 11-plus qualifiers. The decision in 1992 to open a new Catholic grammar school in Belfast may add to the pressures.

Lagan's governors are determined, as Criterion 3 of the 1991 and 1992 admissions policies states, that 'the College will apply its admissions criteria in such a way as to preserve its all-ability nature'. However, their commitment to this principle received a serious setback in 1992 when the Department for Education in Northern Ireland insisted that the mechanism for applying Criterion 3 be removed; the High Court judge upheld the decision and ruled that only grammar schools in Northern Ireland may use academic criteria under the 1989 Order. Trying to ensure a pupil intake across the whole ability spectrum has not proved easy.

Two sixth-form students quoted in the 1992 prospectus exemplify Lagan's academic achievement. 'At Lagan College we're taught that everyone has the ability to succeed, if they're given the opportunity', commented one boy. 'Even though I'd failed in the 11-plus, I was encouraged all the way and have just finished my GCSEs: 2 As, 3Bs, and 2Cs.' A sixth-form girl wrote: 'I failed my 11-plus, but that wasn't an obstacle for me at Lagan College. I got good GCSE results: 5As, 1B, 2Cs, and I'm now completing my International Baccalaureate (IB) studies and planning to go to university.' If Lagan can boast such heartening results with these pupils, its success with a broader range of ability should enable it to enhance its future reputation and standing.

Curriculum issues

The Northern Ireland Curriculum comes into force gradually over the next few years, following the Education Reform Order 1989. It provides for a framework of six Areas of Study (English, Mathematics, Science and Technology, Environment and Society, Creative and Expressive Studies, and Language Studies), within which the 'Contributory Subjects' cover similar ground to the core and foundation subjects of the National Curriculum. In addition, there are cross-curricular themes, such as Cultural Heritage and Education for Mutual Understanding, which are specific to Northern Ireland, as are modifications (e.g. in English) for Irish-medium schools.

This new common curriculum means that the historic divergence in curriculum structure reflected in segregated Protestant and Catholic schools is gradually being diminished. The agreements in common syllabuses for history and religious education encourage new thinking. The challenges met by Lagan in its early years to devise a common curriculum for its own pupils may show it to have been a leading force in the field, and now in a position to help other schools in this area.

The establishment of post-16 provision in 1987 has been, without doubt, the most important decision on the curriculum made by the governors in Lagan's later years. Although the first sixteen pupils to stay on after the fifth year followed only one-year O-level resit and work preparation courses, the college stated as early as 1986 that it planned to introduce A-level study as soon as numbers became viable. This, as the principal's newsletter of June 1986 pointed out, would also give some pupils a second chance of improving their academic qualifications if they needed to do so.

However, if Lagan was to attract a truly all-ability intake, it had to devise a curriculum which could satisfy parents' and pupils' higher academic aspirations, particularly in Northern Ireland where the grammar schools with reason take pride in advertising their Oxbridge successes. There seemed little chance of Lagan being able to compete in the short term in this demanding A-level market-place.

175

At the same time, the British government was also reviewing its post-16 curriculum. The 1988 Higginson Report's attempt to break out of the strait-jacket of 2–3 A-level specialisms and to broaden the post-16 framework was widely welcomed in educational circles, although Margaret Thatcher's advisers eventually decided to pursue the development of the A-level 'gold standard', complemented by AS levels and vocational diplomas, rejecting the specific recommendations of the Higginson committee.

Meanwhile the European dimension was becoming increasingly important as EC funding began to make an impact in both the Republic and Northern Ireland. The European Studies Project, within the cross-curricular theme of Education for Mutual Understanding, was introduced into all Northern Ireland schools to encourage a 'new common identity' for Ulster people as Europeans beyond the sectarian divide. Vivian McIver, the staff inspector responsible for EMU, commented in a paper, 'EMU and the challenge of a new Europe' (given to the DENI Summer School conference in August 1990): 'It is in this multicultural, cooperative Europe that our young people will live, work, travel and settle.' The EC's role in breaking down barriers and enhancing co-operation between member countries may be even more significant in Northern Ireland than elsewhere. As Moxon-Browne pointed out in 1983, 'In the Anglo-Irish context, any mitigation of the stark dilemma for Ulstermen of choosing to be either of one nation or the other, must be welcomed' (p. 165).

In its need to establish academic credibility and to obviate invidious comparisons with established grammar school sixth forms, Lagan College decided to explore the avenue of the International Baccalaureate (IB). The 1990 prospectus stated:

> In September 1990 the College will begin teaching the International Baccalau-reate, a two year university entrance course ... the curriculum of the I.B. has a number of unique factors which makes it a more balanced and coherent course of study than A level.

Although accepted by all higher education institutions as equivalent to A level for admission purposes, the IB is generally used by colleges with a particular international dimension. In some degree Lagan had already established extensive European and American links through the major fund-raising campaign of Sister Anna. Enhancing those links with school exchanges in Spain and Belgium seemed a natural progression. Again, to require the continuation of a modern European language, mandatory for all IB students as 1992 approached, seemed wholly appropriate.

The 1992 prospectus also stressed Lagan's involvement in a group of twelve schools representing each country in the European Community, for which it was to be host in 1994:

Through increased contact with continental Europe, they [the pupils] will be able to see the positive values of their own community within the wider context of Europe.

How far the IB course has been successful is difficult to evaluate at this early stage. Of the 22 students who entered the examinations in May 1992, 15 progressed to higher education. The HMI report, reviewed in the *TES* (25 January 1991), commented that, in comparison with A levels, 'there was greater opportunity and therefore better achievement in independent research and originality' and IB students attained 'higher standards in oral skills' than their A-level counterparts. There is little doubt that it is academically demanding and that continuing with subjects at the higher level and at the subsidiary level places great pressure on a number of students: some prefer to transfer to college for traditional A levels. The requirement to include a balance of arts and science subjects may be commended (see *Education*, 23 November 1990); but it makes it difficult for those who find themselves more capable in one area than the other.

In addition, as the one-year sixth form curriculum is being restructured across Britain (e.g. with new BTEC and RSA courses), so Lagan has seized the opportunity to offer a broader curriculum to students of all ability beyond GCSE (e.g. RSA GNVQ [General National Vocational Qualification] level 2 in Business and Finance). This should encourage more students to continue their studies into Lagan's sixth form.

Religious education and chaplaincy

RELIGIOUS EDUCATION
The 1990 prospectus declared:

> The broad aims of Religious Education at Lagan College are to help pupils from diverse religious traditions, and from none, to reflect upon the meaning of human existence; to develop knowledge, understanding, and tolerance of the beliefs of others; and to understand more fully their own religious tradition.

Over its first ten years the key principles of Lagan's RE programme changed little. The joint heads of RE, one Protestant (currently Presbyterian) and one Catholic, continued the tradition of a common academic RE syllabus taught to mixed classes, complemented by the denominational care for which the chaplains were normally responsible.

The common syllabus, originally devised on the St Bede's, Redhill model, for the first-year pupils included an introduction to the Christian community as seen in the Bible and the lives of individuals, the main Christian festivals, and the life of Jesus; it also involved a carefully planned visit to three different churches, Roman Catholic, Church of Ireland and Baptist/Presbyterian/Methodist/or non-subscribing Presbyterian.

The Catholic teacher commented that, when he visited the Presbyterian church with his mixed class, some of the children were understandably more at home than he was, but were keen to point things out to him. By contrast, he confessed he found it all too easy to slip into Catholic language in discussing the visit to the Catholic Church. When he asked his class to describe the tabernacle, the Protestant children looked mystified: what was self-evident to him was not to them. Clearly these visits were a learning experience for both teacher and pupils.

The RE programme for the second and third years included Church history and 'ethical and moral life issues' (particularly linked with the Ten Commandments) and the study of world religions (Islam in the second-year and Judaism in the third-year course). All pupils followed the GCSE syllabus leading to the qualification in religious studies at the end of the fifth year. Although parents were reminded of their legal right of withdrawal, 'the College believes that understanding different religious beliefs and practices is a vital component of Integrated Education and would strongly encourage parents not to withdraw their children' (1990 prospectus). The 1992 survey (McEwan *et al.*) of parents' views on integrated education showed that 82 per cent approved of their children's RE programme: 'They should remain good Catholics or good Protestants but respect each other's religion and culture.'

The previous Catholic head of RE, recently seconded to the first controlled school to become integrated in order to develop the RE programme along more inter-denominational lines, was reported in a *Church Times* interview (28 June 1991): 'Teenagers have very little interest in doctrinal issues—like young people everywhere, they are more concerned with moral questions, how to behave.' That issues of religious doctrine tend to be more the concern of parents than children was reflected in the views of his Protestant counterpart at Lagan who felt, in common with many RE teachers, that it was 'difficult enough interesting young people to take RE as a serious subject'; she had to be sensitive to the children's development, since (in common with single-denominational schools) pupils generally felt less receptive to specific Church teaching as they grew older.

An important development was the publication, on 26 June 1992, of the new common core syllabus in religious education, agreed after some two years' work by representatives of the four main Churches (Roman Catholic, Presbyterian, Church of Ireland and Methodist). In his speech to the Church of Ireland General Synod on 19 May 1992, Archbishop Robin Eames described the Churches' agreement as 'a moment of historic change'—a not overstated view if one bears in mind the divisive entrenchment caused by the issue of religious education earlier in this century. He further commented:

'It is remarkable how we have been able to trust each other in producing the syllabus. It shows a new respect for the other traditions—a major step forward.'

The synod's education adviser explained in June 1992: the syllabus

> acknowledges the unavoidable facts that Roman Catholic schools deliver RE within a confessional framework ... whereas RE in a controlled school must be Bible-based and not distinctive of any denomination. I believe the core programme in RE permits both types of schools to meet with integrity the specifications of the curriculum and the expectations of the communities served by these schools.

While accepting the recommendations for additional guidance on RE for children with special needs and specific internal assessment of pupil progress, the government also wished to advocate the inclusion of the study of world religions, so that 'young people should be led to view the beliefs of others with tolerance, understanding, and respect'. This new syllabus was introduced for pupils in the first year of the first three Key Stages from September 1993 and for the first year of Key Stage 4 from September 1994, to allow time for the preparation by the Northern Ireland Secondary Examinations and Assessment Council of a new GCSE syllabus.

The impact of this common core RE syllabus on Lagan's RE programme must yet be assessed, but clearly many of its principal elements were already in place. The effect of having a syllabus agreed by all the Churches could only enhance Lagan's confidence in providing appropriate RE to mixed classes of children from all the denominations. The principal, himself an RE teacher, commented that, although the common core syllabus seemed more like a step backwards in educational terms because of its apparent repetitiveness and narrow focus on the Christian faith, in ecumenical terms it was a real step forward.

DENOMINATIONAL CARE

After ten years, one area which was undergoing a radical rethink was that of denominational care, particularly in respect of the role of the college chaplains. The work of the six honorary chaplains (Baptist, Church of Ireland, Presbyterian, Methodist, non-subscribing Presbyterian, Roman Catholic) on a part-time basis since 1981 was complemented by the appointment of two full-time chaplains in September 1992, one Roman Catholic, the other Protestant. The 1992 prospectus reported that 'the size of the College and the demands on the time of these (honorary) chaplains has led the Governors to the decision'. How has the chaplains' role evolved to this point?

The 1990 prospectus included statements from both Protestant chaplains and the Roman Catholic chaplain which illustrated the different approaches. The first specified:

Our aim is to develop an understanding of our own denomination and the strengths and weaknesses of ALL traditions in an imperfect world ... The role of the chaplains is to be at hand and develop as a friend and confidant so the issues which concern the pupils can be discussed in a way not possible within a classroom situation.

The Catholic statement explained that

the emphasis in the chaplain groups is on caring about our faith. What is specifically Catholic is taught under the following broad headings: Human Life, Sacraments, Liturgical Year, Honouring Mary, Praying for the Dead. . . . A lively Catholic presence in Lagan College is not a sign of division, but a measure of understanding and enjoying who we are as Catholics, in order to understand those who are affiliated to other Churches and so learn to live in harmony and freedom.

The arrangements by which chaplains had contact with their respective pupils meant that the children were withdrawn in small groups from RE classes on a rota system. In practice, only the Roman Catholic chaplain, Sister Clarke, developed a formal arrangement by which each Catholic pupil met her once a fortnight for one class period. In 1984–85 she saw 56 children in seven groups; in 1989–90 she was meeting 227 children in twenty-three groups (figures drawn from the Catholic chaplain's report, 1984–90). Because she had accepted early retirement from the Catholic teacher training college, she was able to give considerable time to her chaplaincy work, although not as official representative of the hierarchy. Nevertheless, she was keen to emphasize that her relationship with the bishop and parish priests had improved, now that the Catholic Church was prepared to admit that integrated schools were 'experimental' rather than unacceptable.

The Presbyterian chaplain conceded that, because of too many parish pressures, he did not get into Lagan often enough. When he came, about once a month, he usually saw twelve pupils withdrawn from two classes for about twenty minutes. He found that detailed denominational teaching was generally inappropriate since, like pupils in other schools, they often lacked basic knowledge of Christianity, a view shared by the Catholic sister. His aim therefore was to build relationships with the children that were different from staff–pupil classroom relationships, but he acknowledged how inadequate his time for this work was. Since he helped at Lagan in a purely private capacity, not as a representative of his Church, there was little more that he could do. When asked whether the Church could officially appoint him, he reiterated the familiar theme that the Protestant Churches were unlikely to support integrated schools since, unlike controlled schools where they had transferors' rights, they were granted no influence on the governing body. He had a personal commitment to Lagan, developed through his friendship with the principal and enhanced after his daughter became a pupil.

The recent record of the other Protestant chaplains was uneven. For example, the previous Baptist minister's irregular visits contrasted with the subsequent chaplain, whose more reliable contribution was encouraged also by his own daughter's attendance at Lagan. The non-subscribing Presbyterian maintained regular contact with her small number of pupils. However, the Church of Ireland minister hardly ever visited Lagan; his predecessor in the parish took his pastoral role more seriously, starting for example a lively Thursday Club to which children could 'come and ask anything' of the chaplains, who took it in turns to run the weekly lunchtime meetings; the club has stopped since his departure. One third-year girl admitted that she had not seen her Church of Ireland chaplain apart from one meeting in her first year, though she would have liked to see him since 'the Presbyterians always used to go out to see Sister Clarke' (*sic*). Her parents expressed surprise that this was less than they had been led to expect from the prospectus; but they were not too worried as they were all committed church attenders each Sunday. The Church of Ireland bishop acknowledged that it was for the individual minister to manage his own parish work, and that the current incumbent did not see the voluntary link with Lagan as a priority. Nevertheless in 1991–92 the bishop took the trouble to visit Lagan personally twice within six months to see for himself a Christian integrated school.

There was some danger that the teaching staff might see chaplains as 'mere functionaries' who have little to do with the teaching process other than to disrupt it by withdrawing pupils and taking time out of examination classes. One chaplain commented: 'I am not unwelcome in the staffroom. I'm just not necessary to what the staff are doing.' Staff, expressing views at a residential weekend in March 1988, saw the chaplains' role as more pastoral than for denominational instruction. They wished for greater integration of the work of chaplains and teachers, and welcomed the recent provision of a chaplains' room within the school to mark a recognition of their role in the Lagan community. The proposal to appoint two full-time chaplains was generally well received. One group acknowledged the difficulties a single Protestant chaplain might face: 'while he/she could not speak with authority on individual Church policies, it should be possible for someone who related well to young people to function successfully as chaplain to all our Protestant pupils, consulting Church representatives as and when necessary.' The deputy principal recognized that it was unrealistic to expect the Protestant chaplain to be 'all things to all Protestants', but he thought there was some pan-Protestant dimension which could usefully be explored. The new appointments from 1992, combining some teaching with pastoral commitments to staff and pupils, have strengthened the staff–chaplain relationship.

Another aspect under review was the chaplains' link with parents. The Protestant children generally saw their denominational links primarily through their Sunday schools and parish churches. Catholic parents, on the other hand, 'lack confidence in their own ability to hand on the faith' (Catholic chaplain's report, February 1990), and the parish generally expected the school to cover catechetical instruction. Looking back over six years, Sr Clarke regretted that 'parental awareness of the chaplaincy provision remained minimal ... with a corresponding absence of support from them, even at a personal level, about their children's needs'. This may 'stem from lack of communication, but they could be challenged by the school to co-operate in their own interests'. An apparent reduction in the anxiety felt by current Catholic parents as compared with parents in the early years might perhaps be explicable in terms of a higher degree of confidence that Lagan has not undermined their children's faith, as is evidenced by Lagan pupils completing their education as practising Roman Catholics (see Irwin, 1991).

The Catholic RE teacher reflected that most Catholic parents seemed to look to Lagan to provide specific Roman Catholic education. But it often appeared more to do with 'cultural expectations' than with purely doctrinal matters: it was expected that the children would grow up with a clear Catholic identity as much as with a personal faith. The Catholic chaplain independently agreed; although the 'faith issue' was important, she acknowledged that the children were keen 'to retain their sense of belonging to the cultural tradition which has been part of their family for generations'. She found that day or weekend retreats (at Rostrevor in 1985 and 1989 or Corrymeela in 1988, for example) were particularly effective in supporting the pupils' Catholic identity, though they happened too infrequently; the pilgrimage to Knock in June 1989 'generated a lot of enthusiasm, because the children had a new sense of their own Church at prayer'.

Meanwhile, the Catholic authorities, while insisting that integrated schools do not qualify as 'Catholic schools' for true Catholic families, reluctantly accepted integrated education as an 'experiment', if parents want it. 'Integrated education has now an opportunity to demonstrate its capacity to deliver its ideals. I am quite happy to await the results' (Cardinal Daly, interviewed for *Fortnight* magazine, 13 September 1991). The marked defensiveness exhibited by all the Churches ten years previously appeared to be succeeded by a fragile tolerance; it may be that they were reluctant to appear hesitant in their support for the principle of parental choice, since this might make central government less sympathetic to their claim for equality of treatment and additional funding.

A joint head of RE summed up the *raison d'être* for chaplains in his paper to the staff residential conference in March 1988:

> Chaplains are signs of our wanting to belong to the wider Christian family. They are one way of expressing the desire that, denominationally, we wish to be fully ourselves. They provide an important focus of identity for pupils and, ideally, a valuable supportive pastoral role.

His colleague in the RE department, who had been involved in the working party on chaplaincy, emphasized the importance of the two teacher/ chaplains appointed in 1992 working as a team in an open, non-dogmatic collaboration: their job descriptions also highlighted the importance of close liaison with the honorary chaplains and the local parishes.

WORSHIP

The issue of worship was addressed in different ways as the school developed. Before moving into its new buildings, Lagan had no proper assembly hall in which to hold corporate acts of worship, so that assemblies tended to be classroom based. The prospectuses consistently stated that 'as a Christian school, Lagan College has regular worship. This is intended to allow pupils and staff to take part in appropriate acts of worship and to express together their sense of belonging to a Christian school.' This included celebrating the main Christian festivals and stressing 'issues important to the nature of the College such as peace and reconciliation and justice, concern for others and responsibility for the "two-thirds" world' (1992 prospectus).

To encourage all staff to feel confident in leading class worship, the RE department and chaplains drew up some guidelines for prayer, which were discussed at the staff conference in 1985. These guidelines highlighted two particular sensitivities in a joint Protestant/Catholic school: the making of the sign of the Cross, and the doxology to the Lord's Prayer, in Ireland generally used only by Catholics and Protestants respectively. It was suggested that it would be appropriate to allow time for pupils to make the sign of the Cross at both the beginning and the end of worship, if the teachers did not use it themselves, and that 'since there are no doctrinal reasons to the contrary, Roman Catholic pupils should be encouraged, but not forced, to join in saying the doxology when it is added'. (Perhaps both groups would be reassured by being aware of the great antiquity of both usages in Church history.)

These guidelines were reconsidered at the staff conference in March 1988. Many felt that new staff had not been inducted into form prayers, and that the college 'had lost some of our more overt Christian practices, e.g. prayer or meditation at form-time, before start of lessons, before staff meetings, etc.' It was noted that 'at one time we felt there was an over-emphasis on Christian worship in the College; since then we have gone too far in the other direction.' As a result of the conference, the *Amended Guidelines for Prayer at Lagan College* was published in May 1988, and outline examples were included as part of the new staff induction programme. The principal explained that form prayers were scheduled to take place at midday registration, but admitted that, as in most schools, it is 'taken more seriously by some form tutors than others'. Inevitably as the staff increases in size, it can no longer be assumed that they are a cohesive group meeting each other daily with a common mind and practice. The induction programme is crucial if staff are to share in the school's Christian ethos and its overt expression in school worship.

Other regular services were held at Christmas and in the week of prayer for Christian Unity in January, using both Catholic and Protestant Church buildings. Lagan's requests to use two different Catholic churches in 1987 and 1989 were explicitly refused by the parish priest after consulting the bishop. He expressed courteous regrets, but continued:

> It is the policy of the Church, not only in Ireland but all over the world to encourage parents to send their children to Catholic schools, because these are the best means to help them to pass on their faith to their children. To grant use of————to Lagan College could be taken as implying a certain amount of approval and this could confuse Catholic parents about their responsibility to Catholic education. (Letter of 6 November 1987)

The Catholic chaplain in 1990 expressed optimism that such problems were 'likely to be resolved in coming years with the development of better relationships'. Meanwhile Lagan continued to use the Catholic Clonard monastery for appropriate celebrations, where the pupils and staff always received a warm welcome.

Another issue in Christian schools with more than one tradition is the eucharist. Unlike other ecumenical Church schools in Britain, eucharistic worship was never part of Lagan's experience. The centrality of the mass or holy communion, as explored for example at St Bede's, Redhall, opened up lively debates about permissible practice within the code of canon law; but at Lagan the issue was even more contentious. 'The Governors have long been aware that the celebration of the Sacraments, particularly the Eucharist, in an ecumenical school in Northern Ireland is a sensitive matter' (minutes of governors' meeting, 9 September 1992). This is no doubt due in part to the strong Protestant traditions of Northern Ireland where, even in the Church of Ireland (the Church of John Bramhall and Jeremy Taylor) communion services are normally celebrated only once a month, in contrast with the weekly parish eucharists normal in the Church of England and where in many Churches that could not be called Anglo-Catholic there is a daily celebration. In other Protestant Churches communion may be taken only once a year. Admittedly when one remembers that medieval Catholic canon law had difficulty in requiring the laity to communicate more than once a year,[20] the divergence can come to look almost like a convergence. But the difference between Protestant practice and the weekly Catholic mass is marked. The principal commented: 'The eucharist is divisive enough among Protestants; they can't even agree about candles.' Nevertheless, once the new chaplains become established in post, this may be an area to explore further, perhaps drawing on the experience, where relevant, of ecumenical schools elsewhere in Britain.

Meanwhile, school worship remains central to the life of a Christian school. As the Catholic chaplain wrote in her 1990 report:

> The experience of singing and praying together, hearing and reflecting on the word of God, sharing something of religious significance, is what young people need at this stage of faith development.

Community relations

No less than in its early years, ten years on Lagan College emphasizes community links with parents, with other educational establishments, and with the Churches. Yet in some ways the issues have changed: Lagan is no longer dependent for its daily survival on direct 'hands-on' parental involvement. Nor as an expanding, oversubscribed school can it be so easily ignored by the Churches, its feeder primaries, and secondary competitors.

PARENTAL LIAISON

While there are still many parents living in polarized sectarian residential areas who courageously send their children to Lagan on the special buses from the city centre, there are increasing numbers who, while wanting Christian values and an integrated ethos, also want a 'good school' for their offspring. Others from mixed marriages or non-practising religious families see integrated education as a welcome alternative to segregated denominational schools. In contrast to the early days when it opened its doors to all-comers (within the 60:40 denominational parameter), Lagan now has to operate a careful balance in choosing its intake to ensure an appropriate cross-section of pupil ability, denomination, and social class.[21]

---

[20]'At least at Easter': Fourth Lateran Council (1215), canon 21 (Tanner, 1990, p. 245).

[21]*Education*, 2 March 1990 and 14 August 1992: 'Most integrated schools have waiting lists of Catholics who cannot be admitted for want of Protestants to maintain their essential 60:40 denominational ratio.' As the pressure for places increases, Lagan is inevitably encountering parental resentment when a child is refused admission because of the policy of

185

Table 5.1 Admissions balance since 1987

Year	Protestant %	Catholic %
1987–88	52	48
1988–89	56	44
1989–90	53	47
1990–91	52	48
1991–92	50	50
1992–93	51	49

In 1992, for example, 51 per cent of Lagan's pupils were Protestant, 49 per cent Catholic, and over 40 per cent from working-class backgrounds (see Table 5.1). Because of oversubscription, Lagan's 1992 prospectus even recommended that parents complete a pre-application form at any time, which 'will help to give a child some priority at the time of transfer from primary school'.

In Northern Ireland, parents have a high regard for education, but the pressure at secondary transfer is considerable. The principal recalled an example of parents' special pleading after their child's pet rabbit died on the night before the first admissions test and, by a singular misfortune, the replacement rabbit died on the night before the second test. Another head of a Protestant voluntary grammar school remarked: 'The vast majority of parents show a concern for their children which, in some parts of England, is not in evidence' (*Seven Days* magazine, 20 November 1988).

As in most schools, 'parents whose children are admitted to the College are expected to support the College in its policies with regard to homework and discipline'. They are also 'encouraged to take the opportunity to be involved in the education of their children and in the life of the College', particularly through their elected Parent Council and governor representatives. In the early years, the Parent Council—a statutory committee (unlike most parent–teacher associations)—provided a lively arena for the discussion of ideas. One founder parent commented that 'it worked reasonably well', but another admitted that it was also 'quite contentious' because parents were personally so involved: she recalled that some parents were offended when the first principal 'refused to have masses of parents helping around the school, but she was obviously right'. Two Lagan parents are still elected to represent each year group, which provides an effective forum for parental consultation. Balancing the commitment and 'emotional moti-

maintaining a balance. Tony Spencer recognized this issue back in 1987: it may 'mean that potential pupils from one ethnic-religious community have to be put on to a waiting list until recruitment from the other community catches up' (Osborne et al., 1987b, p. 108).

vation' of founder parents with the enhanced management role of the professional staff is crucial to the school's development and in line with government policy of harnessing parental power constructively (see Dunn, 1989).[22]

In supporting the children's religious nurture, the role of parents is of paramount importance. Most Church schools would endorse the vital three-way partnership of home, parish and school with its shared Christian values. For the Catholic parents at Lagan, who received no encouragement and in some cases obstruction from their parish priests, the link with the school in respect of religious education and catechesis was even more essential.

Mgr McCaughan commented: 'The home, the church, and the school work in harmony in a parish, and if any of these are missing, a gap is created which an integrated school cannot fill' (Education, 2 March 1990). One parent interviewed for the 1992 survey by McEwan commented that their decision to send a child to an integrated school caused problems: 'I have an uncle who is a parish priest and it went down like a bomb.'

Particular efforts have continued to support Catholic parents. Whereas in the early years Lagan seemed more concerned with reassuring parents, ten years on the college seemed less defensive and even active in encouraging them to become more involved in their child's religious nurture (see the Catholic chaplain's report, Clarke, 1990).

RELATIONSHIPS WITH OTHER EDUCATIONAL INSTITUTIONS
These relationships are gradually developing as Lagan is now able to be less protective of its own interests and survival. The 1991 prospectus states:

> The College welcomes cooperation with other post-primary school and further education colleges in its vicinity. It does so to make optimum use of scarce facilities and teaching resources, and to broaden the social contacts of its pupils. The College seeks regular use of publicly provided facilities and services, e.g. Library service, Museum service, Leisure centres, Area Board and District Council playing-fields.

[22]In another integrated school, the council was initially open to all parents. But after it was 'hijacked' by a small clique, it started acting as a second board of governors, which caused considerable problems for the management. In yet another instance, the previous principal bitterly commented that the benefits of parental involvement could be exaggerated: his school was founded by 'strong-minded and persuasive characters' convincing the parents with 'jargon and high-flown waffle' that 'theirs would be a fine school and that anything was possible, without having the courage or self-discipline to detail for the parents the sheer hard work and the degree of finance that would be required in order to achieve even minimal progress' (cited in Caul, 1990, p. 62).

187

However, while Lagan may appear more open and confident, some of its neighbouring schools have expressed uncertainty and even hostility to this new concept of integrated education. Unlike nineteenth-century attempts at mixed Protestant/Catholic schools (e.g. Greencastle in 1812), Lagan College had to start, reluctantly, outside the established dual system. Yet unlike the independent Christian schools recently founded by the Free Presbyterians, it does not wish to be separated, let alone isolated, from the mainstream. Ironically perhaps, its very definition as a DENI 'grant-maintained integrated school' has labelled it as a third category, distinguished from 'maintained' or 'controlled' sectors and thereby different from its neighbours. The deputy director of the Council for Catholic Maintained Schools argued that since it was bound to become just another school system, it would inevitably undermine the Roman Catholic system.

It could plausibly be argued that in Northern Ireland separate religious schooling is more a symptom than a cause of sectarian division, and that, while separate schooling sustains and reinforces the division, the heart of the problem lies in the cultural context of different religious communities (Haldane, 1986). Such a view is presupposed by republicans, for example Bernadette Devlin McAliskey, who is suspicious of integrated schools, 'on the grounds that education is one area where those of the nationalist tradition have control over their own lives and therefore not an area to be yielded lightly'.[23] Parents of both communities considered that 'The Orange Order and the Republican Party can take more blame than segregated education'; 'there is an awful lot that goes on in people's homes that would have a lot more influence on the children than the school system' (McEwan et al., 1992).

Moreover, educationists are also divided on the issue of whether integrated schooling can heal the deep wounds of years of sectarianism. Headteachers in Enniskillen, interviewed on the ITV programme *Borderlines* in 1989, reflected on their community in the aftermath of the murderous bomb blast of November 1987, and commented that the need was to work for co-operation rather than integration. They recognized the importance of education as a 'very stable factor' in Northern Ireland, but saw 'integrated education' as yet another source of division, tending to 'cream off the middle-class children'. However, in the same programme, representatives of the Enniskillen Together movement, founded in 1988 out of 'the collective guilt of the community', expressed the view that 'integrated education is one of the answers', since the segregation of all schools along religious lines inevitably exacerbates community divisions. Their efforts succeeded in obtaining planning permission, mobile classrooms and the necessary teachers in only four months, allowing the opening of an integrated primary

[23] Mary Kenny, *Tablet*, 10 February 1990.

school in September 1989.

Staff and principals from segregated secondary schools in Belfast revealed considerable scepticism and anxiety about the effects of integrated education. All of them felt that, although 'someone has to do something about sectarianism', Lagan College does not get to the heart of the problem, since the children who attend Lagan 'have no religious hang-ups anyway'; and 'how many new disciples are they bringing in?' What were more effective, they argued, were the inter-school links and cross-curricular developments, for example in sport or public speaking and Education for Mutual Understanding. One teacher, however, suggested that such links had been far more extensive before the Troubles started in 1969, and another admitted that 'you cannot always publicize such links for fear of adverse reactions from parents'.

Similar interviews with primary school principals, reported in the *British Journal for Religious Education*, supported these strategies for improving community relations, adding the view of one headteacher: 'Each system could then pursue its own specific aims without threatening the other; there would be no necessity for compromising beliefs' (Morgan *et al.*, 1992, p. 172). The apparent fear that integration means compromising beliefs is directly addressed by Lagan in its publicity material: 'It is not part of the aim of Lagan College to produce some watered-down or synthetic version of the Christian faith in pursuit of a false eirenicism' (1992 prospectus, p. 4). The headteacher quoted evidently assumed that compromise of 'truth' is simply unavoidable with the best will in the world. Lagan irritates by putting a question-mark against the assumption.

While these negative perceptions are real enough, they seemed to be based on hearsay or what people read in the newspapers. Little effort had been made to verify them.

> Opting for contact with other schools did not extend to establishing links with the local integrated school. Only one of the nine principals had visited it; only one expressed his intention of meeting its principal. The remainder had had no contact whatsoever. One principal said that this was because they were probably trying to ignore it. (Morgan *et al.*, 1992, p. 172)

The hope commonly expressed to this researcher that cross-curricular links will bring about reconciliation may not be so effective in practice. One Protestant primary teacher acknowledged that cross-community contact was 'useful', but thought its effectiveness limited, since it needed to be reinforced by regular contact between Catholic and Protestant children using the same shops, swimming pools and so on. He described the Education for Mutual Understanding (EMU) programme as too vague to prevent teachers from avoiding difficult questions which might challenge pupils' or parents' views. The materials were, he thought, wishy-washy, and the compulsory training 'a dreadful waste of time'. However, he acknowledged the usefulness of jointly organized residential trips where a Protestant child shared a room with a Catholic: 'Back in the school playground, at least he can say that the child of "the other religion" doesn't smell when the other children make playground comments.' In the *Tablet* (16 February 1991), Duncan Morrow argued that EMU is deliberately vague on the practical details of contact between schools 'so as to allow for local differences, hesitations, and difficulties'.

The director of the Council for Catholic Maintained Schools, as we have noted, believed EMU and Cultural Heritage offered a much better chance of achieving results than integrated schools. His deputy Mr McCavera commented that inter-school visits broke down the inbuilt fear of the other community, and allowed teachers to meet for the first time; if the exchange was arranged over some distance, children might even stay in each other's houses. This mixing was better than integrated education because the children remained rooted in their own community where they were likely to spend their adult lives. EMU was 'the only way to get into ghetto areas'. This optimistic view was not shared by another influential Catholic, an RE lecturer at St Mary's training college in Belfast, who criticized the message behind EMU that 'if you act more tolerantly, things will get better'. He felt that this analysis did little to tackle the real question of why people feel and therefore act the way they do: if there was no common view of what the problem is, it was not surprising that churchmen and politicians could go no further than polite conversation. Like integrated schools, it did nothing to address the social divisions based on pseudo-ethnic and religious labels and the different levels of access to power and wealth (a viewpoint also reported by Duncan Morrow's *Tablet* article of 16 February 1991).

On the Protestant side, Ian Paisley's Democratic Unionists were concerned that EMU was an attempt to de-Protestantize children by taking them to Roman Catholic churches and teaching them Gaelic songs. More surprisingly, the education adviser for the Church of Ireland's General Synod thought that the divisions between Catholic and Protestant schools paled into insignificance beside the gulf between the grammar and secondary-intermediate sectors, and that it was really 'a waste of time transporting children to visit each other's schools' (*Education*, 22 May 1992). Comparable frustration is expressed by curriculum developers: 'The educational consequences, particularly in Belfast, of the increasing social and intellectual segregation of children at eleven into different educational institutions raised grave doubts as to the validity and value of DENI and Area Board INSET programmes to undertake whole school educational development' (Crone and Malone, 1983, p. 164).

Despite considerable public expenditure (a budget of £200,000 in 1987, £325,000 in 1988, and £450,000 in 1989) and the government's requirement that from 1992 EMU must be taught as a cross-curricular theme within the Northern Ireland Curriculum, the view that EMU can heal conflict is felt to be over-optimistic.[24] One inspector commented: 'We cannot expect clearly measurable progress in the short term. Schools and teachers cannot do it all.' The constraints on curriculum time, the apprehension of parents, and the impact of violence in society all limit effectiveness. But 'children need to be given opportunities to come to terms with diversity and to recognise that both similarities and differences exist in the family, in school, and in the wider community'.[25]

How effective EMU and other cross-community curricular initiatives are in comparison to the full experience of integrated education is hardly proven. Secondary teachers surveyed in 1992 (Smith and Robinson, 1992) considered that policy development in EMU had a low priority and was implemented in widely different ways: most declined to include ecumenism as a dimension of EMU since it drew the curriculum into the potentially contentious issues of religious belief. Dr Colin Irwin expressed his doubts (in an interview on BBC 1, *The Heart of the Matter*, 7 July 1991) on the ground that, by contrast with the daily social interaction in integrated schools, cross-community links were too infrequent and did not penetrate to a sufficiently deep level. His research into social integration had suggested that, if the informal aspects of formal education (such as peer group, the school's community role) were effective influences, 'schools like Lagan College may have the potential to produce a far more positive effect on the improvement of inter-community relations in Northern Ireland than EMU alone' (Irwin, 1991, p. 90). Assuming, however, that segregated education is likely to continue into the foreseeable future, the links at least can be said to be 'fascinating attempts to achieve something intrinsically very difficult' (Dunn, 1990a, p. 16).

Although much of the good practice learnt at Lagan has been written into these cross-curricular initiatives, funding for cross-community contact links has ironically hitherto been denied to Lagan. When the principal bid for money to support a residential experience for children, he was told that 'it was not for integrated schools because they were already linked'.

Alongside their critical views on integration at Lagan expressed in personal interviews, staff in neighbouring Belfast secondary schools also dis-

[24]One Protestant primary school used the funding for inter-school links as 'a way of getting extra money for computers'; although they produced a newspaper with the Catholic school, 'we gained very little from the contact'. In an interview of March 1992, the Joint Council of Churches spokesman criticized computer purchases to send electronic mail to each other as 'absurd abuse'!

[25]Conference in October 1989 on 'Community and the Curriculum' (Coolahan, 1990), p. 7.

missed Lagan as a middle-class phenomenon, founded by middle-class parents who really wanted a grammar school for their children who had failed the 11-plus. After all, it called itself a 'college' and in the early years offered O levels like a grammar school type of curriculum. Yet it was not the only school to open its doors to 'all religions': Methodist College had for example 10 per cent Catholics. These sharp views are matched by research findings from primary schools, where some principals dismissed the 'class-specific gesture' of integrated schools as futile; it merely removed from the system 'those parents and children whose liberal views acted as the necessary leaven'.[26]

At least in the case of Lagan these views are based on a mistaken assumption. Colin Irwin's research showed that the social class structure of Lagan's pupil intake was 42 per cent working class and 58 per cent middle class (1991, p. 129). He acknowledged that 'perfection in this matter is impossible to achieve in practice', but emphasized that Lagan College has a better social mix than most schools, since it made strenuous efforts to attract children from 149 feeder primary schools, representing the more sectarian working-class residential areas of Belfast as much as more integrated middle-class communities. This strategy was confirmed by the principal, although he admitted that it was not possible to guarantee an appropriate social mix through the admissions criteria: 'I expect the situation remains much as it was in Colin Irwin's research, i.e. 40–45 per cent working class—in Belfast that also means no job' (personal letter, September 1992).[27] A Catholic teacher wryly commented that his own preconception of Lagan having mainly 'middle-class kids' was knocked on the head as soon as he walked in to teach his first class.

A real problem for Lagan lies in combating these accusations of elitism. The media have been helpful in publicizing Dr Irwin's findings. Writing in *Fortnight* (8 June 1991), Robin Wilson commented:

> Dr Irwin realises that he has to slice through a rich thicket of obfuscatory myths constructed by the defenders of the status quo. But he hacks away at them, including the notions that integrated schooling is middle-class, that those who attend don't need it, and that it doesn't work. His research at Lagan shows clearly that it isn't, they do, and it does.

Nevertheless the college also needs the effective publicity of good examination results if it is to compete with grammar schools, because traditionally

---

[26]Morgan *et al.* (1992). The principals conceded that Lagan offered a particular kind of education for children difficult to place elsewhere or those from mixed marriages.

[27]Unemployment figures cited on Channel 4 (18 July 1992) revealed 1 in 7 out of work; these included 9 per cent of Protestant men but 23 per cent of Catholic men.

parents have seen the 11-plus as the key stepping-stone to success in life, especially if they come from working-class backgrounds.[28] Convincing these parents that Lagan can help their children to achieve their full potential, while avoiding the stigma of elitism and divisiveness if it is perceived as a quasi-grammar school, is a precarious balancing act.

Northern Ireland's education community, as elsewhere, is under pressure from falling pupil roll numbers and financial stringency. In such circumstances, it is sometimes easier to point the finger at Lagan College down the road than to tilt at the windmills of government bureaucracy. The reduction in the birth rate (34,000 in 1964 to 27,000 in 1983, according to Compton in 1987) combined with the 10 per cent increase in the proportion of children attending grammar schools has greatly concerned Belfast secondary-intermediate school principals. In personal interviews, they anticipated more amalgamations and resented a cut in their 'special allowances'; they suspected conspiracy in the widening of the ability range of grammar schools: 'In the past only grade 1s got into Methody, but nowadays even some 2s get in.' They suggested that the boys' secondary schools, with their street gang culture, were even more difficult to handle if the more motivated boys and their parents transferred to integrated or grammar schools; and single-sex girls' schools were understandably reluctant to amalgamate with such boys' schools to create more administratively viable mixed secondary schools. For these principals, therefore, the establishment of new integrated schools only exacerbated their problems.

The primary principals interviewed by Morgan et al. (1992) threw into relief two concerns. First they considered the 'perk' of offering transport to and from integrated schools as an 'unprofessional method of recruitment', tantamount to poaching, and discerned no commitment to idealistic principles if a 'perk' was needed to give parents a motive to choose integrated schools. This reported view seemed misinformed since all children, including Lagan pupils, are automatically entitled to free bus transport if they live more than three miles from school, an entitlement which in Northern Ireland (unlike England) has not yet been questioned.

Secondly, these principals resented the fact that integrated schools were

[28]Middle-class parents with ready cheque books have been used to buying 10 per cent of the places in grammar schools for children who failed the 11-plus; at the end of each school year the child is tested to see whether he/she is up to the standard required for a free school place. The question whether the grammar school academic curriculum is appropriate for an individual child's ability is seldom asked. Perhaps an even more prickly issue, recognized by Mr McCavera of the Council for Catholic Maintained Schools, is that in Belfast up to 7 per cent of Roman Catholic parents send their children to Protestant grammar schools in the hope that they will face less discrimination in their adult lives (e.g. as rugby players instead of Gaelic footballers).

able to use charitable donations to establish nursery units, an expense justified by an official of the Northern Ireland Council for Integrated Education on the ground that parents need to 'become used to the idea of integrated education from the child's early years'. The desirability of nursery provision for all is on the political agenda, and it may be that the success of integrated nurseries will encourage an extension of such good educational practice to the segregated sector.

The question of government funding is even more contentious. While Lagan College had to raise 15 per cent of its capital costs as a voluntary maintained school from 1984 (putting it on the same footing as Catholic maintained or voluntary grammar schools), the suspicion that it was receiving favourable treatment was reinforced when the 1989 Order allowed it to become grant maintained with 100 per cent funding. Of the primary principals included in Morgan's survey, 'most regarded this kind of funding as highly irresponsible in a time of financial cutback' (Morgan et al., 1992, p. 175). Both secondary and primary teachers in segregated schools argued that this money was unlikely to be new money, and was better spent supporting the already well-established schools with their long-delayed capital building programmes. The Catholic schools in particular felt reason to complain that they still had to find the 15 per cent for capital projects, and the government's 85 per cent clawback arrangement meant that the funds from a closing Catholic school could not be automatically rechannelled into other Catholic school capital projects. Their sense of the injustice that integrated schools should be politically favoured with 100 per cent support, especially since this policy had not been democratically proposed in the election manifesto,[29] even led to the Catholic bishops pursuing an unsuccessful action in the High Court against the 1989 Order.

Fr Denis Faul, speaking at Maynooth in February 1989, argued that the government's 'attacks on Catholic education by the underfunding and the financial advantages given to Integrated Education are part of a failure to cherish the two traditions equally. . . . The whole emphasis is on looking at the Protestant tradition' (Faul, 1989). The agreement in November 1992 that Catholic schools would no longer have to provide their 15 per cent contribution was greeted with parallel indignation by the Ulster Teachers' Union who, sceptical of the government's promise of extra money, thought that financial cuts were likely in controlled school budgets as a consequence. The spokesmen of the Irish Council of Churches were equally concerned about the effect of government policy on controlled schools.

As integrated schools establish themselves as a viable alternative on the scene, it is perhaps not surprising to find anxiety or antagonism among

---

[29]Only the Alliance party committed itself to supporting integrated education in its manifesto.

those who feel pressured or threatened by their existence. The very fact of their creation implies a negative criticism of the existing establishment. Moreover, 'there's nothing like a whiff of success for making enemies', observed Seamus Dunn (1990a, p. 14). Morgan *et al.*'s survey of primary school principals concluded:

> Paradoxically, in its anxiety to ensure their success, the government may have placed them even further beyond the pale. If integrated schools claim a strong commitment to the community, they cannot afford to be oblivious to the attitude they themselves generate. . . . Integration is about the destruction of myths, not, as seems a very real danger at present, about the creation of new ones. (1992, p. 176)

Lagan is far from oblivious. It has made considerable efforts to involve the college in the local community and beyond. Archbishop Robin Eames in June 1992 observed that, although he was unsure how far integrated schools would have an effect on community relations, he recognized Lagan College as 'not as much on the outside as I used to think'. Lagan is aware of the danger of a 'holier-than-thou' attitude towards its segregated neighbours, but breaking down the barriers of prejudice and suspicion has to be a two-way process. It has never claimed to be the answer to Northern Ireland's problems, and knows only too well that it must work in close partnership with its community for the future benefit of its children.

4. LOOKING TO THE FUTURE

'Not to develop is to die', commented Phil Dineen (*Tablet*, 21 May 1983) at the time headteacher of St Bede's, Redhill. Perhaps for Lagan College that has to be even more true. Its existence originated in a demand for change, in a feeling that institutionalized segregation must be intolerable in fact and consequence because of its role in perpetuating distrust and alienation. Such a school cannot stand still. But external and internal pressures impose restraints as a result of which its progress and future development were and are more a matter of hypothesis than secure prediction.

The situation of the school was naturally seen in religious terms. 'There's no givenness about what we're doing', said the principal in 1992; 'no one took us up to the top of the mountain and showed us the promised land. Like Abraham, we set off in faith and we don't know when we've got there. It is like being on a pilgrimage; we are learning as we go.' It would be easy for the college to sit back, even to stall, as it settles into its new buildings. But as the deputy principal commented, we must keep moving in our exploration of religious experience, accepting the importance of continuity within our traditions, yet facing up to the opportunity for rethinking what might be changed: the polarized alternatives of entrenched fundamentalism or wholesale rejection have created unnecessary tension by implying that reform must mean that what went before was inherently wrong. People need to be persuaded that they can still recognize the value of the past, while believing in progressive development which may yet allow them a more open and positive attitude to change.

What then are the issues to be addressed for the future? The principal acknowledged Lagan's foundations to be well laid; but he felt that the school needed to develop further its three key principles:

As a Christian school, it had to clarify and revaluate its overt and hidden curricula. As an all-ability school, it had to ensure proper differentiation according to pupils' learning needs. As an integrated school, it had to maintain the balance in admissions of gender, class, and denomination, while also enhancing the development of cultural diversity. It was no longer crying as a prophetic voice in the wilderness but, more in the tradition of Nehemiah, was building up and strengthening its community ethos.

In order to achieve this, its programme of religious education was under review in the light of the new common core Agreed Syllabus for Northern Ireland, to safeguard an appropriate academic study of the subject (not invariably the case in Roman Catholic schools), balanced by more specific denominational teaching within the respective traditions (not generally the case in Protestant schools). As the two new full-time chaplains explored their role in the college, they were in a position to enhance the importance of collective and shared school worship, while encouraging the pupils' understanding of their own denominational and sacramental traditions.

But a Christian school is characterized by more than just its religious education. It is also about developing a Christian ethos in which the different traditions are recognized, valued and brought closer together. 'It is the challenge of creating school communities where unity consists of reconciled diversity and not uniformity', said the principal. Duncan Morrow, writing in the *Tablet* (16 February 1991) agreed: 'Parents of children at integrated schools have discovered that integrated education is about open acknowledgement of differences, not about assimilation by the back door.' It was a danger, recognized by the staff and the principal, that in the midst of coping with a new building, new curricular initiatives, and financial management responsibilities, the focus on the Christian ethos unintentionally slips down the list of priorities.

The college also recognized the importance of 'Laganizing' the staff, many of whom previously worked in segregated schools but deliberately chose to come to Lagan to escape the ethos of sectarianism. A Protestant teacher commented that in her previous school there was 'a marked atmosphere of bigotry among the staff, let alone the children; it would be strange to go back now into a Protestant school'. A Catholic teacher added that establishing a Catholic ethos in her previous school in deprived west Belfast was extremely difficult. When she saw the Lagan post advertised, she thought 'Now there's something I'd like to be part of'. The Catholic staff have their future career prospects in the Catholic schools put in jeopardy because they have defied the policy of their Catholic teacher training colleges, which are committed to training Catholic teachers for Catholic schools. The principal frankly regretted that in staff appointments he could sometimes be disappointed by the range and quality of Catholic applicants; the best teachers in that tradition might hesitate to apply to Lagan. Moreover, no less than in its early years, Lagan also has to ensure that teachers who have previously worked in a selective system are retrained to teach across the ability range, to provide appropriate differentiation for all Lagan's pupils.

Harnessing staff idealism and creating a professional team are a challenge for any school. The principal reflected that the minimal level of interstaff bickering was in part due to their relative youthfulness but, more importantly, 'because they shared a common sense of purpose'. Holding on to that purpose and maintaining a Christian vision in the midst of contemporary educational pressures cannot be easy.

Any evaluation of the development of an integrated school in Northern Ireland must take into account political, ecclesiastical, economic, educational and community issues. But the school's success or failure depends on the children themselves. This chapter therefore concludes with the pupils' views on Lagan College. What difference has the school made to the attitudes of the children by the time they leave?

The children's view

There can be little doubt that Lagan's achievement in diminishing the sense of community polarization is real. One 13-year-old boy in the school, a Protestant whose father was killed by a paramilitary group ten years ago, commented: 'I never knew a Catholic before I came here. I didn't trust them because they were from the other side. But not any more. We fight about some things here now, but not about being Catholics and Protestants.' And one of the teachers observed: 'It is wrong to assume children are miniature versions of adults. To them it is natural that people should get on together.'

The 1992 prospectus quoted one boy who commented: 'Are we really so strange? It's a pity that the trust and friendship generated in Lagan College is not extended across the whole community.' A girl added: 'Coming to Lagan College has helped me to make friends from all denominations. Not only does the school benefit the pupils, but also their parents; they've got the chance to meet other people from across the divide.'

At the 1992 Cambridge conference on ecumenical education, the principal of Lagan emphasized that it was not enough just to track a child's academic attainment, as with National Curriculum assessments at 7, 11, 14 and 16. What also mattered was whether ecumenical schools increased children's understanding and acceptance of other Christian traditions: for example, did they still have friends later in life from a communion other than their own? How much were they involved in their local parishes and ecumenical groups after leaving school? Colin Irwin's 1991 research provided some indications in his analysis of these attitudes among present and past pupils. His results showed that 71 per cent of new first-year pupils had no friends from the 'other' community;[30] that five years on, pupils had more friends from the 'other' community than from their own; and that past pupils maintained a significant percentage (44 per cent) of friends from the 'other' community, in contrast to similar students at the integrated university (12 per cent):

> Graduates of Lagan College make lasting friendships in, and acquire a better understanding of, the 'other community' to a degree that is not achieved by their contemporaries in segregated schools. (Irwin, 1991, p. 86)

Irwin argued that, because humans acquire their primary in-group identity in the years leading up to and including puberty, integrated secondary schools can have a more lasting effect on social behaviour than is seen if a child, educated in an integrated primary school, transfers to a segregated secondary school. (At Lagan only five pupils in the first-year intake of 1990 came from an integrated primary school.) He also found that schools had more influence on a pupil's friendship patterns than the housing area in which they lived. Lagan's role in providing the social opportunity for the establishing of these new friendships and the expression of these social values may be indispensable. Certainly Irwin's findings suggest that Lagan pupils have a better understanding than segregated pupils of the motives of the various groups, both Catholic and Protestant, involved in the conflict, particularly since 'group stereotypes can be brought into question on an almost daily basis' (ibid., p. 66). One Catholic boy commented: 'Before I came to this school I thought different about Protestants, but now I know them, I don't know why people are fighting. There's no point.' Because the hidden curriculum is more influential than the overt curriculum, integrated

---

[30]Yet 48 per cent of children from Catholic schools had no non-Catholic friends; 86 per cent of those from Protestant schools had no non-Protestant friends.

education may have the potential to be more effective than curricular initiatives like Education for Mutual Understanding alone. The religious institutions which 'promote their own members' interests at the expense of others' must lose their moral authority to secular initiatives or to 'the moral authority of parents who choose to send their children to integrated schools'. Irwin concluded that 'segregated education contributes to the polarisation of the two communities, while integration brings the communities closer together, through increased friendship and mutual understanding' (ibid., p. 97). The head boy of 1991–92 reflected, in Lagan's prospectus, 'Seen from outside Northern Ireland, it would sometimes seem that the situation is without hope; but to come and be part of Lagan College shows that view is simply wrong'.

There remain innumerable problems. It probably does not help Lagan College to be held up by the media as being a model for all integrated education in Northern Ireland. The school is one way of doing it, not necessarily the only way. It has suffered wounds. One of the founder parents of the All Children Together (ACT) movement created great bitterness when he broke away in 1984 to form the Belfast Trust for Integrated Education (BELTIE). He favoured rapid expansion in both primary and secondary sectors, while ACT insisted on prioritizing the secure establishment of Lagan College and Forge Primary School. BELTIE was a leading advocate for the establishment of the National Council for Integrated Education (NICIE) in 1987, which was recognized by the government as the chief co-ordinating body in the matter. The result was that Lagan College found itself marginalized outside this official network, and felt wary of committing itself to an organization that had the potential not merely to facilitate but to impose control on the future development of integrated education. Although Lagan's governors finally decided to join NICIE in autumn 1992, healing the abrasions created by the differing convictions of the early pioneers is important if the Lagan 'flagship' is not to find itself adrift on a different sea, but is to have the opportunity to influence the debate on future developments. Even so, Lagan's principal has argued that the school should not be regarded as an exclusive model by which other integrated schools are measured, but as a 'parable' capable of wider interpretations.

The years of hesitation and apparent coolness towards the pioneers of integrated education on the part of the Northern Ireland Office have not made it easy for Lagan College or other integrated schools in the province. Such caution may, as I have ventured to suggest, be in part explained by the political desire not to offend the Roman Catholic hierarchy or intransigent Protestants more than is utterly necessary. In a society already widely suspicious of Westminster's good intentions towards Ulster, proposals for a change in the structure of educational provision must be a matter where the government is unlikely to lead except, like the Duke of Plaza Toro, from

199

in the rear. Behind the caution there is an evidently long experience that initiatives from England do not easily flourish in Irish soil.[31]

Lagan has established a reputation across Northern Ireland as an integrated school which takes religion seriously. The challenge it poses to the Churches is well summarized by the general secretary of the Irish Council of Churches, a former Stormont Minister of Community Relations:

> The Irish Churches institutionally seem at times to lack compassion on some of the most sensitive areas of life affecting the young. For example, when Protestant and Catholic parents join together to educate their children inside a framework which is Christian and interdenominational, they are often left without the spiritual understanding and support which their courage and ecumenical witness deserve. As such systems grow (and they will), rich opportunities for cooperation between Christian educationists may be lost forever, with secular influences standing to gain. (Bleakley, 1989, p. 2)

The joint schools model, like St Bede's, Redhill, which brings together Churches in England, is not a model that Lagan can copy in its entirety. The principal commented that Bishops Patrick Walsh and Gordon McMullan were technically right when they insisted that the Roman Catholic Church school cannot partner a Church of Ireland school because the Anglicans have no schools themselves, only transferor's rights. Both Churches recognize that the problems of Northern Ireland are more to do with politics and economics than education. As one Roman Catholic spokesman said: 'Don't use children to solve Northern Ireland's problems.' But if the Churches were serious about children's Christian education, they should be working out their own requirements for safeguarding their specific interests in integrated schools rather than distancing themselves.

The heady mix of politics and religion militates against rapprochement and ecumenical dialogue in which there is real listening to one another. The country is renowned for its high level of churchgoing among the people. On both sides of the confessional divide, many practising Christians do not

---

[31]The Anglo-Irish Agreement showed that the British government was not prepared to accept deadlock indefinitely and at least persuaded the Unionists to attend tripartite talks in Lancaster House in July 1992. The British ambassador to Dublin in 1985 reflected in a personal interview (July 1992), that the turning-point came when the Unionists realized that the Conservative government was no longer committed to 'British Ulster' at any price, and would accept the decision if the majority in the province were to vote for union with the Republic. By November 1992 when the talks ended, all parties stated that they had at least achieved agreement on the main points of disagreement. Sir Patrick Mayhew told Parliament: 'Progress has been made. Six months in the history of Ireland is but an evening gone.' The more recent joint declaration by Albert Reynolds and John Major renewed the debate into 1994.

often recognize that, when they pray for the unity of Christ's Church, actions are as important as words. Ecumenism is not infrequently met with a groan of apprehension at the prospect of the flood of paper it can produce and the inevitably technical nature of parts of the theological discussion. But in Ireland, of all places, the dialogue is no abstract discussion but a road along which Protestants and Roman Catholics can refuse to travel only if they are determined to perpetuate the rancour and violence of the present.

6

Conclusion

The search for unity and ecumenical concern are a necessary dimension of the whole of the Church's life. (John Paul II, address to the Roman Curia, 28 June 1985)

The divisions between the Anglican and Roman Catholic Churches weaken the Churches' witness: 'human folly and human sinfulness have at times opposed the unifying purpose of the Holy Spirit' (Pontifical Council, 1993, para. 18). The evidence we have considered suggests that this disunity influences Christian education as much as other spheres of the Churches' mission.

The two joint Church secondary schools with which we have been concerned see themselves as powerful witnesses to the ecumenical theme that the divisions of the past can no longer be accepted without question. They challenge the historical polarity of Protestants and Roman Catholics in education, as well as representing a significant ecumenical project in their own right. In conclusion, let us consider the evidence they offer in answer to key questions for ecumenical education.

1. What are the circumstances under which joint Church schools come into being and in which they survive and flourish? In both case studies a combination of the courageous and inspired vision of the founders and creative pragmatism was clearly vital to the schools' success. In both schools, the support of parents and staff committed to the ecumenical venture created an atmosphere of Christian charity and goodwill which allowed anxieties to be shared and explored; far from exacerbating the tensions inherent in new ventures, Christian understanding brought together all those involved to the benefit of the school community and provided a framework in which common understanding could be developed.

However, if both schools were inspired by an ecumenical idealism, they differed in practical motivation. For Redhill, the initial incentive was to create a viable sixth form and establish a strong Church secondary school in the local area; for Belfast, the desire was rather to create an alternative choice both to secondary intermediate schools and to segregated education generally, enabling the Lagan 'experiment' to gain widespread recognition.

Secondly, we may ask, how essential was the support of the Churches in the process? Certainly in Redhill, unlike Belfast, the backing of the diocese, deaneries and local parishes as well as the LEA was critical in establishing firm foundations. St Bede's took care to bring the Churches 'on board', ensuring that anxieties were responded to sensitively and reassurances offered; through their Christian Education Committee, the governors continue to keep this area under review. However, the founders of Lagan College demonstrated that the support of the Churches is not always a prerequisite; their lay initiative, backed by majority public opinion, strove constantly for Church recognition, but in the end had to 'go it alone' with neither Church nor government involvement. Their success despite these constraints may be explicable by reference to the somewhat 'apocalyptic' situation of Northern Ireland; in normal circumstances it would probably be difficult to operate a joint denominational school without official Church endorsement. All the same, the success of Lagan remains a tribute to what can be achieved by strong-minded lay Christians.

Thirdly, research evidence points clearly to the commitment of staff as being critical to the schools' effectiveness. First and foremost their willingness to explore perceived problems openly and honestly, not fudging or compromising, but 'grasping nettles' early and working through difficulties, meant that apprehensions and prejudices were brought to the surface in an atmosphere of mutual trust rather than allowed to 'fester'. Evidence of this may be seen in the staffrooms of both schools, where there was noticeably less 'bickering' than in many other institutions. If perhaps some staff had feared, or hoped, that an ecumenical school might throw a hazier light on their religious identity or affiliation, they found on the contrary a higher profile given to RE and a more distinctively Christian ethos than in many single-denominational schools.

In both schools many staff were willing to acknowledge that, although they began with an explicit sympathy with the aims of an ecumenical school, they had often been unexpectedly challenged by others' presuppositions arising from different cultures and histories. Particularly for RE staff and chaplains, it was not enough merely to be interested in ecumenical theology; they had to be fully committed to engaging in genuine and frank dialogue with each other and with the pupils, prepared to learn alongside the children and take risks in order to mature in Christian faith and understanding.

Fourthly, we have seen the central role of religious education in creating successful joint schools. It needs to establish its academic integrity, to challenge the pupils to think seriously about the Christian faith and allow them to deepen their spiritual understanding. RE can develop significantly in the ecumenical context, drawing effective ideas from denominational syllabuses as it evolves common Christian frameworks, moving away from policies that reinforce divisions towards strategies that seek to clarify areas of similarity and distinctiveness.

> A special effort should be made to ensure that the Christian message is presented in a way that highlights the unity of faith that exists between Christians about fundamental matters, while at the same time explaining the divisions that do exist and the steps that are being taken to overcome them. (*Ecumenical Directory*, 1993, para. 190)

The mutual understanding of denominational traditions and cultures in the joint schools strengthened as teaching colleagues, especially in their RE departments, were prepared to take time to grow in self-awareness and to share their apprehensions and uncertainties. This process, facilitated by effective chaplaincy support, deepened rather than undermined personal faith and denominational commitment.

Fifthly, how essential was the role of the chaplains? Both case studies indicated that where they were prepared to commit the time to establishing effective relationships with young people, chaplains could contribute much to the pastoral care of pupils and staff, the imaginative development of liturgical celebrations and helpful liaison with the local parishes and community. In both schools, difficulties had been experienced with individual appointments and Lagan, unlike St Bede's, had been dependent on the goodwill of honorary chaplains; yet each school was seeking to develop the role further. It would be ironic if the increasing Free Church involvement in St Bede's accentuated denominational distinctions within Protestantism (e.g. through separate chaplains) while Lagan was moving to a more inclusive Protestant chaplaincy alongside the Roman Catholics.

Sixthly, the case studies suggest, more generally, that the challenge of the joint school is to demonstrate to all concerned that unity involves not dilution down to the lowest common denominator, but enrichment through complementarity of perspectives; not passive tolerance but real growth in Christian insight. Cardinal Hume himself was clear: 'To make progress in unity, we must approach each other in openness and with total honesty.

Unity is gift ... it is also growth' (1988a, p.137). At the deeper level, it involves a rediscovery of familiar tradition alongside fresh perspectives on ideas neglected or underdeveloped over past centuries. Providing reassurance for Roman Catholics who fear dilution of their doctrinal tradition and Anglicans or Free Church members apprehensive about autocratic indoctrination takes time and patience, so that confidence can be built up and diversity acknowledged without defensiveness. At Lagan, since so much depended on the parents' commitment to integrated education, it was important to involve them in first-hand experience of the school if they were to overcome the long-standing prejudices of their segregated communities. In both schools considerable resources were invested to demonstrate that a joint school, in spite of its distinctive culture, was also a fully Anglican/ Protestant or Roman Catholic school like its single-denominational counterparts, but with that all-important 'value-added' ecumenical dimension.

2. *What was the joint school's contribution to the life of the Churches?* By inviting Church representatives to attend major school events and lead assemblies or worship (both eucharistic and non-eucharistic), the schools encouraged greater confidence in more active inter-denominational co-operation among local clergy, whose previous involvement in practical ecumenism may have extended only to well-meaning prayers during annual Christian Unity week.

In Redhill the annual Year 8 parish day stimulated appropriate ecumenical links as clergy worked with each other as well as the pupils, thus demonstrating the school's effectiveness in enhancing local ecumenical partnerships; the role of the two chaplains was also critical to wider relations with the Churches. In Belfast's polarized Christian community, however, only a few clergy were courageous enough to jeopardize parish harmony or risk appearing disloyal to their own denominational schools by publicly endorsing integrated schools. Undoubtedly this served to limit the influence of ecumenism in the surrounding community, although effective support was offered on an unofficial or individual basis.

There were signs that this policy of cool detachment, especially but not only on the part of the Roman Catholics, was leading to a more secular ethos in some integrated schools where Church support was negligible. If ecumenical issues were discussed in schools, the Churches found them less 'threatening' in a single-denominational context; early research, however, suggests that mutual Christian understanding is more positively enhanced by the integrated school experience. The potential of such schools to break down barriers and promote conflict resolution is considerable.

However, *Future in Partnership* pointed out:

> Whilst there may already be joint schools between the Church of England and the Roman Catholic Church or with the Free Churches, the ecumenical model is

205

yet to be fully explored. The educational backroom boys raise questions of ownership, Trust Law, and difficulties of sharing places on governing bodies. (National Society, 1984, p. 100)

Such caution was demonstrated by the dioceses in 1992 when St Bede's considered widening its foundation to include Free Church representation, and pointed up some of the constraints of official Church affiliation. Lagan, on the other hand, may ironically have had more freedom to develop its own contribution to the Churches through 'unofficial' resources provided by religious orders and honorary chaplains. Certainly Lagan established itself from the start with a wider Protestant representation than just the Anglican Church of Ireland, showing the advantages of lay leadership in exploring new pathways for Christian co-operation along which the Churches might follow. Alan Brown of the National Society has observed,

> To the outsider it must seem that Anglican paternalism and Roman Catholic protectionism are the biggest obstacles to ecumenical schools. ... Can all the Churches display sufficient confidence in themselves and be prepared to be vulnerable enough to trust each other in order to loosen the fears of denominationalism? (Brown, 1988, pp. 46–7).

Religious education and nurture have a significant part to play in this process of building up confidence and valuing the enriching diversity of Christian education. As Peter Sedgwick suggests,

> The Church school will be a witness ... to divine grace present in the secular world, where people are led to develop their own potential and the proper diversity of society is affirmed. Ecumenical church schools offer a vision of religious disclosure and nurture which could be of great value in a future secular culture. (Sedgwick, 1992, p. 263)

Leslie Francis also argues that the theology of Christian nurture needs 'to look afresh at the possibilities and problems inherent in a system of ecumenical Church schools operated as a distinctive Christian alternative to a predominantly secular system of county schools' (1990).

3. What therefore should be the contribution of joint schools to education and society at large? Certainly where they are successful, they offer a valuable witness to the wider community that Christians can work together for good, in contrast to the world's inter-religious conflicts portrayed in the media. Joint schools have immense potential to heal deep social divisions and the scars of still unreconciled memories of past persecution and residual marginalization, especially relevant in Belfast. Educating young people to see Christian service as a normal part of their *curricula vitae*; to challenge vested interests and seek reconciliation by accepting rather than confront-

ing diversity; to recognize the value of Christian fellowship, confident in their own religious identity without falling back into denominational defensiveness: this is the challenge posed by joint schools to the education system and secular society. In the process, they have to guard against the pressures of exclusivity arising from parental choice and oversubscription, and be conscious of the dangers of creating an alternative Christian educational ghetto.

An additional contribution of St Bede's lies in its example to other Christian schools within the 'dual system' that ecumenical co-operation is vital to Christian witness. Yet Lagan offers something more: by helping to bring about a change in the law to permit integrated education, it has shown itself to be a 'beacon' of reconciliation for all Northern Ireland's schools and their divided communities. By creating an inclusive 'haven' in a society divided by selective and segregated education, Lagan attracts a variety of Christians and non-Christians into one community. The government has been convinced enough to give 100 per cent funding to integrated grant-maintained schools and provide financial support for the Northern Ireland Council for Integrated Education to promote schools like Lagan. Even if it does not wish to be thought the answer to Northern Ireland's problems, Lagan's success is important for a society searching for signs of hope. Edward Hulmes' reflection is apposite:

> Whether or not Christian education can serve as an instrument for reconciling and for accommodating differences between individuals and groups in this country, not to speak of the wider world of Europe and beyond, depends humanly speaking on the determination of Christians to reflect in their own lives something of the dynamic unity of God, who not only wills that human beings be at one with each other, but also provides the means. (Hulmes, 1992a, p. 305)

4. Joint Church schools: has their time now come? These schools remain relatively few in number nationally even after twenty years of 'experimentation'.[1] The 1988 and 1993 Education Acts have shown clearly that Church leaders need to work more closely together if the 'dual system' is to survive and Christian education is not to be hijacked by individual and sectarian interests in response to the pressures of secularization. Churches with a commitment to ecumenism need to put their theology into practice in the service of education.[2]

[1] In 1992–93, there were eight joint secondary schools in England, one non-denominational and one associated sixth form. In Northern Ireland there were four integrated secondary schools but many more primary schools.

[2] A senior spokesman for Lambeth Palace commented privately that joint schools were one of the 'success stories' of recent Anglican/Roman Catholic dialogue in England.

In a 1989 survey of opinion among English diocesan bishops about the role of joint schools (English Anglican/Roman Catholic Committee paper 90/6), most were favourably disposed to ecumenical co-operation in education. One Roman Catholic bishop commented that difficulties about discussing the issues of joint schools arose from insecurity or feeling threatened, both of which he acknowledged were the consequences of 'a limited vision or a lingering pride'. One Catholic diocesan adviser was convinced that the schools needed to 'take ownership of a joint Christian vision that will meet the needs of both communities'. Cardinal Hume has commented: 'Christian ecumenical schools have broken new ground and may well be a significant indication of a way forward' (1988a, p. 111). In Belfast, such schools would undoubtedly be assisted by a more positive commitment from the Churches in a society torn apart by social and religious divisions, but the difficulties are considerable and complex.

This study has offered some optimistic indications for the future: first in the strengthening of political alliances between the Churches over the important educational legislation of 1988 and 1993; secondly in the reaffirmation of common Christian values and culture in contemporary secular society and the attempts to support effective religious education in the classroom.

The two joint school case studies have shown in their different ways that mere dialogue between Churches is not enough: it must lead to Christian unity in action. Such action owes a debt to theologians and Church leaders who since the Second Vatican Council have sought to clarify important areas of difference and convergence, but young people of future generations need to experience this ecumenical vision for themselves, preferably during their formative years at school, if they are to retain those convictions in later life and play their part in moving the Church towards unity in Christ. At a time when ecumenical co-operation is official Church policy, often strongly supported by lay Christians in their own communities, the opportunities presented to expand the number of ecumenical Church schools should be seized.

An ecumenical school is unlikely to succeed if it is taken merely to embody indifferentism. But if diversity of custom, liturgy and theological tradition is compatible with authentic unity at the level of essential faith, then joint schools point the way for a future liberated from entrenched hostility and distrust, with beneficial consequences for a harmonious, civilized society.

Archbishop Robert Runcie presents the challenge: 'in the early years of Christian ecumenism, enthusiasts for unity thought that if Christians of different denominations learned more about one another, they would come to discover that what united them far outweighed what divided them. There was truth here, but more recently we have come to appreciate diversity within the Christian Church and seen it as enrichment rather than enfeeblement.... We must move from dialogue to partnership ... the rich diversity of religious traditions and communities is one of God's greatest gifts to his world.'[3]

[3] Address to the Inter-faith Network, 29 November 1990.

Bibliography

Abbott, W.H. (ed.) (1966) *The Documents of Vatican II*, London: Geoffrey Chapman.

Abrams, M., Gerard, D. and Timms, N. (eds) (1985) *Values and Social Change in Britain*, London: Macmillan.

Adelman, C. (ed.) (1984) *The Politics and Ethics of Evaluation*, London: Croom Helm.

Adie, M. (1990a) 'Restoring responsibility', *Education*, 14 December.

Adie, M. (1990b) 'Basic or marginal', *Education*, 21 December.

Adie, M. (1993) 'Value inadequate', *Education*, 29 January.

Akenson, D.H. (1973) *Education and Enmity: The Control of Schooling in Northern Ireland 1920–1950*, Newton Abbot: David and Charles.

Aldrich, R. and Leighton, P. (1985) *Education: Time for a New Act?* London: Bedford Way Papers 23.

Alves, C. (1991a) *Free to Choose*, London: National Society.

Alves, C. (1991b) 'Just a matter of words? The religious education debate in the House of Lords', *British Journal of Religious Education*, vol. 13, no. 3.

Anglican Consultative Council (1984) *Towards a Theology for Inter-faith Dialogue*, London: Church House Publishing.

Angus, L.B. (1988) *Continuity and Change in Catholic Schooling*, London: Falmer.

Archbishop's Commission on Urban Priority Areas (1985) *Faith in the City*, London: Church House Publishing.

Armstrong, D. (1985) *A Road Too Wide*, London: Collins.

Arthur, J. (1991) 'Catholic responses to the 1988 Education Reform Act: problems of authority and ethos', *British Journal of Religious Education*, vol. 13, no. 3.

Arthur, J. (1992) 'Policy and practice of Catholic education in England and Wales since the Second Vatican Council', DPhil thesis, University of Oxford.

Ashraf, A. (1987) 'Education of the Muslim community in Great Britain', *Muslim Education Quarterly*, vol. 5, no. 1.

Aspin, D.N. (1983) 'Church schools, religious education and the multi-ethnic community', *Journal of Philosophy of Education*, vol. 17, no. 2.

Astley, J. (1984) 'The role of worship in Christian learning', *Religious Education*, vol. 79, no. 2.

Astley, J. (1988) 'Theology and curriculum selection: a theoretical problem in teaching Christianity in religious education', *British Journal of Religious Education*, vol. 10, no. 2.

Astley, J. and Day, D. (eds) (1992) *The Contours of Christian Education*, London: McCrimmons.

Attfield, D.G. (1991) 'The challenge of the Education Reform Act to church schools', *British Journal of Religious Education*, vol. 13, no. 3.

Aunger, E.A. (1981) *In Search of Political Stability: a Comparative Study of New Brunswick and Northern Ireland*, Montreal: McGill–Queen's University.

Ayel, V. (1981) 'Shifts in catechesis 1950–1980' (trans. G. Rummery), *Word in Life*, August 1981.

Baker, J.A. (1984) Paper for Furrow Trust.

Ball, S. and Troyna, B. (1987) 'Resistance, rights and rituals: denominational schools and multicultural education', *British Journal of Education Policy*, vol. 2, no. 1.

Bander, P. (ed.) (1968) *Looking Forward to the Seventies*, London: Colin Smythe.

Barritt, D.P. and Carter, C.F. (1962) *The Northern Ireland Problem: A Study in Group Relations*, Oxford: Oxford University Press.

Beck, G.A. (ed.) (1950) *The English Catholics 1850–1950*, London: Burns Oates.

Beck, G. (1955) *The Case for Catholic Schools*, London: Catholic Education Council.

Birmingham (1975) *Agreed Syllabus of Religious Education*, Birmingham: City of Birmingham Education Committee.

Bishops' Conference of England and Wales (1979) *Memorandum on School Chaplains*, London: Education Commission.

Bishops' Conference of England and Wales (1981) *Signposts and Homecomings: the Educative Task of the Catholic Community*, London: St Paul Publications.

Bishops' Conference of England and Wales (1988) *Evaluating the Distinctive Nature of the Catholic School*, London: St Paul Publications.

Blake, N. (1983) 'Church schools, religious education and the multi-ethnic community: a reply to David Aspin', *Journal of Philosophy of Education*, vol. 17, no. 3.

Bleakley, D. (1989) *Northern Ireland: More than a Holy War*, London: BCCI.

Boal, F.W. and Douglas, J.N.H. (eds) (1982) *Integration and Division: Geographical Perspectives on the Northern Ireland Problem*, London: Academic Press.

Board of Education (1988) *Children in the Way: New Directions for the Church's*

Children, London: National Society and Church House Publishing.

Board of Education (1991) *All God's Children*, London: National Society.

Board of Education (1992) *Response to the Department for Education Consultation on RE and Collective Worship*, London: General Synod of the Church of England.

Boyle, J.J. and Francis, L.J. (1986) 'The influence of differing church aided school systems on pupil attitude towards religion', *Research in Education*, no. 35.

Bridges, D. (1985) 'Non-paternalistic arguments in support of parents' rights', *Journal of Philosophy of Education*, vol. 18, no. 1.

British Council of Churches (1976) *The Child in the Church*, London: British Council of Churches.

British Council of Churches (1981) *Understanding Christian Nurture*, London: British Council of Churches.

British Council of Churches (1989) *Worship in Education*, London: British Council of Churches.

Brooksbank, K. (ed.) (1980) *Educational Administration*, London: Councils and Education Press.

Brown, A. (1987) *Religious Education and the Pupil with Learning Difficulties*, Cambridge: Cambridge University Press.

Brown, A. (1988) 'Church, school and ecumenism', in V.A. McClelland (ed.) *Christian Education in a Pluralist Society*, London: Routledge.

Brown, A., Barrett, V., Cole, O. and Erricker, C. (1987) *The Shap Handbook on World Religions in Education*, London: CRE.

Byrne, A. and Malone, C. (1992) *Here I Am*, London: Collins.

Cairns, E. (1987) *Caught in the Crossfire: Children and the Northern Ireland Conflict*, Belfast: Appletree Press.

Cameron Commission (1969) *Disturbances in Northern Ireland*, Belfast: HMSO, Cmnd 532.

Carlisle Commission (1971) *Partners in Education: the Role of the Diocese*, London: National Society and SPCK.

Carr, W. and Kemmis, K. (1986) *Becoming Critical: Education, Knowledge and Action Research*, London: Falmer.

Catechism of the Catholic Church (1994) London: Geoffrey Chapman.

Catechism of Church Law (1984) London: Catholic Truth Society.

Catholic Commission for Racial Justice (1984) *Learning from Diversity*, London: Catholic Media Office.

Catholic Hierarchy (1976) *The Directory on Ecumenism in Ireland*.

Caul, L. (ed.) (1990) *Schools under Scrutiny*, London: Macmillan.

Chadwick, P. and Gladwell, M. (1987) *Joint Schools*, Norwich: Canterbury Press.

Chapman, C. (1990) 'Pluralism and British schools: asking the right questions', *Spectrum*, vol. 22, no. 1.

Chichester Project (1982–85), ed. John Rankin, *Christianity as a World Religion*, London: Lutterworth.

Chilver Report (1980) *The Future Structure of Teacher Education in Northern Ireland* (An interim report of the Higher Education Review Group), Belfast: HMSO.

Chilver Report (1982) *The Future of Higher Education in Northern Ireland* (Report of the Higher Education Review Group for Northern Ireland), Belfast: HMSO.

Christian Education Movement (1991) *Planning RE in Schools*, Derby: CEM.

Clark, P.L. and Round, E. (1991) *The Good State Schools Guide: the Only Parents' Guide*, London: Ebury Press.

Clarke, D. (1990) *Report on the Catholic Chaplaincy in Lagan College 1984–1990*.

Cohen, B. (1982) *Means and Ends in Education*, London: Allen and Unwin.

Cohen, L. and Marion, L. (1980) *Research Methods in Education*, London: Croom Helm.

Coke, Sr M. (1983) 'Recent historical summary of Catechetical Renewal and its implications for RE', *British Journal of Educational Studies*, vol. 31, no. 1.

Cole, W.O. (ed.) (1978) *World Faiths in Education*, London, Allen and Unwin.

Cole, W.O. (ed.) (1986) *Religion in the Multi-Faith School*, London: Hulton.

Compton, P. (ed.) (1981) *The Contemporary Population of Northern Ireland and Population-related Issues*, Queen's University Belfast Institute of Irish Studies.

Congar, Y.M.J. (1967) *Priest and Layman*, London: Darton, Longman and Todd.

Congregation for Catholic Education (1988) *The Religious Dimension of Education in a Catholic School*, London: Catholic Truth Society.

Connelly, G. (1984) 'The transubstantiation of a myth', *Journal of Ecclesiastical History*, vol. 35. no. 1.

Coolahan, J. (ed.) (1990) *Community and the Curriculum*, conference proceedings, Belfast: Cooperation North.

Cooling, T. and Oliver, G. (1989) *Church and School*, Nottingham: Grove Books.

Corbishley, D. (1980) *Christian Unity: What Happens Next?* London: Catholic Truth Society.

Cormack, R.J. and Osborne, R.D. (eds) (1983) *Religion, Education and Employment: Aspects of Equal Opportunity in Northern Ireland*, Belfast: Appletree Press.

Cormack, R.J., Osborne, R.D., Reid, N.G. and Williamson, A.P. (1984) *Participation in Higher Education: Trends in the Social and Spatial Mobility of Northern Ireland Undergraduates*, London: Final Report SSRC Funded Project HR 6846.

Council for Catholic Maintained Schools (1990) Paper on *Catholic Education*.

Council for Catholic Maintained Schools (1991) *Response to the SACHR Report on the Financing of Schools in Northern Ireland*.

Cox, H. (1965) *The Secular City*, London: SCM.

Cox, E. (1975) *This Elusive Jesus*, London: Marshall Educational.

Cox, E. (1983) *Problems and Possibilities for Religious Education*, London: Hodder and Stoughton.

Cox, E. (1987) 'The relation between beliefs and values', *Religious Education*, vol. 82, no. 1.

SCHOOLS OF RECONCILIATION

Cox, E. and Cairns, J.M. (1989) *Reforming Religious Education: the Religious Clauses of the 1988 Education Reform Act*, London: Kogan Page.

Cox, E. and Skinner, M. (1990) 'Multi-faith religious education in church primary schools', *British Journal of Religious Education*, vol. 12, no. 2.

Cracknell, K. and Lamb, C. (1984) *Theology on Full Alert*, London: British Council of Churches.

Craft, M. (1984) *Education and Cultural Pluralism*, London: Falmer.

Credo: a Catholic Catechism (1983) London: Geoffrey Chapman.

Crone, R. and Malone J. (1983) *The Human Curriculum*, Belfast: Farset Cooperative Press.

Cruickshank, M. (1963) *Church and State in English Education*, London: Macmillan.

Cruickshank, M. (1972) 'The denominational school issue in the twentieth century', *History in Education*, 1, pp. 200–13.

Culham College Institute (1987) *The Way Ahead?* November conference report.

Culham College Institute and St Gabriel's Trust (1992) *RE—the Way Ahead*, June conference report.

Cunningham, R.F. (1989) *The Education Reform Act 1988 and Catholic Schools*, London: Catholic Education Council for England and Wales.

Dale, A.T. (1972) *The Bible in the Classroom*, Oxford: Oxford University Press.

Darby, J. (1976) *Conflict in Northern Ireland*, Dublin: Gill and Macmillan.

Darby, J. (1986) *Intimidation and the Control of Conflict in Northern Ireland*, Dublin: Gill and Macmillan Davis.

Darby, J. and Dunn, S. (1987) 'Segregated schools: the research evidence', in R.D. Osborne, R.J. Cormack and R.L. Miller (eds) *Education and Policy in Northern Ireland*, Belfast: Policy Research Institute.

Darby, J., Murray, D., Batts, D., Dunn, S., Farren, S. and Harris, J. (1977) *Education and Community in Northern Ireland: Schools Apart?*, Coleraine: New University of Ulster.

Day, D. (1985a) 'Religious education forty years on', *British Journal of Religious Education*, vol. 7, no. 2.

Day, D. (1985b) 'Suspicion of the spiritual; teaching religion in a world of secular experience', *British Journal of Religious Education*, vol. 7, no. 3.

Department for Education (1992a) *Choice and Diversity*, London: DfE.

Department for Education (1992b) *Religious Education and Collective Worship: a Consultation Paper*, London: DfE.

Department for Education (1994) *Religious Education and Collective Worship* (Circular 1/94), London: DfE.

Department of Catholic Education and Formation (1991) *On Appraisal in Catholic Schools*, 2nd edition, London: DCEF.

Department of Education and Science (1988) *School Governors: a Guide to the Law: Aided Schools*, London: DES.

Department of Education and Science (1989) *The Education Reform Act 1988:*

214

Religious Education and Collective Worship (Circular 3/89), London: DES.

Department of Education for Northern Ireland (1982) *The Improvement of Community Relations: the Contribution of Schools* (Circular 1982/21), Bangor, Co. Down: DENI.

Department of Education for Northern Ireland (1988a) *Education in Northern Ireland: Proposals for Reform*, Bangor, Co. Down: DENI.

Department of Education for Northern Ireland (1988b) *The Way Forward*, Bangor, Co. Down: DENI.

Donley, M. (1992) 'Teaching discernment', in B. Watson (ed.) *Priorities for Religious Education*, London: Falmer.

Dummett, A. and McNeal, J. (1981) *Race and Church Schools*, London: Runnymede Trust.

Duncan, G. (1990) *The Church School*, London: National Society.

Dunn, S. (1986a) *Education and the Conflict in Northern Ireland: a Guide to the Literature*, Coleraine: Centre for the Study of Conflict.

Dunn, S. (1986b) 'The role of education in the Northern Ireland conflict', *Oxford Review of Education*, vol. 12, no. 3.

Dunn, S. (1986c) 'The education debate in Northern Ireland: the integrated option', *Education Studies*, vol. 75, no. 3.

Dunn, S. (1989) 'Integrated schools in Northern Ireland', *Oxford Review of Education*, vol. 15, no. 2.

Dunn, S. (1990a) 'Inter-school links', paper to conference October 1989, Co-operation North.

Dunn, S. (1990b) *Multicultural Education in the North*, Coleraine: Centre for the Study of Conflict.

Dunn, S. and Smith, A. (1991) *Extending School Links*, Coleraine: Centre for the Study of Conflict.

Dunn, S., Darby, J. and Mullan, K. (1989) *Inter-School Links*, Coleraine: Centre for the Study of Conflict.

Durham Report (1970) *The Fourth R: the Report of the Commission on Religious Education in Schools*, London: National Society and SPCK.

Earl, W.J.H. (1984) 'The 1944 Education Act: forty years on', *British Journal of Religious Education*, vol. 6, no. 2.

Ecumenical Commission for England and Wales (1968) *Intercommunion*, London: Catholic Truth Society.

Ecumenical Commission for England and Wales (1974) *Memorandum on Christian Schooling*, London.

Ecumenical Commission for England and Wales (1979) *Memorandum on Joint Schools*, London.

Ecumenical Directory (1993): see under Pontifical Council.

Egan, J. (1988) *Opting Out: Catholic Schools Today*, Leominster: Fowler Wright.

Egan, J. and Francis, L.J. (1986) 'School ethos in Wales: the impact of non-practising Catholic and non-Catholic pupils on Catholic secondary schools',

Lumen Vitae, vol. 41, no. 3.

Elliott, J. (1979) 'The case for school self-evaluation', *Forum*, vol. 22, no. 1.

English Anglican/Roman Catholic Committee (1990) Paper on *Joint Schools* (90/6).

Equal Opportunities Commission for Northern Ireland (1981) *Formal Investigation into Further Education in Northern Ireland*, Belfast: Equal Opportunities Commission.

Fahy, P.S. (1980) 'The religious effectiveness of some Australian Catholic high schools', *Word in Life*, vol. 28, no. 2.

Fahy, P.S. (1992) *Faith in Catholic Classrooms*, London: St Paul Publications.

Farmington Institute (1987) *Critical Openness*, Oxford: Farmington Institute.

Faul, D. (1989) 'The Church's task: justice, the perfection of charity', address at Maynooth, 28 February.

Faulkner, B. (1978) *Memoirs of a Statesman*, ed. J. Houston, London: Weidenfeld and Nicolson.

Felderhof, M.C. (ed.) (1985) *Religious Education in a Pluralistic Society*, London: Hodder and Stoughton.

Ferguson, J. (ed.) (1981) *Christianity, Society and Education*, London: SPCK.

Field, F. (1989) *Opting Out: an Opportunity for Church Schools*, London: Church in Danger.

Flannery, A. (ed.) (1981) *Vatican Council II: the Conciliar and Post-conciliar Documents*, 5th edition, Leominster: Fowler Wright.

Flude, M. and Hammar, M. (eds) (1990) *The Education Reform Act 1988: its Origins and Implications*, London: Falmer.

Flynn, M.F. (1975) *Some Catholic Schools in Action*, Sydney: Catholic Education Office.

Flynn, M.F. (1979) *Catholic Schools and the Communication of Faith*, Sydney: Society of St Paul.

Flynn, M.F. (1985) *The Effectiveness of Catholic Schools*, Homebush, New South Wales: St Paul Publications.

Foxe, J. (1563) *Acts and Monuments*, 4th edition ed. J. Pratt (1877), London: Religious Tract Society.

A Framework for Devolution (1982), London: HMSO, Cmnd 8541.

Francis, L.J. (1983) 'The logic of education, theology and the church school', *Oxford Review of Education*, vol. 9, no. 2.

Francis, L.J. (1985) *Rural Anglicanism*, London: Collins.

Francis, L.J. (1986a) *Partnership in Rural Education*, London: Collins Liturgical Publications.

Francis, L.J. (1986b) 'Denominational schools and pupil attitudes towards Christianity', *British Educational Research Journal*, vol. 12, no. 2.

Francis, L.J. (1986c) 'Roman Catholic secondary schools: falling rolls and pupil attitudes', *Educational Studies*, vol. 12, no. 2.

Francis, L.J. (1986d) 'Are Catholic schools good for non-Catholics?', *Tablet*, 15

February.

Francis, L.J. (1987a) *Religion in the Primary School*, London: Collins Liturgical Publications.

Francis, L.J. (1987b) 'Measuring attitudes towards Christianity among 12- to 18-year-old pupils in Catholic schools', *Educational Research*, vol. 29, no. 3.

Francis, L.J. (1987c) 'The decline in attitudes towards religion among 8–15-year-olds', *Educational Studies*, vol. 13, no. 2.

Francis, L.J. (1990) 'Theology of education', *British Journal of Educational Studies*, vol. 38, no. 4.

Francis, L.J. (undated) *Christianity and the Child Today* (Occasional Paper 6), Oxford: Farmington Institute.

Francis, L.J. and Egan, J. (1987) 'Catholic schools and the communication of faith', *Catholic School Studies*, vol. 60, no. 2.

Francis, L.J. and Egan, J. (1990) 'Catholic school as "faith community": an empirical enquiry', *Religious Education*, vol. 85, no. 4.

Francis, L.J. and Thatcher, A. (1990) *Christian Perspectives for Education: a Reader in the Theology of Education*, Leominster: Fowler Wright.

Freire, P. (1972) *Pedagogy of the Oppressed*, London: Penguin.

Gallagher, J. (1986) *Guidelines: Living and Sharing our Faith*, London: Collins.

Gallagher, J. (1988) *Our Schools and Our Faith*, London: Collins.

Gallagher, A. (1989a) *The Majority–Minority Review: Education and Religion in Northern Ireland*, Coleraine: Centre for the Study of Conflict.

Gallagher, A. (1989b) 'Education in a divided society: research issues and questions', in Cooperation North (1989).

Gallagher, E. and Worrall, S. (1982) *Christians in Ulster 1968–1980*, Oxford: Oxford University Press.

Gardner, P. (1988) 'Religious upbringing and the ideal of autonomy', *Journal of Philosophy of Education*, vol. 22, no. 2.

Gay, J.D. *et al.* (1982) *The Debate about Church Schools in the Oxford Diocese*, Abingdon: Culham College Institute.

Gay, J., Kay, B., Perry, G. and Piper, H. (1989) *Church Primary Schools in the Diocese of London: a Report on the Views of the Headteachers*, Abingdon: Culham College Institute.

Gay, J., Kay, B., Newdick, H. and Perry, G. (1991a) *A Role for the Future: Anglican Primary Schools in the London Diocese*, Abingdon: Culham College Institute.

Gay, J., Kay, B., Newdick, H. and Perry, G. (1991b) *Schools and Church: Anglican Secondary Schools in the London Diocese*, Abingdon: Culham College Institute.

General Synod of the Church of England Board of Education (1984) *Schools and Multi-cultural Education*, London: Church House.

Goldman, R. (1964) *Religious Thinking from Childhood to Adolescence*, London: Routledge.

Goodall, N. (1972) *Ecumenical Progress 1961–71*, Oxford: Oxford University Press.

Greeley, A.M. (1982) *Catholic High Schools and Minority Students*, New

Brunswick, NJ: Transaction Books.

Greeley, A.M. and Rossi, P.H. (1966) *The Education of Catholic Americans*, Chicago: Aldine.

Greeley, A.M., McCready, W.C. and McCourt, K. (1976) *Catholic Schools in a Declining Church*, Kansas City: Sheed, Andrews and McMeel.

Green, R.H. (1982) *Church Schools: a Matter of Opinion*, London: Southwark Diocesan Board of Education.

Green, R.H. (1983) *What Are Church Schools for?*, London: Southwark Diocesan Board of Education.

Greer, J.E. and Francis, L.J. (1991) 'Measuring attitudes towards Christianity among pupils in Catholic secondary schools in Northern Ireland', *Educational Research*, vol. 33, no. 1.

Grimmitt, M. (1991) 'The use of religious phenomena in schools', *British Journal of Religious Education*, vol. 13, no. 2.

Groome, T.H. (1980) *Christian Religious Education*, San Francisco: Harper and Row.

Groome, T.H. *et al.* (1988) 'The spirituality of the religious educator', *Religious Education*, vol. 83, no. 1.

Guba, E.G. and Lincoln, Y.S. (1981) *Effective Evaluation*, San Francisco: Jossey-Bass.

Habgood, J. (1990) 'Are moral values enough?' *British Journal of Educational Studies*, vol. 38, no. 2.

Haldane, J. (1986) 'Religious education in a pluralist society: a philosophical examination', *British Journal of Educational Studies*, vol. 34, no. 2.

Haldane, J. (1988) 'Religion in education: in defence of a tradition', *Oxford Review of Education*, vol. 14, no. 2.

Hamilton, D. (1976) *Curriculum Evaluation*, London: Open Books.

Hamilton, D. *et al.* (1977) *Beyond the Numbers Game*, London: Macmillan.

Hamilton, D. *et al.* (1991) *Violence and the Communities*, Coleraine: Centre for the Study of Conflict.

Hammersley, P. (1989) 'Development in faith development theory', *British Journal of Religious Education*, vol. 11, no. 3.

Hammond, P.E. (1988) 'Religion and the persistence of identity', *Journal for the Scientific Study of Religion*, vol. 27, no. 1.

Hampshire (1978) *Religious Education in Hampshire Schools*, Winchester: Hampshire Education Committee.

Harbison, J.I. (ed.) (1983) *Children of the Troubles: Children in Northern Ireland*, Belfast: Stranmillis College Learning Resources Unit.

Harbison, J.I. (ed.) (1989) *Growing Up in Northern Ireland*, Belfast: Stranmillis College.

Hart, C. (1991) *From Acts to Action*, Newcastle upon Tyne: CATS Trust.

Hastings, A. (1968, 1969) *A Concise Guide to the Documents of the Second Vatican Council*, vols 1 and 2, London: Darton, Longman and Todd.

Hastings, A. (ed.) (1991) *Modern Catholicism: Vatican II and After*, London: SPCK.

Hastings, A. (1993) 'Catholicism and Protestantism', *One in Christ*, vol. 1.

Hayden, G. (ed.) (1987) *Education and Values*, London: University of London Institute of Education.

Hayes, M. (1990) *Address to Summer School Conference, Stranmillis College*, Belfast: DENI.

Heenan, J. (1971) *Not the Whole Truth*, London: Hodder and Stoughton.

Heskin, K. (1980) *Northern Ireland: a Psychological Analysis*, Dublin: Gill and Macmillan.

Hewstone, M. and Brown, R. (eds) (1986) *Contact and Conflict in Intergroup Encounters*, Oxford: Blackwell.

Heywood, D. (1988) 'Christian education and enculturation', *British Journal of Religious Education*, vol. 10, no. 2.

Hickey, J. (1984) *Religion and the Northern Ireland Problem*, Dublin: Gill and Macmillan.

Higgins, A. (1979) *Teaching about Controversial Issues in Catholic Schools* (CARE Occasional Paper 7), Norwich: University of East Anglia.

Higgins, J. (1989) 'Gender and Church of England diocesan syllabuses of religious education', *British Journal of Religious Education*, vol. 12, no. 1.

Higginson Report (1988) *Advancing A Levels*, London: HMSO.

Hill, B.V. (1989) ' "Spiritual development" in the Education Reform Act: a source of acrimony, apathy or accord', *British Journal of Educational Studies*, vol. 37, no. 2.

Hill, B.V. (1990) 'Will and should the religious studies appropriate to schools in a pluralist society foster religious relativism?', *British Journal of Religious Education*, vol. 12, no. 3.

Hirst, P.H. (1972) 'Christian education: a contradiction in terms?', *Learning for Living*, vol. 11, no. 4.

Hirst, P.H. (1974a) 'Moral education in a secular society', *British Journal of Educational Studies*, vol. 24, no. 2.

Hirst, P.H. (1974b) *Knowledge and the Curriculum*, London: Routledge.

Hirst, P.H. (1976) 'Religious beliefs and educational principles', *Learning for Living*, vol. 15, no. 4.

Hirst, P.H. (1981) 'Education, catechesis and the church school', *British Journal of Religious Education*, vol. 3, no. 3.

Holm, J. (1975) *Teaching Religion in School*, Oxford: Oxford University Press.

Holm, J. (1977) *The Study of Religions*, London: Sheldon Press.

Hornsby-Smith, M.P. (1978) *Catholic Education: the Unobtrusive Partner*, London: Sheed and Ward.

Hornsby-Smith, M. (1991) *Roman Catholic Beliefs in England*, Cambridge: Cambridge University Press.

Hornsby-Smith, M.P. and Lee, R. (1980) *Roman Catholic Opinion: a Study of*

Roman Catholics in England and Wales in the 1970s, Guildford: University of Surrey.

House, E.R. (ed.) (1986) *New Directions in Educational Evaluation*, London: Falmer.

Hughes, F. (1990) 'Christian education in recently established Christian schools', *Spectrum*, vol. 22, no. 2.

Hull, J. M. (1975) *School Worship: an Obituary*, London: SCM.

Hull, J.M. (1976) 'Christian theology and educational theory: can there be connections?', *British Journal of Educational Studies*, vol. 24, no. 2.

Hull, J.M. (1980) 'The value of the individual child and the Christian faith', *British Journal of Educational Studies*, vol. 28, no. 3.

Hull, J.M. (1984) *Studies in Religion and Education*, London: Falmer.

Hull, J.M. (1989a) 'Editorial: school worship and the 1988 Education Reform Act', *British Journal of Religious Education*, vol. 11, no. 3.

Hull, J.M. (1989b) *The Act Unpacked*, Derby: Christian Education Movement.

Hull, J.M. (1990) Editorials, *British Journal of Religious Education*, vol. 12.

Hulmes, E. (1979) *Commitment and Neutrality in Religious Education*, London: Geoffrey Chapman.

Hulmes, E. (1989) *Education and Cultural Diversity* London: Longman.

Hulmes, E. (1992a) 'Christian education: an instrument of European unity', in J. Astley and D. Day, *The Contours of Christian Education*, London: McCrimmons.

Hulmes, E. (1992b) 'Unity and diversity: the search for common identity', in B. Watson (ed.) *Priorities for Religious Education*, London: Falmer.

Hulmes, E. and Watson, B. (eds) (1980) *Religious Studies and Public Examinations*, Oxford: Farmington Institute.

Hume, B. (1988a) *Towards a Civilization of Love: Being Church in Today's World*, London: Hodder and Stoughton.

Hume, B. (1988b) 'The future of Catholic schools', address to Catholic headteachers, 19 September.

Hume, B. (1989) 'Catholic schools today', address to National Conference of Priests, 5 September.

Hume, B. (1990a) 'Building bridges', address to the North of England Education Conference, 3 January.

Hume, B. (1990b) 'Transforming the World: a Pastor's Viewpoint', address on Catholic education given in Toronto.

Hume, B. (1991a) 'Recapturing the vision', address to conference on the Future of Post-16 Education in Catholic Schools and Colleges, 27 June.

Hume, B. (1991b) Address to Catholic secondary headteachers in the Archdiocese of Westminster, 24 September.

Hume, B. (1992) Address to the First National Conference on Catholic Education, 13 July.

Hunter, J. (1991) 'Which school? A study of parents' choice of secondary school',

Educational Research, vol. 33, no. 1.

Inge, W.R. (1911) *Speculum Animae*, London: Longmans.

Irwin, C. (1991) *Education and the Development of Social Integration in Divided Societies*, Belfast: Queen's University.

Jamison, C. (1991) 'Catholic schools under fire', *Priests and People*, vol. 5, no. 8.

Jebb, P. (ed.) (1968) *Religious Education: the Downside Symposium*, London: Darton, Longman and Todd.

Jerusalem Bible (1968, 1985 edns) London: Darton, Longman and Todd/New York: Doubleday.

Joint Churches Working Party (1976) *Violence in Ireland*, Belfast: Irish Council of Churches.

Jones, S. (1987) 'The analysis of depth interviews', in R. Murphy and H. Torrance (eds) *Evaluating Education*, London: Harper and Row.

Kemmis, S. and McTaggart, R. (1982) *The Action Research Planner*, Geelong, Victoria: Deakin University Press.

Kerfoot, J. (1985) *Proceedings of the General Synod*, London: Church House Publishing.

Knight, C. (1990) *The Making of Tory Education Policy in Post-War Britain 1950–1986*, London: Falmer.

Konstant, D. (1976) *Religious Education for Secondary Schools*, London: Search Press and Macmillan.

Lambkin, B.K. (1990) *Religion in Ireland: Yesterday, Today and Tomorrow* (trial edition).

Lankshear, D.W. (1992a) *A Shared Vision: Education in Church Schools*, London: National Society.

Lankshear, D.W. (1992b) *Governing Church Schools*, London: National Society.

Lankshear, D.W. (1992c), *Looking for Quality in a Church School*, London: National Society, Southwark Diocesan Board of Education and Culham College Institute.

Lawton, D. (1992) *Education and Politics in the 1990s: Conflict or Consensus?* London: Falmer.

Leahy, M. (1990) 'Indoctrination, evangelization, catechesis and religious education', *British Journal of Religious Education*, vol. 12, no. 2.

Leonard, G. and Yates, J. (eds) (1986) *Faith for the Future: Essays on the Church in Education*, London: National Society.

Lima Declaration (1982) *Baptism, Eucharist and Ministry*, Geneva: World Council of Churches.

Livingstone, J. (1987) 'Equality of opportunity in education in Northern Ireland', in R.D. Osborne, R.J. Cormack and R.L. Miller (eds) *Education and Policy in Northern Ireland*, Belfast: Policy Research Institute.

Lohan, R. and McClure M. (1988) *Weaving the Web*, London: Collins.

London Diocesan Board of Education (1988) *Religious Education in the Diocese of London*, London: Diocesan Board of Education.

London Diocesan Board for Schools (1992) *The Education Bill: Brief Summary and Comments*, London: Diocesan Board for Schools.

Loughran, G. (1987) 'The rationale of Catholic education', in R.D. Osborne, R.J. Cormack and R.L. Miller (eds) *Education and Policy in Northern Ireland*, Belfast: Policy Research Institute.

Lundy, M.A. (1990) 'Adult catechesis in the Roman Catholic Church in Britain since the Second Vatican Council', PhD thesis, University of Manchester.

Mabud, S.K. (1992) 'A Muslim response to the Education Reform Act 1988', *British Journal of Religious Education*, vol. 14, no. 2.

McAdoo, H.R. and Clark, A.C. (1972) *An Agreed Statement on Eucharistic Doctrine*, London: SPCK and Catholic Truth Society.

McCabe, H. (1985) *The Teaching of the Catholic Church: a New Catechism of Christian Doctrine*, London: Catholic Truth Society.

McClelland, V.A. (1988) *Christian Education in a Pluralist Society*, London: Routledge.

MacDonald, B. and Walker, R. (1977) 'Case study and the social philosophy of educational research', in D. Hamilton *et al.*, *Beyond the Numbers Game*, London: Macmillan.

McEwan, A., Salters, J. and Agnew, U. (1992) *Integrated Education: the Views of Parents*, Belfast: Queen's University.

McIntyre, J. (undated) *Multi-culture and Multi-faith Societies: Some Examinable Assumptions* (Occasional Paper 3), Oxford: Farmington Institute.

McIver, V. (1990) 'EMU and the challenge of a new Europe', paper to DENI Summer School conference.

McIvor, B. (1984) Address to Preparatory Schools Conference, Cambridge.

McLaughlin, T. (1984) 'Parental rights and the religious upbringing of children', *Journal of Philosophy of Education*, vol. 18, no. 1.

McLaughlin, T. (1990) 'Peter Gardner on religious upbringing and the liberal ideal of religious autonomy', *Journal of Philosophy of Education*, vol. 24, no. 1.

McLaughlin, T. (1992) 'Christian education and schooling: a liberal perspective', conference paper, Stapleford House, University of Nottingham.

McNeilly, N. (1973) *Exactly 50 Years*, Belfast: Belfast Education and Library Board.

McNiff, J. (1988) *Action Research: Principles and Practice*, London: Macmillan.

McWhirter, L. (1989a) 'Longitudinal evidence on the teenage years', in J.I. Harbison (ed.) *Growing Up in Northern Ireland*, Belfast: Stranmillis College.

McWhirter, L. (1989b) *Longitudinal Evidence on Teenage Years*, Belfast: Northern Ireland Office, Planning and Policy Unit.

McWhirter, L., Duffy, R., Barry, R. and McGuinness, G. (1987) 'Transition from school to work: cohort evidence', in R.D. Osborne, R.J. Cormack and R.L. Miller (eds) *Education and Policy in Northern Ireland*, Belfast: Policy Research Institute.

Marcus, J. (1990) *The Next Step*, discussion paper for St Bede's, Redhill.

Marr, P. (1989) 'Denominational schools: some implications from ARCIC 1', *One in Christ*, vol. 25.

Marthaler, B.L. (1987) 'Dilemma for religious educators: indoctrination or indifference', *Religious Education*, vol. 82, no. 4.

Martin, D. (1967) *A Sociology of English Religion*, London: SCM.

Martin, B. (1981) *A Sociology of Contemporary Cultural Change*, Oxford: Blackwell.

Meakin, D.C. (1988) 'The justification of religious education reconsidered', *British Journal of Religious Education*, vol. 10, no. 2.

Merriam, S. (1988) *Case Study Research in Education*, San Francisco: Jossey-Bass.

Miller, R.L. and Osborne, R.D. (1983) 'Educational qualifications and religious affiliation', in R.J. Cormack and R.D. Osborne (eds) *Religion, Education and Employment: Aspects of Equal Opportunity in Northern Ireland*, Belfast: Appletree Press.

Mitchell, B. (1967) *Law, Morality and Religion in a Secular Society*, Oxford: Oxford University Press.

Mitchell, B. (1968) *Neutrality and Commitment*, Oxford: Oxford University Press.

Mitchell, B. (1970) 'Indoctrination in the Durham Report', *The Fourth R*, Appendix B, London: SPCK.

Mitchell, B. (1973) *The Justification of Religious Belief*, London: Macmillan.

Mitchell, B. (1980a) 'Religious education', *Oxford Review of Education*, vol. 6, no. 2.

Mitchell, B. (1980b) *Morality: Religious and Secular*, Oxford: Clarendon.

Moffatt, C. (ed.) (1993) *Education Together for a Change*, Belfast: Fortnight Press.

Moran, G. (1966) *Catechesis and Revelation*, New York: Herder and Herder.

Moran, G. (1967) *God Still Speaks*, London: Burns and Oates.

Moran, G. (1968) *Visions and Tactics*, London: Burns and Oates.

Moran, G. (1989) *Religious Education as a Second Language*, Birmingham, Alabama: Religious Education Press.

Morgan, V., Fraser, G., Dunn, S. and Cairns, E. (1992) 'Views from outside—other professionals' views of the religiously integrated schools in Northern Ireland', *British Journal of Religious Education*, vol. 14, no. 3.

Morrow, D. (1991) 'Across Ulster's divide', *Tablet*, 16 February.

Moxon-Browne, E. (1983) *Nation, Class and Creed in Northern Ireland*, Aldershot: Gower.

Murphy, J. (1971) *Church, State and Schools in Britain 1800–1970*, London: Routledge.

Murphy, D. (1978) *A Place Apart*, London: John Murray.

Murray, D. (1983) 'Rituals and symbols as contributors to the culture of Northern Ireland primary schools', *Irish Educational Studies*, vol. 3, no. 2.

Murray, D. (1985) *Worlds Apart: Segregated Schools in Northern Ireland*, Belfast: Appletree Press.

Murray, D. and Darby, J. (1983) 'The transition from school to work (2): the

Londonderry and Strabane study: out and down in Derry and Strabane', in R.J. Cormack and R.D. Osborne (eds) *Religion, Education and Employment: Aspects of Equal Opportunity in Northern Ireland*, Belfast: Appletree Press.

Musty, E. (1991) *Opening Their Eyes*, London: National Society.

National Association of Head Teachers (1985) *Religious Education in Schools*, London: NAHT.

National Curriculum Council (1991) *Religious Education: a Local Curriculum Framework*, York: NCC.

National Curriculum Council (1992) *The Spiritual and Moral Dimension*, York: NCC.

National Pastoral Congress (1981) *Liverpool 1980*, London: St Paul Publications.

National Society (1973) *Voluntary Controlled Schools of the Church of England*, London: National Society.

National Society (1984) *A Future in Partnership*, London: National Society.

National Society (1985) *Positive Partnership*, London: National Society.

National Society (1989) *Religious Education*, London: National Society.

National Society (1990a) *The Curriculum: a Christian View*, London: National Society.

National Society (1990b) *Staff for Church Schools: Guidelines on Appointment*, London: National Society.

National Society (1991) *Grant Maintained Status and the Church School*, London: National Society.

Nichols, K. (ed.) (1974) *Theology and Education*, London: St Paul Publications.

Nichols, K. (1978) *Cornerstone*, London: St Paul Publications.

Nichols, K. (1979) *Orientations*, London: St Paul Publications.

Nichols, K. (1992) 'Roots in religious education', in B. Watson (ed.) *Priorities for Religious Education*, London: Falmer.

Nichols, A. (1993) *The Panther and the Hind: a Theological History of Anglicanism*, Edinburgh: T. & T. Clark.

Nordberg, R.B. (1987) 'Curricular integration in Roman Catholic education', *Religious Education*. vol. 82, no. 1.

Norman, E. (1985) *Roman Catholicism in England*, Oxford: Oxford University Press.

Northern Ireland Council for Integrated Education (1991) *Statement of Principles*.

O'Buachalla, S. (1985) 'Church and state in Irish education in this century', *European Journal of Education*, vol. 20, no. 4.

O'Buachalla, S. (1988) *Education Policy in Twentieth Century Ireland*, Dublin: Wolfhound.

O'Connor, D. (1980) 'Reports – "Chocolate Cream Soldiers": evaluating an experiment in non-sectarian education in Northern Ireland', *Curriculum Studies*, vol. 12, no. 3.

O'Hare, P. (1978) *Foundations of Religious Education*, New York: Paulist Press.

O'Hear, A. (1981) *Education, Society and Human Nature*, London: Routledge.

O'Keeffe, B. (1986) *Faith, Culture and the Dual System*, London: Falmer.

O'Keeffe, B. (ed.) (1988) *Schools for Tomorrow: Building Walls or Building Bridges*, London: Falmer.

O'Keeffe, B. (1992) 'A look at the Christian schools movement', in B. Watson (ed.) *Priorities in Religious Education*, London: Falmer.

O'Leary, D.L. (ed.) (1983) *Religious Education and Young Adults*, London: St Paul Publications.

O'Leary, D.L. and Sallnow, T. (1982) *Love and Meaning in Religious Education*, Oxford: Oxford University Press.

O'Neill, T. (1972) *The Autobiography of Terence O'Neill*, London: Rupert Hart-Davis.

O'Neill, M. (1979) 'Towards a modern concept of permeation', *Momentum*, 10 (May), 48–9 (USA).

Orchard, S. (1991) 'What was wrong with religious education? An analysis of HMI reports 1985–88', *British Journal of Religious Education*, vol. 14, no. 1.

Osborne, R.D. (1985) *Religion and Educational Qualifications in Northern Ireland*, Belfast: Fair Employment Agency, Research Paper 8.

Osborne, R.D. (1986) 'Segregated schools and examination results in Northern Ireland: some preliminary research', *Educational Research*, vol. 28, no. 1.

Osborne, R.D. and Cormack, R.J. (1989) 'Gender and religion as issues in education, training and entry to work', in J.I. Harbison (ed.) *Growing Up in Northern Ireland*, Belfast: Stranmillis College.

Osborne, R.D. and Murray, R.C. (1978) *Educational Qualifications and Religious Affiliation in Northern Ireland: an Examination of GCE 'O' and 'A' Levels*, Belfast: Fair Employment Agency, Research Paper 3.

Osborne, R.D., Cormack, R.J., Miller, R.L. and Williamson, A.P. (1987a) 'Graduates: geographical mobility and income', in R.D. Osborne, R.J. Cormack and R.L. Miller (eds) *Education and Policy in Northern Ireland*, Belfast: Policy Research Institute.

Osborne, R.D., Cormack, R.J. and Miller, R.L. (eds) (1987b) *Education and Policy in Northern Ireland*, Belfast: Policy Research Institute.

Partners in Mission Consultation (1981) *To a Rebellious House?* London: CIO Publishing.

Pelikan, J. (ed.) (1970) *Twentieth Century Theology in the Making*, vol. 3: *Ecumenicity and Renewal*, trans. R.A. Wilson, London: Fontana.

Peters, R.S. (1966) *Ethics and Education*, London: Allen and Unwin.

Peters, R.S. (ed.) (1973) *Philosophy of Education*, Oxford: Oxford University Press.

Pontifical Council for Promoting Christian Unity (1993) *Directory for the Application and Principles and Norms on Ecumenism*, London: Catholic Truth Society.

Poole, M.A. (1982) 'Religious segregation in Northern Ireland', in F. Boal and J. Douglas (eds) *Integration and Division: Geographical Perspectives on the Northern Ireland Problem*, London: Academic Press.

Purnell, P. (1985) *Our Faith Story*, London: Collins.

225

Rahner, K. (ed.) (1968) *Sacramentum Mundi*, London: Burns and Oates.

Raphael, T. (1991) *The Role of the Church School in a Multi-faith City*, London: London Diocesan Board for Schools.

Read, G., Rudge, J. and Howarth, R. (1986) *How Do I Teach RE?* London: Mary Glasgow.

Religious Education Council (1989) *Handbook for Agreed Syllabus Conference, SACREs and Schools*, Lancaster: RE Council.

Robinson, A. (ed.) (1988) *Education for Mutual Understanding – Roles and Responsibilities*, Coleraine: University of Ulster.

Rouse, R. and Neill, S.C. (eds) (1954) *A History of the Ecumenical Movement 1517–1948*, London: SPCK.

Sacks, B. (1961) *The Religious Issue in the State Schools of England and Wales 1902–1914*, Albuquerque: University of New Mexico.

Sacks, J. (1991) 'The persistence of faith: religion, morality and society in a secular age', *The Reith Lectures 1990*, London: Weidenfeld and Nicolson.

Sacred Congregation for Catholic Education (1971) *The General Catechetical Directory*, London: Catholic Truth Society.

Sacred Congregation for Catholic Education (1977) *The Catholic School*, London: Catholic Truth Society.

Sacred Congregation for Catholic Education (1979) *Catechesis in Our Time*, London: Catholic Truth Society.

Sacred Congregation for Catholic Education (1982) *Lay Catholics in Schools: Witnesses to Faith*, London: Catholic Truth Society.

Sacred Congregation for Catholic Education (1988) *The Religious Dimension of Education in a Catholic School*, London: Catholic Truth Society.

Salter, B. and Tapper, T. (1981) *Education, Politics and the State*, London: Grant McIntyre.

Schon, D. (1983) *The Reflective Practitioner*, New York: Teachers College.

Schools Council (1971) *Religious Education in Secondary Schools* (Working Paper 36), London: Evans/Methuen.

Sealey, J. (1985) *Religious Education: Philosophical Perspectives*, London: Allen and Unwin.

Sedgwick, P. (1992) 'The sectarian future of the church and ecumenical church schools', in J. Astley and D. Day, *The Contours of Christian Education*, London: McCrimmons.

Selby, D.E. (1976) 'The Catholic teacher crisis 1885–1902', *The Durham and Newcastle Review*, vol. 37.

Select Committee Report on the State of the Poor in Ireland (1830) VII, Cd 589.

Sharpe, E. (1988) *Understanding Religion*, London: Duckworth.

Shipman, M. (ed.) (1985) *Educational Research: Principles, Policies and Practices*, London: Falmer.

Simon, B. (1988) *Bending the Rules: the Baker Reform of Education*, London: Lawrence and Wishart.

Simon, B. and Chitty, C. (1993) *S.O.S. Save our Schools*, London: Lawrence and Wishart.

Simons, H. (1980a) 'The evaluative school', *Forum*, vol. 22, no. 2.

Simons, H. (ed.) (1980b) *Towards a Science of the Singular*, Norwich: CARE Occasional Paper 10.

Simons, H. (1987) *Getting to Know Schools in a Democracy: the Politics and Process of Evaluation*, London: Falmer.

Slee, N. (1989) 'Conflict and reconciliation between competing models of religious education', *British Journal of Religious Education*, vol. 11, no. 3.

Smith, A. and Robinson, A. (1992) *Education for Mutual Understanding: Perceptions and Policy*, Coleraine: Centre for the Study of Conflict.

Snook, I.A. (ed.) (1972a) *Concepts of Indoctrination*, London: Routledge.

Snook, I.A. (ed.) (1972b) *Indoctrination and Education*, London: Routledge.

Socialist Educational Association (1981) *The Dual System of Voluntary and County Schools*, London: Socialist Education Association.

Socialist Educational Association (1986) *All Faiths in All Schools*, London: Socialist Education Association.

Spencer, A.E.C.W. (1968) 'Religious education today', in P. Jebb (ed.) *Religious Education*, London: Darton, Longman and Todd.

Spencer, A.E.C.W. (1987) 'Arguments for an integrated school system', in R.D. Osborne, R.J. Cormack and R.L. Miller (eds) *Educational and Policy in Northern Ireland*, Belfast: Policy Research Institute.

Stake, R. (1985) 'Case study and the social philosophy of educational research', in J. Nisbet, J. Megarry and S. Nisbet, *World Year Book of Education*, London: Kogan Page.

Strudwick, V. (1986) *What Are Church Schools For?* Oxford: Oxford Diocesan Council for Education and Training.

Swann Report (1985) *Education for All: The Report of the Committee of Inquiry into the Education of Children from Ethnic Minority Groups* (Cmnd 9453), London: HMSO.

Swanwick Declaration (1987), London: British Council of Churches.

Tanner, N.P. (1990) *Decrees of the Ecumenical Councils*, London: Sheed and Ward.

Taylor, J. (1664) *A Dissuasive from Popery* in *Whole Works*, ed. R. Heber and C.P. Eden, vol. 6 (1849), London: Longmans *et al.*

Taylor, M.J. (1991) *SACREs: Their Formation, Composition, Operation and Role in RE and Worship*, Slough: NFER.

Temple, W. (1942) *Christianity and Social Order*, London: Penguin.

Thacker, J., Pring, R. and Evans, D. (eds) (1989) *Personal, Social and Moral Education in a Changing World*, Slough, NFER-Nelson.

Thiessen, E.J. (1985) 'A defense of a distinctively Christian curriculum', *Religious Education*, vol. 80, no. 1.

Thiessen, E.J. (1990) 'Indoctrination and religious education', in L.J. Francis and A. Thatcher (eds) *Christian Perspectives for Education*, Leominster: Gracewing/

Fowler Wright.

Tilby, A. (1979) *Teaching God*, London: Collins.

Tomlinson, S. (1990) *Multicultural Education in White Schools*, London: Batsford.

Trew, K. (1986) 'Catholic–Protestant contact in Northern Ireland', in M. Hewstone and R. Brown (eds) *Contact and Conflict in Intergroup Encounters*, Oxford: Blackwell.

Trew, K. (1989) 'Evaluating the impact of contact schemes for Catholic and Protestant children', in J.I. Harbison (ed.) *Growing Up in Northern Ireland*, Belfast: Stranmillis College.

Troyna, B. and Carrington, B. (1990) *Education, Racism and Reform*, London: Routledge.

Tulasiewicz, W. and Brock, C. (eds) (1988) *Christianity and Educational Provision in International Perspective*, London: Routledge.

Turner, I.F. and Davies, J. (1982) 'Religious attitudes in an integrated primary school: a Northern Ireland case-study', *British Journal of Religious Education*, vol. 5, no. 1.

Walford, G. and Jones, S. (1986) 'The Solihull adventure: an attempt to reintroduce selective schooling', *Journal of Education Policy*, vol. 1, no. 3.

Walker, R. (1986) 'Three good reasons for not doing case studies in curriculum research', in E.R. House (ed.) *New Directions in Educational Evaluation*, London: Falmer.

Walkling, P. (1980) 'The idea of a multicultural education', *Journal of the Philosophy of Education*, vol. 14. no. 1.

Walsh, P. (1983) 'The church secondary school and its curriculum', in D. O'Leary (ed.) *Religious Education and Young Adults*, London: St Paul Publications.

Walsh, P. (1993) *Education and Meaning*, London: Cassell.

Watson, B. (1987) *Education and Belief*, Oxford: Blackwell.

Watson, B. (ed.) (1992) *Priorities for Religious Education*, London: Falmer.

Webster, D. (1985) 'Commitment, spirituality and the classroom', *British Journal of Religious Education*, vol. 8, no. 1.

Wedderspoon, A.G. (ed.) (1966) *Religious Education 1944–1984*. London: Allen and Unwin.

Whitehead, A.N. (1932; 1970) *The Aims of Education* (first published 1932), London: Allen and Unwin.

Whyte, J. (1990) *Interpreting Northern Ireland*, Oxford: Oxford University Press.

Wilkins, R. (1992) 'Identifying the educators', in B. Watson, *Priorities for Religious Education*, London: Falmer.

Wilkinson, J., Wilkinson, R. and Evans, J.H. (1985) *Inheritors Together: Black People in the C of E*, London: Board of Social Responsibility.

Wilson, B. (1982) *Religion in Sociological Perspective*, Oxford: Oxford University Press.

Wilson, J.A. (1987) 'Selection for secondary education', in R.D. Osborne, R.J. Cormack and R.L. Miller (eds) *Education and Policy in Northern Ireland*. Belfast: Policy Research Institute.

Wilson, J.A. (1989) 'Educational performance: a decade of evidence', in J.I. Harbison (ed.) *Growing Up in Northern Ireland*, Belfast: Stranmillis College.

Wood, P. (1990) 'Indoctrination and religious education in infant schools', *British Journal of Religious Education*, vol. 12, no. 3.

Yarnold, E. (1989) *In Search of Unity*, London: St Paul Publications.

Yates, J. (ed.) (1986) *Faith for the Future*, London: National Society and Church House Publishing.

Young, R. (1988) 'Critical teaching and learning', *Educational Theory*, vol. 38, no. 1.